STAR WARS
INSIDER™

ALIENS, CREATURES, AND DROIDS

TITAN
WWW.TITAN-COMICS.COM

Star Wars Insider
Aliens, Creatures, and Droids

ISBN: 9781785851964

Published by Titan
A division of
Titan Publishing Group Ltd.,
144 Southwark Street,
London, SE1 0UP

© 2019 Lucasfilm Ltd. and ™
All Rights Reserved.
Used Under Authorised User.

No part of this publication may be reproduced, stored in a retrieval
system, or transmitted, in any form or by any means, without the prior
written permission of the publisher.

A CIP catalogue record for this title is available from the British Library.

First Edition November 2019
10 9 8 7 6 5 4 3 2 1

Printed in China.

Acknowledgments
Titan would like to thank the cast and crews of the *Star Wars*
saga. A huge thanks also to Brett Rector and Michael
Siglain at Lucasfilm, and Eugene Paraszczuk, Shiho Tilley, and
Christopher Troise at Disney for all of their invaluable help in putting
this volume together.

Please note:
The interviews and features collected in this volume were originally
printed in *Star Wars Insider*, some of which date back over 20 years. In
order to maintain the originalty of the material, we have not modified
the content unless absolutely neccesary.

Disney · **LUCASFILM**

STAR WARS INSIDER™

ALIENS, CREATURES,
AND DROIDS

CONTENTS

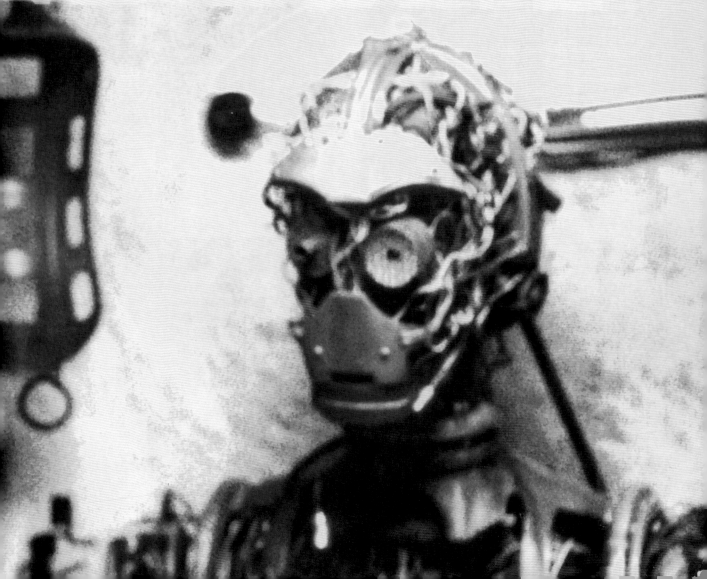

ANTHONY DANIELS
NUTS AND BOLTS

STAR WARS LEGEND ANTHONY DANIELS TALKS ABOUT MEETING HIS FANS,
THE RETURN OF C-3PO, AND THE POSSIBILITY OF DONNING THE GOLD SUIT
AGAIN FOR EPISODE II   by Scott Chernoff

ONE OF THE MOST STARTLING

and successful visual designs of the new *Star Wars* film is Doug Chiang's fantastic re-imagining of C-3PO, the prototypical protocol droid presented in all his glory. It's a bold take on Ralph McQuarrie's original design, and one of George Lucas' strongest signals that his new prequels mean business. By putting a fresh face on one of the saga's oldest friends, *The Phantom Menace* revealed new layers in the history and development of one of the most powerful icons of the *Star Wars* saga, the one Han Solo so eloquently dubbed, "Goldenrod."

But no matter what you call Threepio (as he's come to affectionately be known), there's no question that his prevalence as one of the most beloved characters in the *Star Wars* universe can only be due to the talents of actor Anthony Daniels.

Sure, C-3PO's gold costume and mask made a permanent visual impression on the minds of a few generations, but it's Daniels' performance that imbues Threepio with the surprisingly deep reservoir of feeling that has carried the character through not only all four *Star Wars* movies but also a never-ending stream of starring roles in TV commercials, cartoons (1985's *Droids*), and other projects.

Indeed, Daniels' contributions to the creation of C-3PO are by now *Star Wars* legend – it's no secret that Lucas had originally wanted Threepio to speak with a Brooklyn accent and the attitude of a used car dealer. The plan was to have Daniels play the part on the set and have another actor dub the voice later. But Daniels' take on the character – the odd British accent, more butler than bluster, and a fallback setting on fear – felt too right, and ultimately Lucas realised there was no need to change a thing.

Of course, there's more to Anthony Daniels than C-3PO. The actor portrayed a unique pathologist on the acclaimed British series *Prime Suspect* and the elfen Legolas in the animated *Lord of the Rings*. He's also got his own company that produces live entertainment events and interactive experiences all over the world. But of course, Anthony Daniels is most closely associated with the role he had to be talked into taking back in 1976. As Threepio, Daniels kicked off the classic trilogy, delivering the trilogy's first lines of dialogue and quickly establishing his character as a supplier of information ("Did you hear that? They've shut down the main reactor") and a classic scaredy cat ("We'll be destroyed for sure. This is madness! We're doomed!"). Whether fretting over freeing his master from the trash compactor or nervously telling his trusty counterpart R2-D2, "Let the Wookiee win," Daniels gave the classic trilogy some of its funniest moments.

It's a measure of how far things in the *Star Wars* universe have come that although Chiang's concept of Threepio in Episode I as a see-through puppet manipulated by an unseen operator did not call for an actor inside a suit, Lucas still felt it necessary to call Anthony Daniels to the Leavesden Studios set to voice the character again. It was more than just protocol – he couldn't imagine C-3PO any other way.

HOW DO YOU LIKE THREEPIO'S NEW LOOK?
I quite like it – I think nudity is *in*. I think there's a new liberalism here. I think he looks terrific. If you see the actual costume, it's stunning, because it looks like it actually works. Of course, it's immensely unwieldy and has a life slightly of its own, but hey, that's been C-3PO all the way along.

WAS IT SURREAL SEEING THREEPIO, AND BEING THREEPIO – BUT NOT BEING INSIDE OF HIM?
Well, first of all, I was thrilled to be involved in the movie at all, because there was no law that said I had to be.

WELL, THERE WAS IN *MY* MIND.
Oh, that's very nice, but George has the ability to do what he wants with it, so he could have thought, "Nah, let's do something new." So I felt pretty good about being asked to be associated again.

Yes, it did feel slightly strange, but because he is so different, physically, in this one, it wasn't that much of a jolt. And as I said, just to be there at all – you know, when I did *Star Wars* 23 years ago, I never expected there to be a second *Star Wars*, and then there was. And then there was a third. Then, I didn't expect the re-release. I didn't expect a new series. And I've never expected all the spin-offs I've done over the 20-odd years. Each one comes as a new surprise – sometimes a surprise, sometimes a shock. Depends on what the script is.

But it's a job, as we know, that I didn't originally want, and to have it last this long gives me a tremendous feeling of warmth – both to the movies and to Threepio. It's kind of

nice to belong. I think the thing Threepio really wants in life is to belong. And I guess he does. Unfortunately, he belongs to Anakin Skywalker.

WHAT DID YOU THINK WHEN YOU FIRST LEARNED ANAKIN HAD BUILT THREEPIO?
George explained the story to me. He said, "You were built by Anakin," and I thought, "Oh, that's really nice, because Alec Guinness was so supportive to me on the earlier movies." I thought it fitting that Threepio was built by Sir Alec.

Two days later, I suddenly thought, "Wait a minute, Alec played the *other* one." It's true. I'd completely forgotten that Anakin Skywalker was Darth Vader. I was shocked and horrified. I tried to call George and say, "You have to rewrite the entire movie!" But then I thought, "This is quite neat. The last person from whose hand you would expect Threepio to come would be Darth Vader's. At least he did *something* right."

You know, years ago, I wrote an article in the *San Francisco Chronicle*, outlining how Threepio came from the ghastly planet Croydon where machines are built. And I reckoned that Threepio'd been in this factory on a conveyor belt, and it got stuck in the conditioning zone, and that's why he's a little odd. George wrote me a letter saying, "This is great – more." So to find out Threepio was not a fault on a conveyor belt gave me a little buzz – though I'd been wrong all these years!

WHEN DID YOU FIRST SEE EPISODE I, AND WHAT WAS YOUR REACTION?
I'd seen chunks of it when we were working on it, and during the music dubbing, because I was hanging out at the studio – well, it was warm in there and they had hot coffee. I was very impressed by what I saw, but it didn't make any sense – it was just bits. Then I finally saw it on arriving in Salt Lake City at the equivalent of 4 o'clock in the morning my time in, I have to say, not the best cinema in the world.

But in spite of these things, I enjoyed it immensely – well, I would say that, wouldn't I? It actually did keep me awake to the end. Even with jet lag, I could sit back and know that I was in pretty safe hands. I thought so many things were good, like Jake Lloyd – I was pretty pleased with that because he is a neat kid. Also, just to know how things like the battle droids have been done, and to see how amazingly realistic they were – it tells you how good the actors are at pretending all that stuff's there, because that's quite difficult. It was *beyond* blue screen.

photos by Lucas Gilman

GOLD STAR: Anthony Daniels, sporting his now-famous gold jacket, struts his stuff as Master of Ceremonies at the *Star Wars* Celebration in Denver.

Of course, there's obviously a major, major fault – a glaring mistake – in the movie.

NOT ENOUGH C-3PO?

Absolutely. But apart from that – excellent. George said to me, "People are going to say Threepio isn't in it enough." But then he's right about a lot of things.

When I talked to him about the slight quirkiness and the movements [of this Threepio], he said, "He's just been built by a nine-year-old, what do you expect?" Right! You'll notice that he's really quite polite to R2-D2. And Artoo naturally comes back with, "Hey, you're naked." You know, Artoo's a real class act sometimes.

YOU'VE SAID THAT FOR *EMPIRE* YOU WERE CONCERNED ARTOO AND THREEPIO WERE SEPARATED.

Yes, and they gave me Harrison Ford instead – pretty good Artoo substitute. It was a very good dramatic coupling. His spikey approach with Threepio's need for everything to be proper worked extremely well. And that bit where Harrison keeps tapping C-3PO on the shoulder, telling him to do this and that, until Threepio just turns and gives Harrison this look that says, "You insufferable jerk" – I'm pretty proud of Threepio for doing that.

But I do feel Artoo works well with Threepio. On their own, neither is much use, really. I think they need each other. Maybe George will think of putting us back together. But you know, I'm always amused, because most of the time I couldn't even see R2-D2, so I would have to feel where he was. I was sort of grappling him on the set.

SO DID SOME OF THREEPIO'S AWKWARDNESS COME FROM YOU NOT HAVING COMPLETE SIGHT INSIDE THE MASK?

> "ANYBODY WHO KNOWS ME KNOWS THAT I AM NOT A GOLD-JACKET-WEARING PERSON. I'M FAIRLY DISCREET. I LIKE JEANS, AND I DON'T GO AROUND SHOUTING MY HEAD OFF SAYING, 'I'M THE GOLD MAN—HERE'S MY GOLD JACKET TO PROVE IT.'"

Oh no, because I had worked everything out. It would be boring to give you a blow-by-blow detail, but I'd rehearse and work out where things were – providing they stayed in the same place. Threepio's strange attitude, I think, is more down to *him*. I don't quite know where it comes from. Can you put the whole of his predicament down to being built by a nine-year-old who wants to go Podracing? I don't know.

IF YOU WERE WRITING THE YOUR *STAR WARS* MAGAZINE COLUMN RIGHT NOW,

WHAT EXPERIENCE FROM SHOOTING EPISODE I WOULD BE THE FIRST THING YOU'D WRITE ABOUT?

They'd been filming for some time before I arrived on the set. Apparently, when I spoke my first line as Threepio, someone whispered, "*Star Wars* has arrived!" That made me feel very proud.

But going to meet George at Leavesden Studios to talk about it all, at the gate house – they had forgotten to say I was coming. "*Who* are you? You're here to see *who*? And you're *who*? Do *what*? *Robot*? *What?!*" And all the time there's an Alsatian snarling at the wheels of my car. Perhaps it was a critic who had not enjoyed my performance reincarnated as a dog – beware! Security was so intense that as I drove out, I decided unkindly to not offer them back the heavy security badge they'd given me, just to annoy them. They're probably still looking for it. And I still have it. I'm so petty!

YOU WERE DEFINITELY WELL-RECOGNISED AT THE *STAR WARS* CELEBRATION.

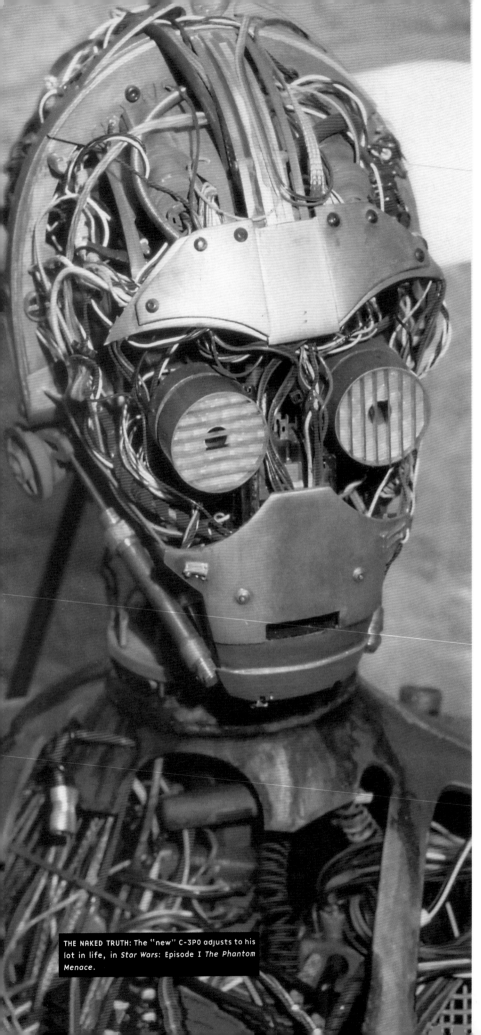

THE NAKED TRUTH: The "new" C-3PO adjusts to his lot in life, in *Star Wars: Episode I The Phantom Menace.*

AS MASTER OF CEREMONIES, YOU WERE SURROUNDED BY THOUSANDS OF PEOPLE WHO KNEW EXACTLY WHO YOU WERE.

I felt the Denver event was just *spectacular.* I thought Dan Madsen's organisation and the generosity of it all was just staggering. I gained so much respect for fans over that couple of days – because, as you know, the conditions were torture. And people behaved magnificently. I had never, ever worked with such a wonderful audience. They could have been sitting there damp and cold, going, "Make me laugh." Instead, they responded to everything, in spite of the rain.

I don't know who had the better time, them or me – despite the puddles pouring over the tops of my shoes. It was a genuine celebration. Beautiful, great experience. I was very glad to be offered the chance to do it. You were doing the business (as master of ceremonies on Stage B), as well.

YEAH, BUT I DIDN'T HAVE THE GOLD JACKET AND THE THOUSANDS OF FANS WHO ALREADY LOVED ME.

The gold jacket was, what can I say? Anybody who knows me knows that I am not a gold-jacket-wearing person. I'm fairly discreet. I like jeans, and I don't go around shouting my head off saying, "I'm the gold man – here's my gold jacket to prove it." But some flip of the imagination made me go and have one made. It felt absolutely right.

YOU SEEMED TO BOND WITH A LOT OF THE FANS THAT WEEKEND.

Denver worked out well for me in that way – I thought, "I made a lot of new friends here." I went around threatening to take away anybody's pass who wasn't smiling as they stood for four hours in the rain, and if they weren't smiling as I lurked up behind in the line, they smiled within seconds of me speaking. That was such a rewarding experience, to have that reaction.

I came away with such a high opinion of *Star Wars* fans. They had come to have a good time. We were giving, but they gave it back. I was very grateful. It's very easy as just an actor in these films to forget why they're so successful, who it is who makes them successful, and it is the fans, their support.

WHY DID YOU DECIDE TO BE AN ACTOR?

Gosh, I don't know. I've never had a choice. You know, if I had a choice and I had a brain, I would have said, "No way." But I just *needed* to do it. There is no logic. Sounds like Yoda, doesn't it?

"There is no logic, just *why*?"

The only time I ever came alive at school was when there was a play production. But the problem was, when I told people that I wanted to be an actor, they were embarrassed. That's why I went into law. It was only when I realised life was pretty unbearable not doing something you really want to do that I had the courage to do it.

HOW FAR DID YOU GO IN PURSUING A LAW CAREER?

Not far at all, because I was so bad at it. But the jump from being a potential lawyer to being a gold robot is staggering, isn't it?

DEFINITELY. SO YOU QUIT LAW SCHOOL AND WENT TO DRAMA SCHOOL?

Yes, I went for three years, and became very good at mime. I was 27 when I became an actor – embarrassing, isn't it? I won a scholarship to the BBC to do radio plays every day of the week. I was thrilled, but then I auditioned for an out-of-town theatre and I two-timed the BBC. From that, I got offered the National Theatre in London, and I was touring with that company when I was asked to meet George.

WAS IT YOUR MIME HE WAS PRIMARILY INTERESTED IN, INITIALLY?

Yes, and that I was an actor who was *cheap*. These things were major considerations.

WAS STAR WARS YOUR FIRST FILM?

I'd been in a very small film called *City of the Dead*, and I'd done TV. But no, I hadn't really been in a film before *Star Wars*, and the whole process was kind of surprising. I was staggered that we would do a scene which seemed total garbage, but then seeing the finished film, I realised what an editor does and how they take three seconds out of that scene – the three seconds that were good. And I was delighted, amazed, to hear R2-D2 speak, thanks to Ben Burtt. I had talked to myself all the way through the filming, so to hear him reply to me was quite odd, really. And it sounded very real. It sounded like we had actually had a conversation – which would have been nice at the time, but hey, you can't have everything.

I was in Death Valley last year on vacation, staying where George and I stayed when we were shooting the road to Jabba's palace, the last scene we did in *Jedi*. It was the very first and last time George rehearsed with me. I suddenly realised he was walking next to

DUELING DANIELS: **Anthony Daniels takes on Jake Lloyd outside the *Star Wars* Celebration last spring.**

photos by Lucas Gilman

"THREEPIO DOESN'T GET IT. HE'S AWARE, SADLY, OF SOMETHING HE DOESN'T HAVE BUT HUMANS DO – PROBABLY A HEART, THOUGH HE DOESN'T UNDERSTAND AFFECTION. HIS OWN BRAND OF LOYALTY COMES PRETTY CLOSE."

me, bent over, being R2-D2 and beeping. It was the happiest time out of all the movies.

IF YOU HAD NOT PLAYED THREEPIO, WAS THERE ANOTHER PART IN STAR WARS YOU WOULD HAVE LIKED TO HAVE PLAYED?

No. It's hard to say this without sounding rude, but the only person I liked in the *Star Wars* script was Threepio, because he was odd – and in any case, I wasn't being offered another part. You know, Harrison and I are not *necessarily* up for the same roles anyway. But I'd already fallen for the picture by Ralph McQuarrie, the rather sad painting of Threepio.

YOUR FIRST IMPRESSION OF C-3PO WAS HIS SADNESS. YET HE'S ALSO A COMIC CHARACTER.

Well, you see, somebody who thinks they're funny is generally not very. But somebody to whom everything that happens is a tragedy and a disaster, that's quite amusing. Nothing for Threepio is easy, and that's a good comic set-up. He's funny because he has no sense of humour. Zero. You never hear him crack a joke, do you? The nearest he gets is when he says, "I'm rather embarrassed, General Solo, but it appears you are to be the main course at a banquet in my honour." That is said with a certain amount of irony. But as a stand-up comic, Threepio ain't gonna do it, you know?

Threepio, being pure machine, is utterly confused by things like the Force and people kissing – anything that is non-mechanical, Threepio doesn't get it. He's aware, sadly, of something that he doesn't have but humans do

– probably a heart, though he doesn't understand affection. His own brand of loyalty comes pretty close. He's a very confused person.

AND YET HE DOES EXPERIENCE FEAR.
Oh, it's about the only thing he does experience. I'm sure one of the laws of robotics is to stay alive, to be *plugged in*. So that is a fairly automatic response, and it's not an emotion, it's a reaction. Whereas love, well, if all he might be in love with is R2-D2, I think it's better he doesn't get involved.

DID C-3PO'S VOICE AND STYLE OF SPEECH COME TO YOU RATHER EASILY, OR IS IT SOMETHING THAT YOU WORKED ON?
It came out of, I think the phrase is, left field. I'd been working with various drafts of the script for six months, but it wasn't until the very first day's filming, Threepio arrived the way he was. I'd done a lot of homework and background thoughts without ever coming to a conclusion.

They just laughed. Also, on something like *The Muppet Show* or *Sesame Street*, it is not unusual to have people in weird costumes, so they know how to treat a person who is.

I think you know "The Holiday Special," *The Donny & Marie Show* – I have this dark museum of memories. I have a whole range of things I laugh at today. Like the Kellogg's C-3POs – the commercials were great, the cereal was … interesting.

YOU'VE WRITTEN FOR C-3PO A LOT – FOR INSTANCE, *THE PROTOCOL OFFENSIVE* COMIC BOOK, WHICH YOU WROTE WITH RYDER WINDHAM.
Very interesting, writing for a comic book. Not at all what I thought it was going to be – it was hard work! You don't just fill in the balloons.

KNOWING THREEPIO AS WELL AS YOU DO, WHAT WOULD YOU LIKE TO SEE FOR HIM IN EPISODES II AND III?

Threepio. He picks up a blaster and takes over the universe. End credits." I gave that to George and he said he'd think about. So if that is what Episode II is about, it was my idea.

But I think for Threepio, I'd quite like him to spend a little more time with Artoo, because I think that was a coupling that worked very well. But I'm not presumptuous enough to tell George how to write.

HAS HE TOLD YOU ANYTHING ABOUT THREEPIO'S ROLE IN EPISODE II?
Well, you know, if I'm the person that can mix up Anakin and Obi-Wan, I'm not the person who's going to give you the best information.

ARE YOU OFFICIALLY SIGNED FOR EPISODE II YET?
Oh, not at all. They know I'll turn up on the day.

WOULD YOU LIKE TO PUT ON THE GOLD SUIT AGAIN?
Oh, I would like to, when Threepio gets his coverings, because his movements are very specific. Threepio is Threepio.

> "GEORGE EXPLAINED THAT HE HADN'T STARTED ON EPISODE II, SO I PICKED UP THE PAPER AND I WROTE: 'ENTER THREEPIO. HE PICKS UP A BLASTER AND TAKES OVER THE UNIVERSE. END CREDITS.'"

It was rather like sitting in a restaurant thinking, "Well, I could have salmon or I could have pork," and it's not until the waiter stands there tapping his pen that you suddenly say, "I'll have the spaghetti." You don't actually make up your mind until you are forced to. Threepio happened in that way. It's almost as though he was in a box waiting to leap out.

I LIKE LISTENING TO HIM SPEAK IN OTHER LANGUAGES, LIKE AT THE DOOR OF JABBA'S PALACE.
Weird, isn't it – "Arto-Day-toa" – and of course I was the only one speaking in that scene at all, because the ball was coming out of the wall, Artoo's silent, and there's me, trying to struggle my way through the scene. Maybe that's why Threepio's always so perplexed, because he's talking to himself the whole time.

YOU'VE PLAYED THREEPIO SO MANY TIMES – THE RADIO DRAMAS, COMMERCIALS, CARTOONS, LIVE APPEARANCES – DO YOU HAVE ANY FAVOURITE THREEPIO PERFORMANCES OUTSIDE OF THE MOVIES?
I think Star Tours is wonderful, and the people at Disney are just magic to work with. I wanted the people at *Sesame Street* to give me a job.

Well, in fact, at the scoring session, George explained that he hadn't started on Episode II, and Rick said, "Of course he has – and here it is," and he picked up a piece of paper and wrote, "Opening credits" and "End credits," with a big gap in the middle. And George laughed. So I picked up the paper and I wrote, "Enter

YOU DID AN INTERVIEW WHERE YOU CALLED C-3PO YOUR BEST FRIEND. DO YOU STILL THINK OF HIM THAT WAY?
I suppose I have a best friend, a human. But I think of Threepio as a much-loved friend, a very loyal friend – somebody I don't want to abandon. He's been a very good friend to me, and I owe him. It's kind of symbiotic. He needs me, and I guess to a certain extent, I need him. ☻

NATURAL COMPANIONS: R2-D2 and C-3PO have their first adventure together in *The Phantom Menace*.

"I KNOW IT'S A STRANGE THING TO SAY, BUT I FELT THAT HE HAD HUMANITY."

That's Anthony Daniels, speaking of his role as C-3PO for the 1980 book *Once Upon a Galaxy: A Journal of the Making of The Empire Strikes Back*. The quote encapsulates not only Daniels' thoughtful approach to acting, but also throws a spotlight on the unique role of robots in *Star Wars*. George Lucas took the robot, a classic sci-fi staple for decades, and created an overlooked underclass with thoughts, feelings and raw emotions ranging from spunkiness to terror. Writing the first *Star Wars* movie in 1975, Lucas even coined a new term for his lively mechanical men.

Since that time, droids have become an indelible thread of the *Star Wars* fabric, as inseparable from the greater saga as a cup of flour is from a freshly-baked loaf of bread. Heroic droids like C-3PO and R2-D2 display a sweeping emotional range, while sinister machines like the Death Star's torture robot are cold, dispassionate, and frightening.

So it should come as no surprise that many new droids will appear in *Star Wars Episode I The Phantom Menace*, and that their roles will be equally wide-ranging. The droids of Episode I—from mechanics to manservants to mercenaries—are just as important as any member of the human cast.

But fans needn't worry—despite a 32 year gap separating the new prequel from the classic trilogy (and a "real world" wait of 16 years!) the droids are reassuringly familiar, yet in the best tradition of *Star Wars*, they still find unexpected ways to surprise and amaze.

PROTOCOL DROIDS

‹ INNATE DIGNITY ›

Anthony Daniels will again have the opportunity to explore See-Threepio's humanity, since the character will be making a repeat appearance in Episode I—his debut, so to speak. But Threepio's "peers" will be appearing as well, and they should be quite familiar to any fan of the *Star Wars* saga. Protocol droids are a crucial component in the machinery of intergalactic relations. They function as consular attachés and personal assistants to big-shot ambassadors and business executives. Accordingly, they are experts in diplomacy, languages, and the social graces.

Among the protocol droids featured in Episode I is the TC series, a line manufactured (in the universe of the saga) by the massive droid conglomerate Cybot Galactica. The droids follow a standard humanoid configuration and seem imbued with an innate sense of dignity. Unlike a certain gold-plated worrywart, TC units are thoroughly unflappable, a factory-installed trait that is reinforced every time the droids undergo a memory wipe.

TC units are quite expensive, as protocol droids go, but the price is worth it due to their undeniable poise and professionalism. Everybody from the pompous officials of the Trade Federation to the efficient legislators in Coruscant's Galactic Senate Chamber employ TC units.

PROTOCOL DROID: With their multitude of functions, the TC series is expensive—but worth it.

photo by Keith Hamshere

BY DANIEL WALLACE

...POPULATE *THE PHANTOM MENACE*

BATTLE DROIDS

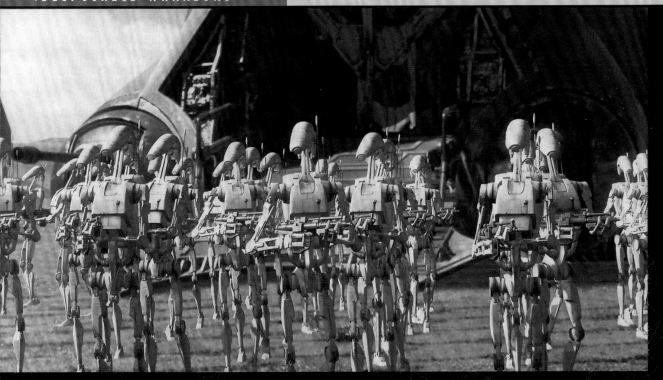

The dehumanization of the enemy is an old cinematic technique—in an air-duel epic, for instance, the good-guy barnstormer has his face uncovered, allowing the audience to see and sympathize with the hero's emotions. The enemy pilot, on the other hand, is often hidden beneath a helmet, scarf, and flight goggles, resulting in an inscrutable, implacable, and much more frightening foe. The original *Star Wars* films employed this technique to great effect, most notably in the person of the black-masked Darth Vader and his legions of emotionless stormtroopers. In fact, stormtroopers

did such a good impression of robotic obedience that children in 1977 could be forgiven for thinking the plastic soldiers *were* droids—a common misconception among the under-10 crowd.

The Phantom Menace takes the dehumanization a step further by pitting the heroes against armies of unstoppable mechanical infantryman. Robotic infantry soldiers have appeared in the expanded universe before, beginning with the 1980 novel *Han Solo and the Lost Legacy*, but this is their first appearance in the *Star Wars* films. Fortunately, computer-generated imagery (under the guidance of

Industrial Light & Magic) has progressed to the point at which a thousand droids can be generated almost as easily as one, eliminating the need for a thousand full-size models or a static matte painting.

In Episode I, these disposable warriors are known as battle droids. The battle droids' masters in the Trade Federation are wealthy cowards—unwilling to risk their own lives, they have built an army to fight in their stead. Battle droids are cheap and easy to produce in great

BATTLE DROID: **Walking weapons, an army of battle droids amasses, ready for a fight.**

numbers, the better to overwhelm their foes on the battlefield. They never tire, never grow hungry, and never question their orders. Battle droids also possess one additional advantage from a moviemaking standpoint—Jedi Knights can use their lightsabers to hack them to tiny pieces without slipping into the realm of excessive blood and gore.

Each battle droid stands nearly two meters tall and possesses a skeletal frame, a duckbill head, and a standard-issue blaster rifle. Their bodies are cast from an off-white alloy, but different classes can be distinguished by colored markings—orange for commanders, blue for pilots, and maroon for security officers.

Additionally, a battle droid's backpack contains a sophisticated comm system, including several transmission antennas and an encryption/decryption computer. The droids are ferried into combat zones aboard armored transport vehicles, but some serve as reconnaissance scouts on single-person repulsorlift flitters called STAPs. A battle droid rides a STAP by gripping the handlebars and leaning precariously off the back end, a position that would be acutely uncomfortable for anyone other than a droid.

Battle droids are overwhelmingly stupid. Battlefield commanders are granted greater intelligence and autonomy, but the rank and file robots are simple drones. Designed to respond to remote command signals, battle droids are powerless without guidance. They work best when assaulting a numerically inferior foe—by attacking *en masse*, they quickly shut down any resistance. If one droid falls, there is always another to replace it.

DESTROYER DROIDS ‹DEVASTATING ATTACKERS›

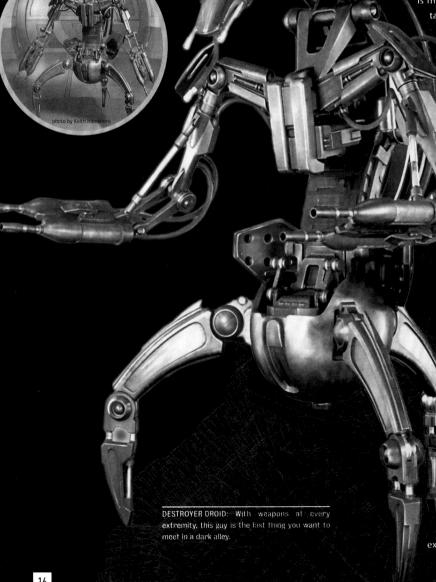

photo by Keith Hamshere

Sometimes, however, a problem arises that even a phalanx of battle droids can't handle. When that occurs, it's time to call in the heavy hitters—the destroyer droids. If a battle droid is the foot solider, a destroyer droid is the Sherman tank. A single destroyer droid can lay waste to an entire battalion of troops, being nothing more than a deadly mobile weapons platform.

Destroyer droids, programmed to be fearless, make perfect front-line combat machines, but only the bounty hunting droid IG-88 represented this aggressive category in the classic trilogy—and audiences never got to see IG-88 strut his stuff. Episode I's destroyer droids, on the other hand, are sent into the thick of the fighting, rolling into position as massive armored wheels. While they are in this configuration these droids are nearly impervious, except perhaps to the blade of a Jedi lightsaber.

When they are prepared to strike, destroyer droids unfold from their wheel mode and become devastating attackers with weapons at every extremity. Destroyer droids have no need to carry blaster rifles, since their lethal laser cannons are built right into their bodies. These droids can also generate their own deflector shields, making *them* extremely difficult to destroy. Fortunately for the peace-loving citizens of the galaxy, destroyer droids are highly expensive and difficult to produce, and only exist in limited numbers.

DESTROYER DROID: With weapons at every extremity, this guy is the last thing you want to meet in a dark alley.

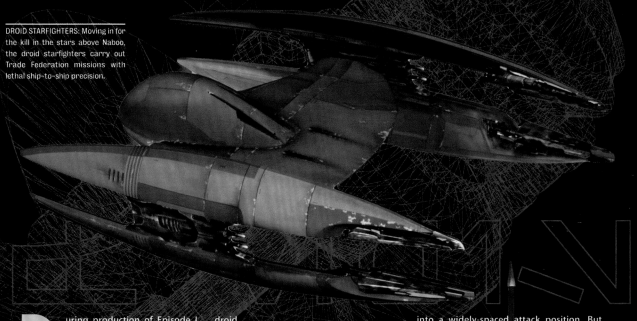

DROID STARFIGHTERS: Moving in for the kill in the stars above Naboo, the droid starfighters carry out Trade Federation missions with lethal ship-to-ship precision.

During production of Episode I, the art department often referred to the Trade Federation droid starfighter as the "vulture droid." The menacing fighter craft does indeed resemble a colossal bird, particularly in its resting and its "walking" modes. Unlike the Empire's deadly TIE fighters, which are flown by space-suited pilot aces, the Trade Federation droid starfighter is nothing more than a huge spacegoing droid.

The cowardly Trade Federation has once again used its considerable wealth to finance an ever-ready fighting force—battle droids rule the ground, but Trade Federation droid starfighters rule the sky. The quick and maneuverable vessels are often stationed aboard Trade Federation battleships for lethal ship-to-ship combat.

When an X-wing fighter enters a combat zone, its s-foil wings split apart and lock into a widely-spaced attack position. But when a Trade Federation droid starfighter does the same, two compartments slide open to reveal weapons powerful enough to make its enemies break and run. The droids function equally well during deepspace dogfights and planetary strafing runs. Like battle droids, Trade Federation droid starfighters are most effective when used in overwhelming swarm attacks.

PROBE DROIDS

The name "probe droid" will undoubtedly sound familiar to any longtime devotee of *Star Wars*. In the opening scenes of *The Empire Strikes Back*, eight Arakyd Viper probe droids are launched from an Imperial Star Destroyer, and one of them succeeds in rooting out the hidden Rebel base on Hoth. *Star Wars: Episode I The Phantom Menace* has its own version of *Empire*'s probot—a much smaller, sneakier little number known as the Sith probe droid.

The Sith "dark eye" probe droid is employed by the mysterious and cunningly evil Sith order for the purpose of spying on their enemies. Each droid is about the size of a basketball, and lacks the dangling claws and manipulative appendages that make the Arakyd Viper so distinctive. But the Sith probe droid has no need for external adornments, since its only mission is to find its target as quickly and efficiently as possible. In fact, in appearance it vaguely resembles the training remote used by Luke Skywalker for lightsaber practice aboard the *Millennium Falcon*.

When cornered, however, or if it is sent on a search-and-destroy mission, the Sith probe droid can lash out with deadly force. The droids have no standard weapons complement, instead possessing a universal internal mount which can accommodate a laser cannon, a stun blaster, a poison-dart needle, or any number of other lethal gadgets. The weapon selected depends on the mission profile, and many Sith probe droids are left unarmed to give them greater speed. The droids have limited autonomy outside their mission parameters and are typically directed via a remote-control comlink.

PROBE DROID: A forerunner of the probot that discovered the Rebel base on Hoth, the Sith "dark eye" probe droid will search—and destroy.

PIT DROIDS

Humor has always been an outlet for droids to express themselves in *Star Wars*. While most other cinema robots stay locked in the homicidal *Terminator* mode—or instead are bland, push-button automatons—George Lucas' creations also serve as an outlet for broad comedy. The two leading droid characters, R2-D2 and C-3PO, bicker like a pair of mynocks with a single power cable between them. And then there was the mouse droid on the Death Star that flees before Chewbacca's roar, and the labor unit in Mos Eisley who takes out a pesky flying probe droid with a good hard swat in the *Star Wars Special Edition*. That tradition of laughter continues in Episode I with the antics of the pit droid.

Pit droids are squat little bundles of energy designed to make on-the-fly repairs to Podracers. Podracing is a dangerous sport, and the high-speed afterburners are prone to breakdown. During long races, the Podracer jockeys often break from the action and pull into the pits to refuel their engines or recalibrate their controls. Pit droids perform these tasks with ease, though they are deployed in such great numbers they are seemingly always underfoot.

Despite their diminutive stature, pit droids can lift many times their own weight. They are extremely durable and cheap to manufacture and maintain, and come in a variety of colors. For easy storage, pit droids can fold up into a compact size when hit on the "nose"—an oversized circular feature located on the front of the head.

Pit droids come by their natural comedic talents quite accidentally. Programmed with a built-in feistiness, they focus on their jobs with the intensity of an angry bulldog. If a pit droid is trying to fix a blown stabilizer, nothing is going to get in its way—not other pit droids, not raceway hazards, not even the droid's own inability to perform the task at hand. The droids will try and try again, but heaven help the poor pit droid who isn't as aggressive or aware as the rest of his comrades. As race spectators (and movie audiences) can attest, watching a stable of pit droids going about their duties can be nearly as entertaining as watching a Podrace itself.

photo by Giles Keyte

PIT DROID: Programmed to work with the determination of an angry bulldog, pit droids attend to Podracers [ABOVE], folding to a compact size when hit on the nose [BOTTOM].

ASTROMECH DROIDS

< PLUG-IN COUNTERPARTS >

By far the most familiar droid class in Episode I is the astromech— the brightly-painted three-legged barrels so endearingly represented by R2-D2 in the classic trilogy. Artoo appears in Episode I as well (played again by stalwart actor Kenny Baker), but he is also supported by dozens of other astromechs, all almost identical in appearance to the droids audiences have loved for over 20 years. It's nice to know that, despite so many changes, some things remain exactly the same.

R2-D2 and other astromech droids are members of the R series, a line of starship counterparts manufactured by Industrial Automaton. Before the climactic battle against the Death Star in *Star Wars*: Episode IV *A New Hope*, dozens of R2 units were seen being lowered via vacuum hoses into interface sockets just behind the cockpits of the Rebels' X-wing and Y-wing starfighters. There, in the droid sockets, the little droids monitor flight performance, maintain efficient energy levels, and fix minor electrical malfunctions. This frees up their pilot masters to handle more important tasks – like shaking enemy bogeys off their six o'clock.

Many of Episode I's astromechs are used in similar fashion, as plug-in counterparts to the Royal Naboo N-1 starfighter. The wickedly pointed N-1, dressed up in bright yellow and shiny chrome, is one of Episode I's most distinctive creations. The familiar R2 unit domes that pop up behind the bubble canopies are a subtle reminder of the consistency of *Star Wars* technology.

Unlike the bothersome setup for X-wings and Y-wings, astromech droids are fitted into Naboo N-1 starfighters from below. This makes it much easier for the droid to get out— after all, if Luke hadn't crashed his X-wing at a convenient Dagobah swamp level, who knows if Artoo would have survived a three-meter fall to the ground? In order to fit into the N-1's cramped interface socket, the droid's legs retract a short distance into its body while its head pops up like a submarine periscope.

Yet in *A New Hope*, Uncle Owen, who was no starfighter jockey, attempted to buy two different astromechs from the Jawa droid auction. What gives? The answer is that the astromech is the *Star Wars* version of the Swiss army knife, able to perform any maintenance task with a bewildering array of retractable tools. R2 units come equipped with everything from buzzsaws to arc

welders and make outstanding mechanics. In Episode I, astromechs are seen making repairs to starships and can even operate in the zero-gravity vacuum of space.

Aliens, Sith Lords, and man-eating monsters—with a rogue's gallery like this, droids may seem to be the *least* exotic creations in Episode I. But the automatic actors are arguably the best thespians of the bunch, delivering their lines with mechanical precision and always hitting their marks. In a contest of terrifying relentlessness or manic comic energy, the droids of Episode I continue to bring their own unique humanity to the *Star Wars* saga. ☉

Daniel Wallace is the author of the books *Star Wars: The Essential Guide to Droids*, *Star Wars: The Essential Guide to Planets and Moons*, and the upcoming *What's What in Episode I*. He wrote about the unseen planets of *Star Wars* in *Insider* #36.

ASTROMECH DROID: The *Star Wars* version of a Swiss Army knife, astromech droids help pilot Naboo N-1 starfighters

R2's DEBUT

ROGER CHRISTIAN WAS ONE OF THE VERY FIRST PEOPLE HIRED BY GEORGE LUCAS TO WORK ON *STAR WARS*, AND WENT ON TO WIN AN ACADEMY AWARD FOR HIS SET DECORATION ON *A NEW HOPE*. HERE, HE TELLS *INSIDER* ABOUT HIS INVOLVEMENT IN CREATING OF ONE OF THE SAGA'S BEST-LOVED CHARACTERS.

Right: R2-D2, the versatile utility droid, equipped with a variety of tool-tipped appendages.

Opposite page: A rough sketch of R2-D2 by George Lucas and Bill Harman; George Lucas standing next to the first prop ever made for *Star Wars*, a wooden R2-D2.

The first R2-D2 took shape in a tiny studio in Kensal Rise in London, when George Lucas came to the U.K. in 1975. Five of us set up shop in a tiny studio, and [art director] Les Dilley and I were given the task of making a mock-up.

"From the script, it was clear that George didn't have a movie without R2-D2 and C-3PO. They were the storytellers. We knew that C-3PO would work because of the robot in *Metropolis* (1927), but R2-D2... He had to be under four-feet tall and we couldn't make him do everything he needed to do using radio-control, so we had to make him work around a small person.

"George hired Kenny Baker, who is 3' 8", and we recruited Bill Harman, the carpenter who made everything for *Monty Python and the Holy Grail*

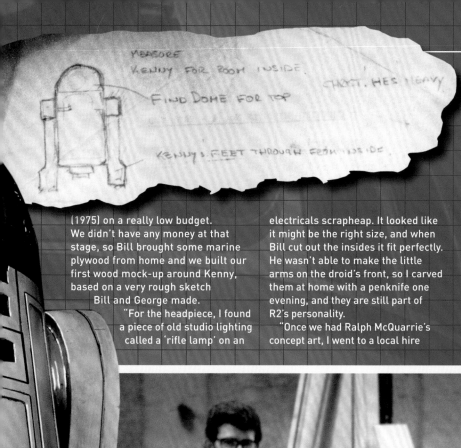

MEASURE
KENNY FOR ROOM INSIDE.
FIND DOME FOR TOP CHRIST. HE'S HEAVY
KENNY'S FEET THROUGH FROM INSIDE.

(1975) on a really low budget. We didn't have any money at that stage, so Bill brought some marine plywood from home and we built our first wood mock-up around Kenny, based on a very rough sketch Bill and George made.

"For the headpiece, I found a piece of old studio lighting called a 'rifle lamp' on an electricals scrapheap. It looked like it might be the right size, and when Bill cut out the insides it fit perfectly. He wasn't able to make the little arms on the droid's front, so I carved them at home with a penknife one evening, and they are still part of R2's personality.

"Once we had Ralph McQuarrie's concept art, I went to a local hire company that specialized in old military equipment, looking for items to match Ralph's painting. I bought several passenger air vents and reading lamps from an old Vickers Viscount turboprop airliner, and various grid pieces and pistons. I stuck them onto the mock-up in accordance with the painting, and they are all still on R2 today.

"While I was doing this, Bill was cutting away at the insides and adding foam padding until Kenny was able to fit inside. He got it so that the frame wasn't digging into him, but it was just too heavy for Kenny to move. When he slotted his boots into the legs, all he could do was make the whole thing shake a little.

"I had also bought a fighter pilot's harness with the airplane scrap, thinking it might be useful, so we fitted that into the body, too. That meant that Kenny could wear R2 like a rucksack and take the weight off his legs. "George came down to watch the first real walking test, and Kenny made the little droid shuffle forward a few steps before falling over on his back. Seeing those few steps, we knew that we had conquered how to make R2-D2 function. As Kenny shook the droid and made its head turn, there was relief all round. From there, we all knew that R2 could be developed as one of the main characters with a truly unique personality." ☻

CINEMA ALCHEMIST
DESIGNING STAR WARS & ALIEN

ROGER CHRISTIAN

MORE TO SAY

Cinema Alchemist is available now.

HAVE YOU?

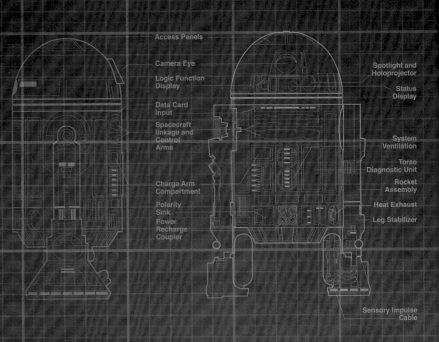

Access Panels
Camera Eye
Logic Function Display
Data Card Input
Spacecraft linkage and Control Arms
Charge Arm Compartment
Polarity Sink
Power Recharge Coupler

Spotlight and Holoprojector
Status Display
System Ventilation
Torso Diagnostic Unit
Rocket Assembly
Heat Exhaust
Leg Stabilizer
Sensory Impulse Cable

THE MAN WHO BUILT R2-D2!

LESLIE DILLEY

Turning concept sketches and designs into solid objects and real environments for a movie is the job of an art director and set decorator. Leslie Dilley, who fulfilled those roles on *Star Wars: A New Hope*, reflects on his part in creating movie history.

WORDS: PAT JANKIEWICZ

Two-time Academy Award-winning production designer and art director Leslie Dilley has overseen a great deal of onscreen destruction during his career. He's created earthquakes in Southern California for *Superman The Movie* (1978), caused traffic chaos in Piccadilly Circus for *An American Werewolf in London* (1981), facilitated an alien invasion in *Invaders From Mars* (1986), and helped destroy civilization as we know it in *Deep Impact* (1998). But it was his creative input as art director and set decorator on the original *Star Wars* film that has become instantly recognizable to generations of movie fans. In fact, the prolific art director's contribution to the iconic movie was officially recognized in 1978, when he was awarded the Best Art Decoration-Set Decoration Oscar for *Star Wars: A New Hope* (1977).

Now a resident of the U.S.A., Dilley—who was born in the Rhondda Valley of South Wales, U.K. in 1941—spent his formative years learning his craft in and around London. An early apprenticeship led to him joining the art department of the prestigious Associated British Picture Corporation (which would later become EMI), where he worked as a freelance junior draughtsman during the 1960s at the legendary Elstree Studios. Little did the aspiring production designer know that, just over a decade later, he would be working at the studios again, on a project that would make cinematic history.

"*Star Wars* came my way in 1975, when I was serving as assistant art director under [production designer] John Barry on *Lucky Lady* (1975), a big Burt Reynolds movie for 20th Century Fox that we were making in Mexico," explains Dilly. "The writers on that movie were Willard Huyck and Gloria Katz, who were good friends with George Lucas, and they recommended he use John Barry for *Star Wars*. That's how it happened—John took the job, and I became the art director on the film.

"My work entailed being responsible for everything visual, everything you saw on the screen, apart from the actors," Dilley says. As such, the art director had a direct hand in creating the worn and lived-in look that has become familiar to fans of the *Star Wars* galaxy, and defines it to this day.

In The Beginning

Although *A New Hope* would break new ground in the movie-making arena, both in terms of box-office success and its influence on the sci-fi and fantasy genres, in the early days of production it was a case of all hands on deck for the handful of personnel initially drafted onto the crew, ▶

▶ and Dilley soon found himself heavily involved in the development of the picture. "The only production people working on the movie at the beginning were John Barry, myself, and a guy named Roger Christian, who went on to become a film director himself," Dilley says of the film's humble beginnings. "There was nobody else—just George Lucas, [producer] Gary Kurtz, and the three of us, and we delivered it all from scratch!"

Lucas and his band of filmmakers settled on North West London as their base of operations from which to bring their epic vision to the big screen, and it saw Dilley return to the stomping ground of his youth. "We were trying to get [the project] off the ground in a place called Lee International Film Studios on Kensal Road, London," he recalls. "That's where we developed R2-D2, C-3PO, and Luke Skywalker's landspeeder. We were also joined by Norman Reynolds, who was doing C-3PO. Norman and I were co- art directors on *Star Wars*."

Reminiscing on how Luke's iconic vehicle came together, Dilley recollects that, "The

"Artoo was developed straight from the drawing board."

03

"I said, 'You've got this job on *Star Wars*, Kenny, and you've got to do it!' To which he replied, 'But we're on *Opportunity Knocks*!'"

landspeeder was a joint effort between all of us. We made this full-size mock-up of it, which George said was much too big. So we cut it down by a third, and that's the lovely little thing you see in the movie."

But Luke's memorable hot rod wasn't the only iconic mode of *Star Wars* transport that Dilley had a hand in creating. "I drafted the plans for the Jawa sandcrawler that you see on Tatooine, and went out to Tunisia with a construction crew to put it up," he reveals. "We put it together in this dried-up salt lake there. The sandcrawler was a really huge set: 120 feet long, 20 feet wide, and 40 feet high."

01 Leslie Dilley (left) with production designer John Barry (right).

02 Dilley's team working on the remote control R2-D2 prop.

03 Actor Kenny Baker enjoying lunch in his R2-D2 costume.

Droid Detail

Perhaps Dilley's biggest challenge was realizing the plucky little astromech droid who would go on to become one of the best-loved characters in the entire saga. "I ended up building R2-D2, which was essentially based on Ralph McQuarrie's illustrations. Artoo was developed straight from the drawing board," says Dilley. "We started out with a cardboard drum, added cardboard arms, and then tried to walk it. It took months to make the whole thing, and we actually came up with different versions of him."

Eventually, Dilley and the team came to the conclusion that the little droid would work most efficiently if he was being operated by someone inside the prop. Of the different versions created during the design and building process, Dilley explains that, "One Artoo-Detoo was built so that a small man could stand inside, and another so that he could waddle, but we could never get one where he could simply walk around in it, because there was never enough room for leg movement! The legs of the person we needed to pilot it would have to be very short."

Dilley realized he needed to find an appropriately sized actor to play the droid. "To find our Artoo-Detoo, we searched everywhere in England for little people," he says. "We brought in some actors who we thought would work, but many of them just weren't strong enough." To operate the prop manually would require an actor with a lot of stamina, as Dilley elaborates. "They had to get inside this thing and walk in it enough to make it waddle around."

After much searching, the team finally discovered their perfect R2-D2 in the form of British actor, Kenny Baker. "We eventually found Kenny, who really did a great job. Kenny had a performing partner named Jack Purvis, who was also in the movie—at that time they were working as a musical double act, playing the xylophone and drums."

For a worrying time, however, it looked as though the production team were in danger of losing their dream droid. "Kenny and Jack were on a show called *Opportunity Knocks*, which was a popular TV talent show in the U.K. at the time," remembers Dilley. "They were going through the rounds of the competition, and were really close to getting somewhere in it, and I sensed Kenny was wavering on *Star Wars*.

"I said, 'You've got this job on *Star Wars*, Kenny, and you've got to do it!' To which he replied, 'But we're on *Opportunity Knocks*!' It took a lot of persuading, but I finally got him to do this Artoo-Detoo thing."

▶

▶ **Dagobah Days**

As technology progressed and advances enabled the R2-D2 props to be remotely controlled more reliably, by the time *Star Wars: The Empire Strikes Back* (1980) rolled around Dilley found himself working with Baker less and less often. But, as he explains, the actor was still a pivotal part of the team, and essential in imbuing the droid with individuality. "Kenny wasn't in every single shot—like he pretty much was on the first film—but he was very important to the character.

"For example, he did all of the stuff on the bog planet of Dagobah, where Yoda was teaching Luke Skywalker the power of the Force. In one scene, Artoo was standing on the side of the swamp, and we wanted him to be reacting to what was going on in a big way. We wanted personality in that reaction shot from this droid—this machine—and the way to do that was to put Kenny Baker inside, bringing his personal movements into it. Kenny was great for stuff like that."

Speaking of Dagobah, if there's one place in the galaxy to which Dilley would happily never return, it's Yoda's swamp planet home.

"I remember that place well, because it played host to one of my most embarrassing moments ever in the motion-picture business," he confesses with a sheepish grin. "I was putting Artoo's head on Kenny Baker, and polishing it up. I finished what I was doing and said, 'You're okay, Kenny!', took one step backwards—and fell up to my waist into the slimy water! It was all set and ready for filming, beautiful, and so the whole crew wanted to shoot me! I have to admit, it was pretty embarrassing."

Dilley's time on *The Empire Strikes Back* was a bittersweet experience to some extent, as the film's original production designer (and Dilley's mentor) John Barry tragically passed away during filming. Norman Reynolds took over as production designer, and Dilley became

04 Building Luke's landspeeder at Lee International Film Studios in London.

05 The lansdpeeder takes shape.

06 The art department: (L-R) Roger Christian, Leslie Dilley, John Barry, Bill Welch, and Norman Reynolds.

"The whole crew wanted to shoot me!"

his art director. The shoot wasn't without its challenges—but this time, it was nothing to do with budgets or uncooperative droids. "I was going to Norway to start preparing the sets for the Hoth sequences, but when they came to take me to the airport, I was so ill, I couldn't go," says Dilley. "I was really sick with a bad throat, and I was choking and could hardly breathe. When I finally got well, Norman said, 'I can't send you out there to Norway, Les. If anything happened to you, I would be in real trouble!' So I stayed back and helped Norman out."

Having worked with many stellar directors including James Cameron and Steven Spielberg, Dilley— who still works as a production designer and art director in the industry at age 78—has fond memories of his involvement with the *Star Wars* saga, and of its creator. "I worked with George Lucas closely on the shooting of that movie," he says in conclusion, "and I found him to be a terrific, friendly guy with a great eye for filming." ☻

BY DAN MADSEN

THE REAL R2-D2...
KENNY BAKER

Although diminutive in size, Kenny Baker is a man of incredible eights when related to personality and character. This British-born actor is best known for adding the "human element" to one of the most famous robots in the world: R2-D2.

With a seemingly unending supply of good humor and charm, and the honest ability to win anyone over, it is not hard to see why this talented actor became one of the most popular characters-from the Star Wars *saga.*

Growing up small in a world full of tall people was not easy, but Kenny faced it head-on with a winning perspective on life and turned what some people would consider a disability into success and opportunity.

Acting and entertaining since he was 16 years old, Kenny has had a long and varied career as a performer, traveling all over the world and touring Great Britain in such shows as Snow White and the Seven Dwarfs.

But it was his diminutive size (three feet tall) even for a dwarf that inspired George Lucas to cast him for the role of R2-D2 since they needed someone very small to fit inside the robot. Kenny wasn't crazy, at first, about being trapped inside a moving mechanical apparatus. But after reading the script and witnessing first-hand George Lucas' unique vision, he admits that he "began to like the little fellow."

Although other mechanical Artoo units were developed for the Star Wars *films which didn't utilize Kenny inside, there is no doubt that Kenny Baker is unquestionably the personality behind the lovable robot.*

Living in London, England, Kenny keeps busy performing in various stage plays that tour Great Britain. He also anticipates R2-D2's return in the upcoming Star Wars *prequels and hopes to be involved with the new series of films.*

The official Star Wars Insider *sat down with Kenny recently and asked him to share with us some of his memories of working on the* Star Wars *trilogy.*

Kenny, what have you been doing lately to keep yourself busy?

I'm doing a pantomime stage play now of *Snow White and the Seven Dwarfs*. I'm playing Dopey. We travel all around England doing this. I've been with this company now for six years doing the same show. We only do it for about six or seven weeks each year but it's fun. I also did *Snow White and the Seven Dwarfs* on ice back in the '60s.

I recall years ago that you were involved in a group called the Minitones.

Yes, we came straight out of *Star Wars* and went straight to Harrah's in Lake Tahoe. We're not

doing that show anymore, though, because my partner, Jack Purvis, was in a car accident and became paralyzed. Jack played the head Jawa in the original *Star Wars*.

We had been doing the Minitones for over 30 years. It's hard for Jack now because he is paralyzed. It's tragic. He's mentally fine but, physically, he can't move. He's frustrated because the body doesn't work but the mind does. He's not going to get any better I'm afraid.

Do you have children?

Yes, I have two sons who both are of normal height. One of my sons works at Planet Hollywood in London. They have these restaurants all over the world now. In the front window of these places they have replicas of C-3PO and R2-D2. They have my name over Artoo and Anthony Daniels' name over Threepio.

George is now working on the early stages of the new *Star Wars* prequels. He's said before that the droids are the only continuing characters throughout the films.

Yes, that's what I've heard, too. You know, years ago, when I was in America and went to see my mother who lives near New Orleans, I was flying back to London and I picked up a *Time* magazine that had Darth Vader on the cover. Inside

that issue was an article by George saying that the only two characters to survive the whole series were the robots because they're not born and they don't die. So I'm hoping to be involved with the next three films.

I get a lot of fan mail still but most of the kids think I'm American. In fact, just about 10 minutes before this interview, I had a father and his son stop me down the street from my house and ask me if "I was Kenny Baker, the man who played R2-D2." Obviously, it's still very popular.

How early did you become involved in the entertainment industry?

It was in the 1950s. I was with a midget review that had 25 other little people. I was playing a harmonica, roller skating and a few other things. There was a lot of variety—it was really vaudeville. We traveled all over England, Wales and Scotland. I was only 16 at the time. I really wanted to be a commercial artist but I don't think I was talented enough. I got into show business and went from one show to the next.

I understand that both of your parents were of average height.

Yes, that's true. I am the only little person in my family. My wife was the same way.

As you were growing up what was the hardest thing to overcome being small?

There wasn't really anything hard to overcome, I just had to adapt to the situation. You just have to stand on stools to open doors and to turn on light switches and so on. It didn't really bother me. I went to a disabled boys school where everyone was disabled in one form or another. But we didn't even think about it. Then I went into show business with 20 other little people.

Was that when you realized that there were others like you in the world?

Well, there were a couple of other little people at my school but I didn't meet so many in one go. There were all ages in that show. I then did ice shows and eventually got into a version of *Snow White and the Seven Dwarfs* where there were seven dwarfs who could skate. I then did *Chu Chin Chow on Ice* and *Peter Pan on Ice* and even toured South Africa with these shows.

I then went into my cabaret show with Jack Purvis which we did for 30 years. When Jack and I played Harrah's in Lake Tahoe we met some really big people in show business: Sammy Davis, Jr., Crystal Gale, Bill Cosby, Willie Nelson, Wayne Newton, etc.

"We had no idea what [*Star Wars*] would become. We all thought it was going to be a lot of rubbish!"

How did you become involved with *Star Wars*?

I happened to be working in the London area and an agent phoned my agent and said that there was a guy in London looking for a little guy to play inside a robot. I don't know what transpired after that, but I was sent to the 20th Century-Fox head office in London for an interview. I actually came to the interview with my partner, Jack Purvis. I got the job right away because they wanted someone small to get into the robot because Carrie Fisher and Mark Hamill were small and they wanted a small robot. I said "I can't just walk into a movie and leave my partner stranded." They said, "Well, we have plenty of work for Jack," and they made him the head Jawa.

What was your first reaction when you found out you were going to play inside a robot?

I wasn't that crazy about it at first. I was doing television in England and I thought to myself that I would rather be a star on television here than stuck in a robot all over the world! I didn't really know the potential of the film at that time—nobody did!

Do you recall when you first saw the design for R2-D2?

Oh, yes. I always liked the look of the robot, it just wasn't very comfortable at first. They had screws going through the robot's head that stuck into my head. I then got wise and told them and they cut

off the screws and put rubber in the top of the head of the robot to stop it scratching my own head.

When you first got inside R2-D2 and they closed the head down, was it a bit claustrophobic?

I thought, "Oh, what have I got myself into?!" You couldn't see much inside, but there was a spy hole to see through. However, the bottom was open so that let a little light in. It wasn't really too bad. I just had to flick some switches and move the head around and wobble the body. The hardest thing was to keep up with everybody, and that's why they developed the remote-control robot. It could keep up with them, I couldn't move fast enough.

Do you recall the first scene you shot as R2-D2?

I think we were doing the scene out in the desert where Threepio and Artoo part ways. It was incredibly hot out there. After that we filmed the scene where Artoo is coming down the canyon and gets caught by the Jawas.

It's amazing to me to think back about the filming of *Star Wars*. We had no idea what it would become. We all thought it was going to be a lot of rubbish! It had all these strange names like Obi-Wan Kenobi and bizarre creatures. It was hard for me to understand, on the first movie, how I was a Rebel yet also a good guy. I didn't quite get it at first. Then we filmed *The Empire Strikes Back* and I understood.

Was the atmosphere on the set of *Empire* different since you all knew then how big *Star Wars* had become?

We all knew each other better by then and we knew we were part of something successful. The cast had been all around the world promoting the movie but I couldn't go because I was with my partner, Jack, working in cabaret in the United States. We missed out on all the good trips with all-expenses paid, stretch limos and big hotels. I did get to go to the Washington premiere for *Empire* and we all flew back on the Concord for the premiere in London with Princess Margaret.

Do you have any special memories from working on *Star Wars*?

Well, in the scene where the Jawas are trying to sell R2-D2 to Luke and his uncle, I was inside the robot and Jack was playing the head Jawa. There were all kinds of robots careening over the desert—about five or six. They were all charging around on the flat desert. It was near an oasis so there was water in the air. One robot crashed into me. Jack was yelling to me, "Lookout! There's a robot coming!" There was nothing I could do about it, it just crashed into me. It tipped me over. We had a lot of funny things happen to us.

What was the filming like in Tunisia?

We stayed at several different hotels and we would wander around when we weren't filming because there was no television, no radio or anything! It was a very primitive area—there wasn't even glass in the windows of our hotel rooms—it looked like biblical times! One day, I was walking along the street, there was no pavement, it was all dirt, and Alec Guinness came along in a Mercedes and said, "What are you doing?" And I said, "Nothing, really." He said, "You want to see an oasis?" I said, "Yeah," so I jumped in the car and I went with he and his wife to see an oasis. That was a nice trip. They are both lovely people. But there was really nothing to do in these places. The money you would get while filming there had to be spent there because you couldn't spend it anywhere else.

Did you work with Harrison Ford?

Oh, yes. They had the large model of the *Millennium Falcon* in the hangar on one of the soundstages in London. It was a massive thing. My kids were little at that time so I took them to see the sets which were on eight stages. Harrison Ford said, "I'll take you around," and took us to see the *Millennium Falcon*. One of my boys said to Harrison, "what will we call you?" They couldn't get their tongues to say Harrison Ford. It was too hard of a name to pronounce at their age. He said, "Oh, just call me peaches!" [Laughter] And to this day, my boys call Harrison "peaches."

Is there anything special you recall about the filming of *Empire* or *Jedi*?

I wasn't involved in the filming in Norway for *Empire*. It's hard to remember specific events because I get the films mixed up sometimes. But I do remember filming out in the Redwoods in California for *Jedi*. We were in the trees and someone noticed a huge branch that was sticking across

another branch—it had been blown off. It was perched between two other branches. These trees were about 250 feet high. If that branch had been blown off by the wind it would have come down like a spear and could have been serious.

They brought in two sharpshooters with rifles and tried to shoot it down but with no luck. The bullets went right through it

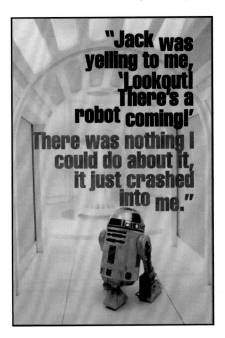

"Jack was yelling to me, 'Lookout! There's a robot coming!' There was nothing I could do about it, it just crashed into me."

because it was rotten wood. In the end, they had to move the whole set because they could not get this huge branch down and they didn't want any accidents. They couldn't risk this six- or seven-foot-long branch falling down 200 or 300 feet on the cast and crew. It was just too risky. It could have killed someone.

I wish that they had utilized me more on *Jedi*. The director, Richard Marquand, told me, before we started filming, that he wanted to really utilize me because George liked it more when I was in R2-D2 because it came to life. But they still didn't use me that much. I actually spent more time on *Jedi* working with the makeup people trying to get the Ewoks' eyes right. I spent most of that movie in the Stuart Freeborn makeup and special effects department trying to get the eyes of the Ewoks to blink. It wasn't easy—it was hard work. I was like the prototype Ewok.

Do you recall working with George Lucas on the first film?

Out of all the directors, I liked George the best. Irvin Kershner was very funny. He

reminded me of Kermit the frog because he sounded like him. I didn't get along with Richard Marquand as well. I don't know why. He didn't seem to use me very much. But with George Lucas as the director you always knew what he wanted. He was very clear and precise. He knew exactly what he wanted. I like that.

But George had the vision of *Star Wars* in his head—he knew it forwards and backwards. I used to sit with George and have dinner when we were filming *Star Wars*. We usually wouldn't chat about the film, we would talk about other things. However, he was always preoccupied with the movies so you didn't get a lot of talk out of him. But I got along very well with both George and Irvin Kershner.

C-3PO and R2-D2 are partners on screen. Would you describe your relationship with Anthony Daniels the same way?

We are not exactly close. I found him to not be an easy guy to get close to. We didn't argue or anything but we were not close friends. I didn't really mix with him socially. Maybe if we are both in the new *Star Wars* movies we will have an opportunity to get to know each other better and we'll have a lot more to relate to. I think the robots will be a good link from the previous movies to these new ones. It will help introduce people to the new films by giving them a bit of something they're used to. I hope they utilize me in the new films.

Another movie you did which was very popular was *Time Bandits*.

That was good fun! I was involved in everything in that movie because we [the little people] were the stars of the movie. To be honest, that was more fun than *Star Wars*. *Star Wars* was more difficult for me to do because I didn't know what it was all about but *Time Bandits* I understood and was just good fun to film. I wish we could have done more of those but the filmmakers wanted to go on to other things. We went all over England to film *Time Bandits*. Jack Purvis played Wally and I played Fidget. The late David Rappaport was in the film as well.

Kenny, you've worked on some timeless films and we appreciate you taking time out for the *Star Wars Insider* to talk about your *Star Wars* experiences.

Well, thank you. I look forward to sharing more experiences with you if I'm in the new *Star Wars* films ... and I love to hear from the *Star Wars* fans! ☺

IN MEMORIAM
KENNY BAKER

1934 — 2016

KENNY BAKER, THE MAN WHO GAVE LIFE AND SOUL TO R2-D2 FROM 1977'S *STAR WARS* THROUGH TO 2005'S *REVENGE OF THE SITH*, HAS DIED AT THE AGE OF 81.

Born Kenneth George Baker on August 24, 1934, in Solihull near Birmingham, England, his career as an entertainer began in 1951 at age 17 when he was invited to join a theatrical troupe. That led to a brief stint with the circus, and then a part in Snow White with Holiday On Ice—the first of many appearances on frozen water. Baker formed a close friendship with fellow little person Jack Purvis, and together the pair developed the Mini-Tones, a stage act they performed until Purvis' death in November 1997.

Baker's first film appearance was in the 1960 Hammer film *Circus of Horrors*, directed by Sidney Hayers. U.K. television appearances in *Man of the World* (1962) and *Dave Allen at Large* (1975) followed, before he was cast as R2-D2 in George Lucas' original *Star Wars* movie (1977).

THE HEART OF R2-D2

Baker became famous for his role as the little astromech droid, despite never being seen on screen. Working inside R2 when internal movement was required, Baker imbued the prop with his own unmistakable character. When R2 was excited, that was Kenny. When he was sad, that was Kenny. Interviewed in 2005, he looked back fondly on his *Star Wars* experience:

"It was an utter explosion around the world. Nothing like it had been seen before. All the merchandise, toys... It was crazy. Fan-mail was pouring in for everyone, and we were being asked for interviews all over the world. People really did take the two robots to their hearts, which was great for Anthony [Daniels, C-3PO] and me. In a sense, R2 really is the pace-keeper of the first movie."

Baker continued to appear in other projects alongside his *Star Wars* work, including *Wombling Free* (1978), based on the popular children's books by

Elisabeth Beresford, in which he played Bungo alongside his wife, Eileen Baker, as Tobermory. Throughout the 1980s, he performed in high-profile film productions such as David Lynch's *The Elephant Man* (1980), *Flash Gordon* (1980), *Time Bandits* (1981, with Jack Purvis), *Amadeus* (1984), Jim Henson's *Labyrinth* (1986), and *Willow* (1988, with Purvis and Warwick Davis).

In the *Star Wars* galaxy, he first reprised his role as R2 in *The Star Wars Holiday Special* in 1978, before immortalizing the droid in cement outside Grauman's Chinese Theatre, and appearing on *The Muppet Show* alongside *Star Wars* co-stars Mark Hamill, Anthony Daniels, and Peter Mayhew in 1980. In *The Empire Strikes Back* (1980) he brought R2 back to the big screen, and he also played a GONK droid (or power droid, if you please). The movie was his favorite, both as a filmmaking experience and as a chapter in the *Star Wars* saga.

"[*Empire Strikes Back* director] Irvin Kershner and I got on very well on set," Baker recalled. "He was such a genuine, nice man. Obviously the first *Star Wars* had been massive, so we all knew this was something to be part of. *Empire* is the darkest chapter, with much more depth to the story and characters."

The year 1983 saw Kenny in a dual role once again: back in action as R2, as well as stealing scenes and a speeder bike as heroic Ewok Paploo in *Return of the Jedi*. After *Jedi,* it was another four years before he climbed inside the astromech once again, to play R2 in the Star Tours theme park attraction. More than a decade later, he returned to the role three more times: in *The Phantom Menace, Attack of the Clones,* and *Revenge of the Sith.*

By the time *The Force Awakens* started filming in 2014, Baker was not well enough to physically portray R2, so instead served as a consultant, sharing his decades of wisdom with the filmmakers. His final performance was in the 2013 short film *One Night At The Aristo.*

Kenny Baker was a convention staple, traveling the globe to attend shows in Europe, the United States, and beyond. His last appearance was at the London Film & Comic Con on July 31, 2016, where he signed autographs for his many fans.

SAYING GOODBYE

Since his passing, Kenny Baker's colleagues have lined up to pay their respects.

His friend of 40 years, Peter Mayhew (Chewbacca), said: "Cherish the times of your life. Here's to you Kenny Baker. The man I made so many memories with, swapped stories with, entertained with, and carried to his hotel room at the end of the night!"

Mark Hamill (Luke Skywalker), tweeted, "Goodbye Kenny Baker. A lifelong loyal friend—I loved his optimism and determination. He WAS the droid I was looking for!"

Lucasfilm president Kathleen Kennedy said, "We're all saddened to learn of Kenny's passing. There is no *Star Wars* without R2-D2, and Kenny defined who R2-D2 was and is. He will be greatly missed."

Jeremy Bulloch (Boba Fett) recalled Baker's love of meeting the fans. "He was an amazing person who only two weeks ago was greeting fans and signing autographs. We will all miss him greatly— what a superstar he was."

Star Wars creator George Lucas also paid tribute: "Kenny Baker was a real gentleman as well as an incredible trooper who always worked hard under difficult circumstances. A talented vaudevillian who could always make everybody laugh, Kenny was truly the heart and soul of R2-D2 and will be missed by all his fans and everyone who knew him."

Everyone at *Star Wars Insider* sends their condolences to Kenny's family, colleagues, friends, and countless fans. He will be much missed but never forgotten. ☙

The Droids o

R ampaging robots were the foot soldiers of *The Phantom Menace*, and once again in *Attack of the Clones* the bad guys have employed a factory-made army to do their dirty work. This time, droidekas and battle droids have been joined by floating assassins, intelligent tanks, and bigger, beefier super battle droids. In light of the newcomers' armour-piercing missiles and rapid-fire blaster cannons, one thing is clear -these guys have obviously never heard of Asimov's First Law of Robotics.

Nevertheless, the killer droids of Star Wars can't really be considered evil. Evil cannot exist without intent, and these push-button warriors simply carry out the wishes of their more sinister masters. (When the battle droids in Episode I disengaged from their master control signal, they went as limp as wet noodles.) Just the same, it's probably overstating the case to say, "droids don't kill sentients, sentients kill sentients." The few Gungan soldiers who survived the Battle of Naboo might disagree.

f Episode II

by Daniel Wallace

It stands to reason that, if droids can be programmed to kill, they can also be programmed to perform more benign tasks. Most of the droids populating the Star Wars galaxy are little more than automated tools. more mindless of these robots, don't choose their stations in life any more than a toaster elects to make toast.

Droids in Star Wars have never been mere appliances, though. From the moment of their screen debut in a blockade-runner's hallway, it was obvious that R2-D2 and C-3PO were fully realized characters. Oroid

personalities develop when the automatons go too long without memory wipes. Their processors start to catalogue life experiences and soon generate a self-aware consciousness complete with personality quirks. "Aware droids" include 2-1B, the Rebellion's soothing medical unit from The Empire Strikes Back. In Attack of the Clones, Obi-Wan's astromech droid R4--Pl 7 continues the tradition of valiant droids.

Deadly, passive, or heroic, the droids of Episode II have a silicon style all their own.

ASN-121
(Zam Wesell's Assassin Droid)

The first direct contact between villains and heroes in *The Empire Strikes Back* is through a mechanized stand-in, namely a spider-eyed Imperial probe droid. This scenario is echoed in Attack of the Clones, itself the middle episode of a trilogy. The ASN-121 Assassin/Sentry droid is smaller than Empire's probe droid, but travels in a similar fashion on an anti-gravity repulsorlift cushion. With its dagger-like cooling vanes, the droid's silhouette resembles that of an Imperial TIE fighter.

The ASN-121 is similar to another *Star Wars* droid, Darth Maui's ball-shaped seeker, in that it has no built-in weaponry. Just like Maui's Sith droid, the ASN- 121 boasts a universal tool mount that can accommodate any number of lethal devices. The final array varies according to the parameters of the mission, but ASN droids used for assassinations commonly carry glasscutters, flame projectors, poison gas sprayers, durasteel drills, long-range blasters, or canisters of kouhuns or other venomous insects. When ASN droids are used for spying or sentry duty, they might carry heat sensors, eavesdropping pickups, stinger blasters, harpoon guns, or tangle nets. If anyone gets too close, the droid can electrically charge its outer shell in a particularly shocking method of self-defence.

The long barrel of her sniper rifle is evidence that Zam Wesell prefers to hit her targets from a safe distance. The ASN-121 is perfect for Wesell's needs, so small that it escapes casual notice and so quiet that it won't even wake a light sleeper (unlike that probe droid from Empire, who seemed to mumble something like "man the defender, defender in the space" everywhere he went). It packs enough power in its fusion generator to scale the highest Coruscant towers and to boost through rush-hour traffic, not to mention its impressive ability to support the extra 63 kilograms of an unexpected Jedi hitchhiker.

ASN-121 Assassin/

R4-P17
(Obi-Wan's
Astromech)

Okay, Mister "Don't-Seem-To-Remember-Ever-Owning-A-Droid," time to fess up. R4-P17 is the cute astromech navigator for Obi-Wan's Jedi starfighter, and the droid and the Jedi Knight have several scenes together in *Attack of the Clones*. In defence of the truth-challenged Kenobi, however, the starfighter and its plug-in counterpart are the property of the Jedi Temple, and therefore -at the risk of invoking the "certain point of view" defence -Old Ben's statement in *A New Hope* is technically true, so far.

Astromech droids have appeared in every episode of the Star Wars saga to date, and that's not even counting astromech hero R2-D2's turns in the spotlight. As readers of *The Essential Guide to Droids* know, the various models of Industrial Automaton's R-series can be identified by their caps.

R2s have domes above their necklines, R3s sport see-through domes, R4s have truncated cones, and RSs have heads that resemble inverted flowerpots. That knowledge, however, won't help you identify R4-Pl 7's curious pedigree.

According to *Episode II Incredible Cross Sections*, R4-P 17 began his operational life as a cone-headed R4 until a malfunctioning trash compactor at the Gyndine shipyards accordianed him into a mini-droid. Anakin Skywalker found the crumpled wreck while inspecting the shipyard's modifications to the Jedi starfighter, replaced the ruined head with an R2's cupola, and used his skills at droid reconstruction to save the ailing R4 from the scrap heap. Restored to perfect working order -but now much shorter -R4-P17 became the prototype for other half-sized astromech droids to be fused into the Jedi starfighter's narrow fuselage. R4's unfortunate trip through the garbage masher had created a new market niche

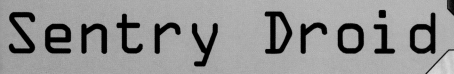

RIC-920
(Rickshaw Droid)

Two-wheeled vehicles pulled by runners, rickshaws (from the Japanese jinrikisha, meaning human-powered vehicle) have been used in Asia as taxis for over 130 years. With the rickshaw droid, *Attack of the Clones'* designers have once again followed a uniquely *Star Wars* road - take an old object (a longsword, a chariot, a World War II fighter plane) and recast it in a fantastic light while retaining its basic functionality. Is a rickshaw the most efficient configuration for an anti-gravity vehicle? Probably not, but neither is a lightsaber the most logical way to harness an energy beam that can cut through anything. These idiosyncratic fantasy elements are what give *Star Wars* its space-opera reality - familiar, yet strange - that we want to visit again and again.

Conceived by George Lucas as a way to convey Anakin and Pad me through the streets of Mos Espa, the rickshaw droid came to life through the imagination of designer Marc Gabbana. Over several iterations, the draft droid became shorter and narrower, and Gabbana gave it a two-piece neck to reduce the similarities to a certain long-necked Extra-Terrestrial who had a cameo in *The Phantom Menace*'s senate scene. The oversized, unicycle wheel, on the other hand, was a part of the rickshaw droid's design from the beginning.

RIC-920, as the rickshaw droid has since been dubbed, is a tough little number built to withstand the gritty sandwhirls of Tatooine. According to *The Episode II Visual Dictionary*, these "unipod droids" haven't changed in centuries.

Among this class of automatons, simplicity of design is matched by simplicity of intellect, so an owner who runs his droids for months without a single break down has little cause to complain that his workers don't know a chessboard from a chainsaw.

RIC-920's operational life revolves around getting paying passengers around the city as straightforwardly as possible (unless its owner programmes in a little deliberate waywardness to drive up fares). The droid's central processor contains street maps and situational-awareness circuitry, while its narrow face is dominated by a broadcast speaker and a tiny "ear" where his mouth should be. His claw-like, three-fingered grippers can perform simple maintenance tasks when taxi duty isn't calling. The balance gyro in RIC's belly is perhaps its most vital piece of equipment, maintaining its equilibrium even when lurching, braking, and cornering while towing the mass of a fully laden rickshaw cart.

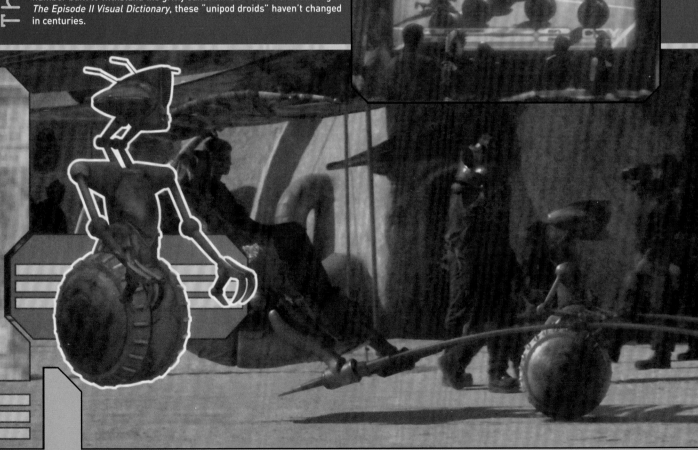

RIC-920 Rickshaw

Super Battle Droid

"They all broken," said Jar Jar, when he saw the Trade Federation's battle droids switch off and crumple to pieces on the grass. Had super battle droids been present at Battle of Naboo, however, the Gungan army might not have survived long enough to sound the retreat. A hundred times more deadly than their progenitors, super battle droids are the newest weapon in the Trade Federation's growing arsenal.

The humiliating collapse of his mechanized army on the plains of Naboo convinced Trade Federation viceroy Nute Gunray to open his pocketbook and shell out the credits for better soldiers. While his lawyers kept him out of prison for his part in the Naboo invasion, his engineers determined what improvements should be made to the bare-bones design of the stock battle droid. They recommended a heavily armoured trooper that would be more resilient to blaster fire and less dependent on the guiding force of the master control signal.

Separatist leader Count Dooku arranged for the production of these robo-killers in the foundries of Geonosis. Nearly a decade after the defeat of automated armies on Naboo, the first super battle droid rolled off the steamshrouded assembly lines. Upon seeing a demonstration of the new droids' destructive power, the penny-pinching Gunray complained that their firing accuracy left something to be desired. Geonosian leader Poggle the Lesser countered by noting the design improvements built into the super battle droid, calling his factory output "the finest army in the galaxy."

Super battle droids look a lot like battle droids, and both of them bear a strong resemblance to the Geonosian species. The similarities are intentional, for the two products are produced by Geonosian engineers at Baktoid Combat Automata plants across the Rim. Fearful victims facing a Trade Federation battalion for the first time have also noted the battle droids' resemblance to dried humanoid skeletons.

Barrel-chested and broad-shouldered, super battle droids are much less likely to be mistaken for skeletons than their spindly brethren.

Though their inner structures are, in fact recycled battle droid frames, their torsos are reinforced with cumbrous acertron armour that protects their sensitive power units and signal receptors. This added bulk prevents super battle droids from folding up on troop transport racks, but it makes them much tougher against concentrated small-arms fire.

The hands of super battle droids look like metal mittens. Their lack of manipulative digits makes the droids useless for manual labour, but they were never designed for any job other than killing. A super battle droid can fire a blaster rifle by activating an "impulse transmitter" wired into its clumsy hands (as opposed to twitching a trigger finger), but usually it deals death from the double-barreled blaster cannons built into each forearm.

Considering the number of battle droids that lost their heads to Jedi lightsabers during the Naboo conflict, the low-profile noggin of the super battle droid might be the most sensible improvement. With its head a mere swelling of equipment above the brawny body, a super battle droid looks a bit like a turtle hiding inside its shell. This configuration gives the super battle droid extra protection for its logic centre and sensor package. It also provides an eerily inhuman silhouette that is much more intimidating than anything developed by the Trade Federation to date.

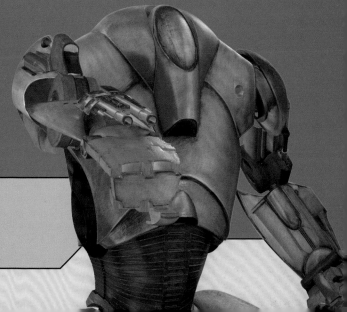

Spider droids

Mercantile Murderers

Count Dooku has lured powerful mercantile interests to the secessionist banner by promising lower taxes and the elimination of trade barriers. The Trade Federation's droid army is notorious to anyone who saw The Phantom Menace. This time around, however, we learn that the galaxy's other business monopolies have built their own robotic killers and aren't shy about using them in defence of their profit statements. *The Episode II Visual Dictionary* provides a close look at these weapons of industry.

The Corporate Alliance is a negotiating body responsible for brokering deals between the galaxy's biggest commercial operations. Headed by Passel Argente, the Corporate Alliance enforces its will with a legion of unstoppable tank droids. Each CA tank droid rolls on a central treaded tire with outrigger wheels for stability. Blaster cannons jut out from the armoured torso, while reception antennae receive orders from the CA central command computer.

Spider droids scuttle through crags and craters on planets under the sway of the Commerce Guild. This conglomerate, which includes the Mining Guild mentioned by Princess Leia in Empire, has a stranglehold on excavating and drilling operations throughout the Republic. Small mines that don't pay the requisite Guild tributes receive a visit from laser-spitting spider droids dispatched by Guild Presidente Shu Mai. A typical Guild spider droid homes in on its targets with a sensor dish hanging from its low-slung body, then fires deadly energy darts from the cannon hidden in the centre of the dish. When fearful victims hole up in their mining tunnels in hope of escape, the Commerce Guild sends in miniature, burrowing spider droids, each equipped with infrared sensors.

The droids commanded by the InterGalactic Banking Clan could be the most dangerous of all. From his headquarters on Muunilinst, IBC chief executive San Hill pragmatically extends financing to parties on both sides of a political conflict - but if one of those parties dares to default on an IBC loan, it's time to send in the Hailfire droids. Hailfire droids are monstrous assault 'mechs, groaning with weaponry and capable of terrifying speed with their huge hoop wheels. Two fanlike pods extend from the droid's compact body, each stuffed with dozens of blistering hailfire missiles. The mere sight of the Hailfire droid's single burning red eye has been known to make IBC opponents break and run. 🌀

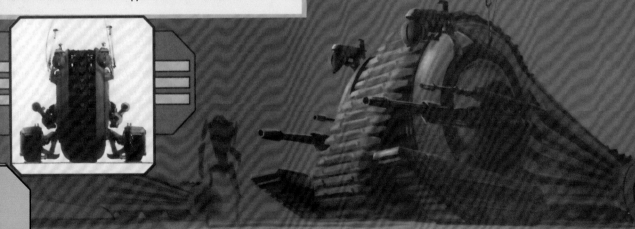

CA TANK droid*

*Appears off-screen in *Star Wars: Episode II Attack of the Clones.*

Um, hello

There can be nothing more cruel for an artiste than for that person (she/he or perhaps he/she - this is a PC column, remember - though what my personal computer has to do with it, I'm not sure - abbreviations can get very confusing - look at C-3PO - what does it mean? But I'm sure you'll understand *TNWCIEIOTIFTMIC* - it saves space *) to slave away, put in heart and soul, finally to see their fruits squashed into oblivion underfoot. Not merely *Not Wanted On Voyage*. NOT WANTED AT ALL! Very sad making. But this I have escaped - thus far at least - in THE NEW WONDER COLUMN. As to the rest of my life, that is another chapter - well, page. OK, paragraph. Anyway, THE NEW WONDER COLUMN seems to have avoided the great trash can in the sky and, to some extent, the ~~censor's~~ editor's blue pencil. (What pencil?—Ed) I used to quite like editors before all this started. I learned that they can take a pile of mediocrity (on which you have laboured, as above) and can make you look so much better by chopping you up and leaving out the bad bits, like Dr Frankenstein - on a good day. But oh, the horror of that phrase, THE CUTTING ROOM FLOOR - the place we all reach, sooner or later. I have been there - and survived - for now.

So remember! You <u>might</u> see it here first ....

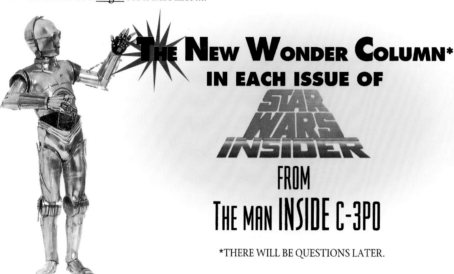

THE NEW WONDER COLUMN*
IN EACH ISSUE OF
STAR WARS INSIDER
FROM
THE MAN INSIDE C-3PO

*THERE WILL BE QUESTIONS LATER.

Gosh!

I made it!

Far from being edited out of *Star Wars* in any way, long after we'd finished filming, I actually recorded some <u>extra</u> lines, by myself in a broom cupboard in London. The resulting tape was biked to the airport to be inserted somewhere in LA (of course, I mean inserted in *the movie* in a studio somewhere ...etc - I was just making the sentence a bit shorter to save paper but now realise that I might have confused you - I certainly confused me). If you listen carefully there is a slight acoustic mismatch behind the new lines. It's in the Control Room scene. I think it's where I, sorry, Threepio, no, me, I say, *The tractor beam is coupled to the main reactor in seven locations.* I seem to remember that SOMEONE and <u>certainly not</u> THE MAN RESPONSIBLE FOR EVERYTHING had forgotten to say what a *tractor beam* was actually <u>for</u> and the scene could have sounded like an item from *Farming For Beginners*. So they snuck in the explanation via me/him. What I

Out of control!

had originally said was something like, *Oh my goodness* or possibly *if we could just get on with this scene then I can take off this ridiculous costume and go home and play Shakespeare in front of the mirror.*

But no, sometimes there isn't room for everything and everyone that got shot (moviewise, that is) to make it to the screen and even with the tightest shooting ratio (that's a technical phrase that I once heard and have always wanted to throw into a conversation but somehow I've never met anyone to whom it might be a relevant remark - until now - hopefully. But what does it mean? - (Whilst we're at it, what does *crossing the line* mean and *pump the dolly* ? And what <u>does</u> the *best boy* actually do that's better than anyone else?) (Must be rather odd when people ask you what you do for a living and you reply *I'm a best boy*. Bet that shuts them up! Mind you, when I tell people what I do for a living, it has the same effect.) (Then there's a whole list of other words I'd eventually like to find a use for, like pulchritudinous and verisimilitude and plectrum - but perhaps another time.) Anyway, where was I - oh yes - some dearly loved items can get left out of even the humblest movie - not that humble is an option at Lucasland - ever - OK!

Frozen out!

I suppose you might describe the trilogy as a great omelette *(see Cantina Cuisine No 98 for more great omelette ideas)* into which many eggs must be cracked but some get dropped on the floor and left there. But when I spotted this about to happen to some footage of me in *TESB*, towards the end of my first entrance scene - you know, when I'm telling-off Artoo for warming up the Princess's ice chamber - I approached Paul Hirsch, the editor, in a fit of artistic pique. I had an axe to grind. Paul sat there in the murk of the cutting room. His hands, wrapped in white cotton gloves, punctuated the shadows like those of some scrupulous serial killer. He lurked darkly against bins of film strips, including some of my favourites - strips of me. I faced him. *Why,* I boldly demanded, glancing nervously at THE FLOOR in case I was about to crush myself underfoot, *why, when nothing of my gilded performance had ever been edited out before, had he removed the end of the scene where I had been magnificently angry with Artoo and grand. How could he cut that and WHY?* Silence. Nothing. Then suddenly a white glove moved towards me. Blinding light in my eyes. *You were too angry and too grand,* Paul smiled and reangled the desk lamp to illuminate THE FLOOR. Was he making a point? I saw it was completely clean. *It's the first time we see you in this movie,* he said. *That angry - where do you go from there?* Oh, I said. I think he was right. I hate that kind of thing.

Wipe to:

INTERIOR TRASH COMPACTOR: DAY Our gallant blond hero and friends are souping about in assorted debris. The walls are about to close in, crushing out all life as we know it, but we don't know that yet because it's on the next page. Suddenly. strange stirrings underfoot. Liquids bubble. Blond hero disappears beneath boiling minestrone, sucked below by fearsome and utterly terrifying ... what? The studio sculptors and designers had thought and created for weeks. On the way from my dressing room I had frequently walked past a giant, steel armed, mucus green tentacle, a football pitch long. Some design error perhaps, since the scene was set in the rather small Compactor and not actually on a sports field. So then came Idea No.2. Huge! Ovoid! BROWN! We stared at it. SOMEONE and obviously not THE MAN RESPONSIBLE FOR EVERYTHING said it looked like a ....What was the word .... I think it began with a 't.' Anyway, that idea hit the pan. And what did we get? A fearsome and utterly terrifying ... mini periscope and a yard of plastic squid. Later, I saw the big brown thing massively but forlornly dumped on the back lot. I think THE MAN RESPONSIBLE FOR EVERYTHING was right, too!

In the soup!

But I digress (how unlike him, you cry) because those items never got onto film, unlike - TATOOINE DESERT: DAY Band of noble heroes track manfully or in one case, womanfully, through blinding sandstorms whipped by offshore galactic winds as they struggle to the entry ramp of the *Millennium Falcon*. Unspoken emotions fill the eyes of the sensitive but fearless group. We know what dangers lie ahead. Will they ever meet again? We can only guess how they feel. We care. We do.

So there we were in the arid wastes of England's Elstree studios again, but this time on Stage 2. The walls, painted a sandy - well, sand colour, I suppose, blended with the tons of real sand spread on the floor. In one corner stood the *Millennium Falcon*, symbol of freedom, truth and a million merchandise items. On the other side of the stage, were huddled rows of bins filled with sand and pow-

Where are we?

lunch. It worked. The engines still pounded but I could see - just. I could see Camera B right there in front of me where it shouldn't have been. Its deafened clapper-loader was kneeling before the lens, still waiting to mark his slate and as disoriented as was I, especially as he now saw me speeding out of the gloom, clearly about to road-accident him severely. Forgetting the Force, he panicked and dived left but was really saved from a good squashing by a scenic rock which fate or the set designer had placed between us. I never saw the rock, not even after I had careened over it and was lying pancaked on the sand at his knees. I never did make it to the *Falcon*. Like me, the scene made it - to THE FLOOR.

But in happier times, when I first saw *Star Wars*, I was amazed to see Threepio (there is no way round that, I'm afraid) wandering about endlessly at the beginning of the

der From them, crinkled tubes of silver trunking snaked upward on a scaffold to vent themselves in front of an iron curtain of propeller blades, looking like an antique air force, smacked cartoon-like into an invisible wall, and numerous enough to vacuum a vertical lift to the binned debris and very likely, the building itself. I was probably just being a wimp, but if there was nothing to fear, why were all the other actors being heavily muffled, goggled and protected from the oncoming onslaught? *The pieces of your suit will provide protection*, they said. *What about the bits between the pieces?* I said. *What bits?* they said. *Bits of me*, I said. *Oh*, they said.

All we had to do was walk towards the *Falcon's* ramp in a semicircle, in a group, in a sand storm and say *Goodbye* and *May the Force be with You*. Easy. Two cameras. Camera A by the *Falcon* and B, way off in no-man's-land, for a wide shot. Rehearsal discussion finished, I trudged through the sand to our start position near the bins, under the menacing blades. The normally petite Carrie looked like Captain Doughboy in her bulky protective wrappings, whilst Harrison (if it was he) was mummified to anonymity behind assorted bandannas, hoods and goggles. Which left me wondering whether the small piece of gauze taped over the mouth, on the inside of my mask was quite the thing. Would it actually stop me being choked to an early obituary? Hopefully.

"*ROLL CAMERAS A AND B. START THE FANS. MAR........*" That was the last I heard - apart from the magnificent roaring of a hundred planeless propellers trying to take off. The sound was deafening to anything other than itself - I do not exaggerate (I hate that kind of thing, too) - so I was left only with my sight to know that the others had begun to move off in a semicircle as planned. I set out after them but, curse my metal body, I wasn't fast enough. Where had they gone? I began to search. The air was solid with noise and thick with the choking junk spewing out of the tubes. Earth and sky merged into one mass of sensory deprivation (though I could still hear, unfortunately). With no compass bearings, I was flying blind, edging along in my suit, a dense sandy coloured fog clouding any sense of time or space, and that was on the inside. Forget unspoken emotions filling my eyes - I was working in the same room as Mount St Helens. But the show must go on. I had to keep moving.

To clear the gels they had thoughtfully stuck over the eye holes, I blew upwards, bouncing my breath off the interior of the mask and onto the eyes, thankful that I hadn't eaten the garlic bread for

Where are you? Come to that, where am I?

movie. Enter desert right, exit desert left, enter right again, almost as if I were whipping round the back of the screen, like a hard-up theatre group trying to present a whole army with five increasingly breathless actors. The intercutting scenes in the coffee bar on Tatooine that had so been beautifully acted and painstakingly filmed at Elstree had been assigned to the oblivion of THE FLOOR because, I suppose George Lucas couldn't bear to have anything interrupt my brilliant performance. Quite right too. Shame though, because there was a rather pretty girl in those scenes and some years later she dated famous British royal, PRINCE ANDREW for a while. George really blew that one. Could have been Lord George by now. Or even King George. He was in a movie. Mad though.

Just like the time when the wampa ... Oh look. Mickey's little hand is nearly touching his big one, so I think that must mean it's time to say: *That's all folks!*

(Am I'm confusing my cartoons - or am I just confusing? What do you think?)
(Don't push me!—Ed)
PS Who's Ed ?

London, England

Um, hello

What you may not appreciate is the chain of being that connects the ridiculous and unconsidered jottings of my brain to your eyes at this very moment. (Bit of a brain teaser here. I'm writing this NOW and you are reading this NOW. *Now, now,* I hear you cry, *how can this be?* When I get my brain around it, I shall tell you). Anyway, this and other thoughts emanate from where my brain ought to be, through my fingers onto my PC onto my printer onto my fax in London onto the editor's desk in Colorado onto Lucasfilm's desk in Marin County onto a disc in London onto a desk in Colorado onto a layout desk in Minnesota back to me in London (hold on, we're nearly there) onto film and onto a printing press in Wisconsin onto a distributor's pallet onto a plane in anywhere into your mailmale's (or mailfemale's) hand where you live and through your letter box where you see this in all its glory. All for THIS! Is this IT? Is it worth it? Before you answer that, I should point out that I have feelings which can be wounded. For instance: you may remember that I am using abbreviations to save space and therefore, paper. After all, magazines do not grow on trees. Certainly WONDER COLUMNS don't. So last time, I faxed-off my efforts under the ecologically sound heading - USE LESS PAPER. I'm sure you'll agree that we should. But somewhere along the above marathon trail, this simple, caring message had been subtly changed. It eventually returned to me in its printed, proof state, woundingly hurtful. I'm sure it was an accident. I think it was. But maybe not. And maybe you too think this is a *useless* piece of paper.

But if you do - remember! You saw it here first ....

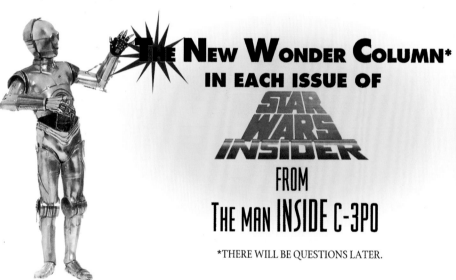

THE NEW WONDER COLUMN*
IN EACH ISSUE OF
STAR WARS INSIDER
FROM
THE MAN INSIDE C-3PO

*THERE WILL BE QUESTIONS LATER.

Gosh!

Perhaps you have found a use for it after all. In England they would wrap deep fried fish and chips in stuff like this. A great leveler, to have your deepest thoughts elevated to the rank of a fast food wrapper, but now that foaming polystyrene and plastic are decorating the streets, poor, primitive old paper is left to a fate like me writing on it (although I can think of even a worse one). However I am now - at last - reminded of why I have got paper on the brain.

You know how the fans of my NEW WONDER COLUMN write to me - well this week, it was the turn of the other one, John Haller to ask me a question. John, as I'm sure you remember, lives in Cold Spring, KY and yet still finds time to ponder those ancient riddles that tease greater brains than mine. But for once I know the answer. I was there. I confess. I was the one what done it.

MIX TO:

INTERIOR ICE CAVERN: HOTH: DAY. Enter Threepio in a hurry. Lots of breathless acting. Actually I wasn't acting. I was breath-

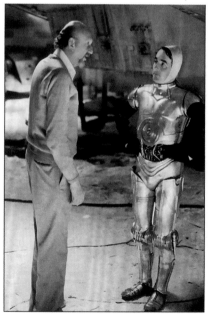

MFIK and ME

less. It was a tight fit in there - not the cavern, the suit. Anyway, shimmying between icy walls glistening with fake coolth, Threepio races towards camera, fleeing from unknown terrors. He pauses, glancing behind. Thinks. Slides right and with a deft swipe of his hand rips a red and yellow sign from the door set in the cavern wall. A look of smugness crosses his gilded features before he skids out of shot clutching the torn paper. *CUT,* said MY FRIEND IRVIN KIRSHNER. And Yes, it was.

So what was all that about and where? You missed it? Well it's survival of the fittest in Cold Springs, KY, so no surprise that eagle-eyed John noted that, whereas this scene made it to the trailer of *ESB*, it didn't make the final cut. Was it something I said? They never expressed any displeasure at my work - not to my face anyway. Was I a failure? Wasn't my ripping up to scratch ? (actually it did go better in Take 1 than Take 2 but that is irrelevant).

What got me was that they had abandoned

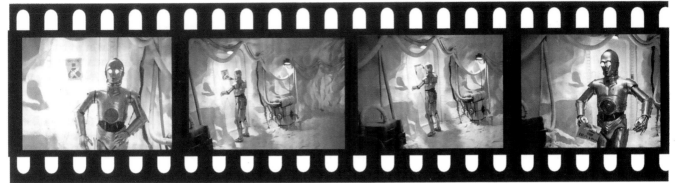

Think...   Aim...   Rip...   Smug...

a scene to THE FLOOR (See Number 3 of TNWCIEIOTIFTMIC for an in-depth look at THE FLOOR), a scene in which I had actually managed to tear a piece of paper off a door. *So what?* you cry. *Piece of paper? Piece of cake!* Have you any idea how inflexible Threepio's hands are! Just about capable of clubbing a careless cameraman but when it comes to the finer things of life like picking out needlepoint or just picking your nose - USELESS. They have all the flexibility and, with Threepio's re-stricted vision, all the accuracy of those amusement arcade cranes standing in their miniature, brightly lit world of gold coloured watches and unprecious rings. You urgently twist the dislocated controls to aim the limp metal jaws over your chosen prize. They drop emphatically over it, pause and close, then swing up - merely stroking the object of your dreams - up and away before they open again to let fall their imagi-nary cargo of wealth and merely emphasise their emptiness. My child-hood was filled with such failures - explains everything really. Anyway, this kind of clumsiness is bad enough on your own, but when you're sur-rounded by millions of dollars worth of directors, producers, cast and crew and the tea lady, all looking at their watches, you will know just how bad that arcade game felt, if you get it wrong (nothing to do with the construction of the suit of course). But I didn't get it wrong. I sighted, aimed, lunged, grabbed and ripped. Great acting or what? (Don't answer that!) And they never used it. And that hurt. Years later, in therapy, they told me it was nothing to do with me at all. But I don't know whether to believe them. If I share it with you, perhaps you can decide.

As you know, Planet Hoth is a grossly inhospitable place. Cold be-yond even the wildest dreams of Cold Springs, KY, and without the lat-ter's obvious charms and fast-food outlets. Hoth suffers from a pest con-

MFIK meets TMRFE

trol problem beyond the dampest reaches of an Ewok's fur. Big, bad and ugly - the opposite of Ewoks - who are short - wampas roam the wastes of Hoth looking for anything that might count as food. Sadly, Ewoks don't visit Hoth much. I mean err... Ewoks are sad because err... they love to go on trips. And anyway Ewoks don't count (err... mathemati-cally that is). Anyway... wampas love Ewoks. So do I. I think we'd better move on....

The story so far... It was a desperate situation. Snow outside (snow inside, come to that) The Empire about to descend on our gallant heroes (there were quite a number by this time). And a gang of wild white wampas out for lunch (as opposed to out to lunch) (Oh, I don't know). Whaming across the drifting ice fields, they had been given a table for twelve in the ice cavern, as above.

Boy, am I ready for a bite!

So there they were, all locked up, when a party of stormtroopers ar-rived, cold and hungry from melting snow and Rebels outside and look-ing for hotter action and a table for eight. They found Threepio instead, who naturally ran away. They pursued. He ran. They pursued. He ...(we get the idea. Ed) CUT TO the cavern scene, as above, as before. What Threepio had noticed was the ... err... notice that the maitre d' had put on the door saying *DANGER. This room is full of wampas. Do not disturb on pain of being the first course in a banquet given... etc.* With a breathtak-ing demonstration of his superb intelligence, our golden hero bravely ripped it away, implying to the pursuing troopers that they were free to enter and take a seat. They did. Big mistake! It was all very exciting. Shame you missed it!

And why did you? I think THE MAN RESPONSIBLE FOR EVERY-THING had found that a gang of wampas is not cheap to have around and, even with a discount, this particular storyline was getting quite out of hand. He made an executive decision and suddenly my brilliant origami act had been for nothing and our one and only wild white wampa was destined to remain that way. Oh well....

Of course TMRFE might have been swayed in his unswerving judgment by events in another scene. INTERIOR ICE CAVERN: DAY (ANOTHER ONE) (ICE CAVERN, I MEAN) (ACTUALLY, ANOTHER DAY AS WELL). Glistening white walls tower above, shimmering in the fierce blue-white lights focused on and around the snowy scene. Melted candle wax, sprinkled with salt crystals, creating a beautiful and extraordinary facsimile of what any self-respecting ice cavern should be. Giant, frozen icicles dripping icily, were really elegantly crafted glass vessels, hand-blown into an unbelievable recreation of nature, or rather, to a completely believable recreation of nature. Inverted and filled with water, slowly weeping through a pin hole at the tip, they completed the utterly convincing scene of permafrost. Convincing ... except for the heat. I remember from my school days, light means heat. (I assume it is still thus) and the number of lamps needed to provide the required dazzle, gave out the kind of heat normally found in a fish and chip shop in August.

The only other giveaway that we were not actually on Planet Hoth but on Stage 3 at Elstree Studios, was that the set was ringed around with police-like barriers in picket lines saying, Do Not Cross, Collapsing Set, Keep Out, etc (there wasn't actually a sign

err... brrrrr...

saying 'etc'. What I mean is there were lots of other indications that this was a place where I wasn't wanted)(rather hurtful, really). For this was the home-base of the wampas, or rather wampa. He or she (rather dangerous to carry out a close inspection, so perhaps, 'it'), was destined to burst through the ice walls, terrifyingly appearing to devour the camera in its onward rush for a taste of Rebel or Ewok.

This was a one-take shot. The kind of destruction planned did not countenance a second go. Three cameras would whirr to record the one-time-only event. The solid cavern walls had been cleverly constructed to be less impenetrable than they looked. Hidden fault lines would cause a great tumble-down, triggered by a double-fisted blow from the belligerent wampa - played by Eric. Eric is a gentle chap but big. Sneaking a look into the wampa's inner ice sanctum behind the ice walls, now revealed him as a giant. He stood on top of large hairy moon-boot type shoes which raised his massive frame almost two feet higher. Shaggy white fur spread across his heavily padded body and down to his huge, vicious clawed hands. With the great razor-toothed head carefully placed on his shoulders and the hair combed down to hide the join, there stood Eric, the Biggest Wampa In The World.

STAND BY. You all right in there, Eric? asked David, the ever resourceful AD (here standing for Assistant Director rather than the incredibly resourceful Anthony Daniels). *Herbumunooaa* said Eric. *You know what you have to do?* asked David. *Hertumunooaa* said Eric, so that was all right. Everything was ready. Barriers gently removed lest any undue vibration should bring the set to an early collapse. Crew at a safe distance.

Me, as always, at a safer one. *ROLL CAMERAS A, B AND C,* called David. *Speed!* they chorused. *ACTION* said MFIK. There was a thud. Fake snow fell off fake ice. Another thud. Deep silence. *CUT* said MFIK.

Well, clearly something had to be done. Teams of set-builders and dressers swarmed over icy surfaces, weakening them to utter fragility under the blazing lights. Time passed. *STAND BY. You all right in there, Eric?* asked David. *Ewaaimaakoodwin* said Eric, rather woollily. *You know what you have to do?* asked David. *Ibnocmmowhawihi*, said Eric, so that was all right. *ROLL CAMERAS A, B AND C,* called David. *Speed!* they chorused. *ACTION* said MFIK. There was a thud. Fake snow fell off fake ice, for the second time. Another thud. Bit more snow. Deeper silence. *CUT* said MFIK.

So they swarmed again and set-to with Plan B. Wires and ropes were attached, invisibly, to key positions in the ice walls. On the given word, out-of-shot crew would heave and haul the ice walls to the ground. Time was running out. Temperatures were running high. *STAND BY ROLL CAMERAS A B AND C,* called David. *Speed!* they chorused quickly. *ACTION* said MFIK. There was a mighty hauling and the walls Jerchoed down in a flurrying cloud of snow and ice. As the fog of white cleared, there stood the Biggest Wampa In The World, magnificently fearsome from his giant taloned feet, to the muscled breadth of his hairy shoulders, above which Eric's severely overheated and reddened face gasped perspiringly at the three cameras busy whirring at him and his wampa head, cradled football-like in his ripping-clawed hands. *Sorry*, said Eric. *CUT* said MFIK.

And it was.

But this wasn't as bad as ... Oh dear... Mickey seems to be sticking his finger in his ear. I think he's trying to tell me something so I'd better be quiet.

PS You will remember the magnificent gift of a Star Wars *Electronic Bank I received from merchandising magnate, Howard Roffman, which I had assumed was stuffed with gold coins. Well fortunately, before I received Stephen (Evansville, IN) Helmbock's advise re explosives (what would the neighbours have said) (and just think of the damage it might cause to the mint condition of the gold!), I had finally got it open. It seemed to be empty. An oversight, perhaps? But then, it's the thought that counts, isn't it.*

PS (i) Isn't it?

Um, hello

It's an awfully long time since I left school but, do you know, I still dream about it - well *nightmare* about it really. Apart from the once yearly drama production, school, as they say, was not my bag. I wasn't clever. (So no change there. Ed) I wasn't good at sport. I was a weed.(So no change th...) yes, thank you... and sport was played every day. So I was miserable - less so on Mondays when we played at being soldiers. We had real, if ludicrously ill-fitting, uniforms and ridiculously oversized rifles. We mindlessly marched up and down. Sometimes we played war games. All manly stuff.

One day I was crawling through the undergrowth on my own, having got separated from my half of the platoon which was searching for the other half that we had deliberately told to go and hide - so that we could seek them, I suppose. Like I said - all manly stuff. Anyway, I spotted movement beyond the bushes and quelling my natural reaction to run away, I hurled myself forward with a terrifying war cry. There was a pause. Then a returning howl, far more frightening - of pure mirth.

The family sat on a florid travel blanket surrounded by the picture-book stuff of a magnificent picnic. They gazed at me in my overgenerous camouflage jacket and pants; mushroomed by an oversized helmet draped in greenery like the Hanging Gardens of Babylon; brown smudges on my face, less blending into the countryside, as looking like the first attempts at applying an unfortunate shade of lipstick, blindfolded, trampolining.

How they laughed. I stood there, confused. They might be the other half of the platoon, cunningly disguised in costumes filched from the Drama Soc. I moved forward to intimidate them. They laughed more. My tin hat fell over my camouflaged eyes and I fell over a bramble. Cunningly, I decided to demonstrate the leopard crawl. I slithered away, back into the comforting undergrowth. Very cunning. Very manly. The howls of laughter pursued me, more hurtful than any enemy fire. At least the green face-paint disguised my blushing cheeks when the entire platoon turned up to see what was going on.

Shortly after this confrontation we had a Grand Inspection by a major general. He swaggered a lot. He made a speech. He told us many things which I have forgotten. But he told us that we *were the sort of chaps who won wars* and I wasn't sure about that as a sentiment. The next day, I resigned.

Which left school-work itself. And the real stuff of my nightmares is the teacher who taught me French - or didn't. We held a mutual dislike for each other; stupid on my part since he had the upper hand - both of them. So I was perpetually doomed. I dream about him still in his chalky-black gown. I dream about the end of term and the test that destroys all joy at the prospect. In this twilight world of learning, my only knowledge is the certainty that I have missed each class and now it's all too late - and I must fail. And then... then I wake up.

So WAKE UP and study the following passage...

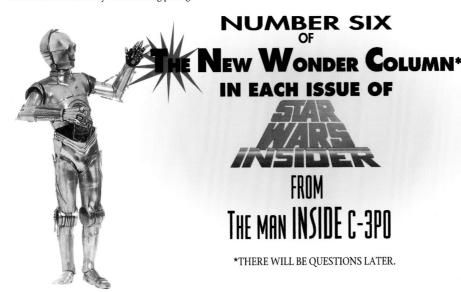

NUMBER SIX
OF
THE NEW WONDER COLUMN*
IN EACH ISSUE OF
STAR WARS INSIDER
FROM
THE MAN INSIDE C-3PO

*THERE WILL BE QUESTIONS LATER.

Gosh!

And here is the first question. No cheating! Ready?

What is *Shadenfreude?*

No cheating I said! If you have just rushed off to get your copy of Number 2 of TNWCIEIOTIFTMIC then you are disqualified - forever. But you clever ones who got the answer right, Well Done! You may take pleasure in the failure of your fellow readers. You may enjoy their discomfort. You may feel... *shadenfreude*, that amazing German invention - enjoyment in another's misfortune. From the letters you write to me, I know that many of you are not strangers to this sensation. You love hearing about things that go wrong on the set. Things that might never reach the screen.

HANDS UP who remembers the following: DEATH STAR - CONTROL ROOM: DAY.

Thank you. HANDS DOWN.

We're in the cupboard. A Trooper still lies on the control room floor, earlier knocked unconscious by H Solo. The door flies up and in rush his trooper chums. And here, I'm going to have to trust you. HANDS UP if you noticed what happens when the troopers arrive. OK. DOWN. All you very clever people who saw it years ago can skip the next bit and may feel a little touch of *shadenfreude* at our stupidity. Right, that's enough! But, for all those who, like

me, didn't see it (I was in the cupboard, remember)... what am I talking about?

In rush the troopers, all most manly and warlike except the one on the right who smacks his head into the door frame. As he totters forward, bemused, matters are not helped by his commander saying *Pick that man up.* And they thought we'd never notice!

Actually stormtroopers are rarely as scary as they look. WIPE TO:

HOTH - INTERIOR ICE CAVERN: DAY: Re-creation of Wampa Ideal Home conditions (For a full description of snow depths etcetera, see Number 3 of TNWCINEIOIFIFTMIC). Enter a whole posse of white clad and booted troopers who all look very threatening until they rush towards camera. Shiny floors covered in snow-look-a-like salt, are not a good idea if you're trying to look manly. They didn't exactly skid to a halt. They just kept on skidding. Before MFIK could shout CUT, the scene looked like the opening day of Bloomingdale's Christmas Sale in the china department. You saw Take 2. So...

WIPE TO:

EXTERIOR FOREST: ENDOR: DAY.

Shining-self-sacrificing-super-hero (C-3PO) leans out from behind a tree and calls, *I say you. Over here. Were you looking for me?* You remember it well.

Ooops!!

Well, in order to get the vast army of troopers to react on cue, they had to be able to hear me. Given that they were at the far end of a tree-lined glade in the tree-filled forest, and given that - when inside, so to speak - when I speak I am inaudible at three feet (you try talking through a hole the size of a matchbox) (used to irritate H Ford like crazy) (irritated A Daniels more than somewhat) - how could I make myself heard? Well, a cunning scheme was employed to link up my radio mike to an amplifier to a loud speaker to broadcast to the troops · *á la* Bob Hope.

ACTION! (through an inferior megaphone) *I say you. Over here. Were you looking for me?* I imperiously echoed around the forest, causing buzzards to lay eggs and gofers to... Anyway...

To a man, each trooper turned and raised his blaster. Terrifying. Then to a trooper, each man began to run towards me along the sylvan path. Thrilling. Unrehearsed, the front one fell over. Mistake. Then another. OK, I thought. Hearing my voice still echoing amongst the mighty trees, I began... *AND NUMBER TWELVE IS DOWN AND IT'S NUMBER THREE IN THE LEAD AT THE FIRST LEAP* (cut) *BUT JUMPING WELL AND COMING UP ON THE OUTSIDE IS NUMBER FIVE WITH SEVEN CLOSE BEHIND AND* (cut) *AS THEY APPROACH THE NEXT HURDLE ITS... AND THERE GOES NUMBER TEN. WHAT A FALL! BUT BREAKING THROUGH WITH* (cut) *A MAGNIFICENT OH NO HE'S DOWN BUT HERE WE HAVE A NEWCOMER RACING TO TAKE THE LEAD...*(**CUT**)!!

Finally the megaphone drowned out my voice but I think I got a round of applause for my race commentary. Sadly Take 2 appeared in the movie too. But it occurred to me that so many people couldn't be falling over for the fun.

I picked up an abandoned helmet and put it on. What was the problem? It had more space than mine. Certainly enough room to swing an Ewok. But when I looked out of the eyes, I couldn't. No wonder they fell over. Swirls of inexpensive green plastic obscured the outside world with defocusing confusion. If you've ever looked down an empty green wine bottle (Not me. Ed) you'll know how it is to be a stormtrooper. No wonder they never hit anyone with their blasters.

But of course, we knew they were going to be a problem from the start.

Armies of extras would arrive at the studio wearing their regular day clothes and go first to the wardrobe department. They walked with pride and enthusiasm. They walked like normal people going to work. But once kitted-out in their threatening white suits of protective body armour, they showed a strange reluctance to move otherwise than in a peculiarly delicate, crab-like way. The trouble? The armour!

The intriguing white design was created in plastic. Made from moulds, the copies were churned-out in hundreds and doled-out to the extras on arrival. They looked great but each edge was unfinished in a knife-like blade - which cut into whichever part of the actor it touched.(I know the feeling). Hence their reluctance to walk normally. Marching was out of the question. They tended to teeter along in a rather unmanly and certainly unwarlike manner. They would cluster in homely groups and discuss solutions to the problem which was achieved with scissors, tape and padding - and endurance. But at least they were ready to face the Rebels.

Though never did they foresee the greater threat that lay ahead.

Wot! No cake?

In those glorious days at Elstree Studios, the days before we began shooting, there was so much to be planned. Stages had to be allotted; sets built; costumes designed; lights rigged; actors hired: locations scouted; etcetera. And all this had to be within the BUDGET - The Word that haunts any producer - The Word that is sacred. Go over The Word and see a world of weeping, and a certain amount of gnashing.

Since its not only armies that march on their stomachs, studio catering is the first thing to get right. This may come as news to some studio caterers. Some get the food wrong - but that is for another WC. Filming on location - meals are the high point of the day. Any day. It's a brave producer who doesn't provide the cast and crew with a more than hearty range of hot - and cold (the union says) - eats. This is often against all the odds if, for instance you're filming in a desert or up a mountain. But somehow quaint and nondescript little vans will turn up, let down their sides and display fish and chips, lasagne and chips, curry and chips, etecetera and chips. And tea. And all for nothing. Well, you don't have to pay for it. But they do. The producers. It comes out of the BUDGET. But only on location. If you're filming in a studio it doesn't count.(For other things that don't count, see No 4 of TNWCIEIOTIFTMIC)

So there I was in the production office at Elstree when APWSBN (ref No 5 of TNWCIEIOTIFTMIC) walks in from America. (Figure of speech in use -

The last straw

Wot, STILL no cake?

Now the troopers know what to do. They rush in formation and form a line to Doris more regimented than anything filmed so far. The brighter ones remember to take off their helmets <u>before</u> they speak and the first in line says his line.

Tea please.

Surprised, Doris asks, *Sugar? Two, please. There you are, dear. Thank you. That'll be four and a half pee. Oh. There. Have you got any less? No, sorry. Never mind. Wait a minute. There you are, dear. Thank you. Thank you dear. Yes love? Tea, please. Sugar? Three please. There you are....* Well you get the idea. (Took the words right out of my mouth. Ed)

Tea's ready!

HOMEWORK ASSIGNMENT:

The Great British Tea Break lasts for fifteen minutes. Calculate the <u>actual</u> time it takes to serve seventy-five stormtroopers a cup of tea plus the occasional cake, receive payment (average spend, the irrationally odd figure of seven and a half pee) and give change to each trooper who is now holding a scalding plastic cup in one hand, his helmet in the other with the occasional cake perched in any available nook. (**NB** You will remember that stormtrooper armour does not have pockets). The ones hopping in line are removing their money from their shoes. Others, oddly writhing, have found an even more private place to hide their loose change. Which may be another reason why stormtroopers show a strange reluctance to move otherwise than in a peculiarly delicate, crab-like way. As I said - all manly stuff.

On the other hand... Oh. Mickey says it's tea time. 'Bye.

he'd arrived some weeks before, by plane). The conversation turned to the subject of refreshments. Naturally a running buffet of drinks and snacks would be available at all times, *à la Amércain*. My mind went towards champagne, caviar and M&Ms but Robert Watts, the Production Manager looked shocked.

Robert is English and is chiefly famous, not for his work on the Trilogy, the Indy films and Roger Rabbit, but for christening me Stardust - he had obviously made a quick assessment of my talents. Years later I felt a thrill when I finally saw my name up in dappled gold neon lights. You will remember where we stayed in Yuma - yes! - The Stardust Motel. Oh well, it was start.

Anyway, RW looked shocked not because of the cost of caviar and champagne (to say nothing of the M&Ms) (actually I'd rather just have M&Ms) but because in England, this is simply NOT DONE! Give food away! This could lead to rioting in the streets - to total anarchy. Or worse. It could inflate the BUDGET. Even worse, it would set a precedent and any film made in the future on England's green would have to provide refreshments gratis. The entire population would become actors just to get a free bun, so there would be no one left to watch the movies so they wouldn't get made and that would truly be the end of civilisation as we know it.

Great Britain is justly famed for its proud traditions and the greatest of all is tea time - tea is what made the (British) Empire *great*. (Why, the very word great contains the exact letters required to make *tea*) (also allowing you, at the same time, to make the word *rg*).

Nothing gets moving on the set before the entire workforce (small 'f') has had a bacon roll (for further discussion on the subject, yet again, see number 5 of TNWCINEIOFIFTMIC re Mon Mothma having a roll with me) and a cuppa. Only then can the day begin. Only then can the expensive studio machine roll into action (bit of a pun there which was actually accidental). The whole process to be replicated at eleven in the morning and four in the afternoon, with bacon being replaced by cakes. But tea, ever. It is known as The Great British Tea Break. But tea and cakes do not grow on trees. *Give them away??*

No! said RW. *Let them eat cake - but let them pay for it!*

Behold the swelling scene:

INT. DEATH STAR - DOCKING BAY. Troops of... er... troops rushing about trying to prevent heroes doing anything heroic by rushing about and firing blasters badly (see above). The scene is not going smoothly. We are behind schedule. We need another take. Suddenly the awesome interior of the Death Star grows silent. A presence is felt and now seen across the vast expanse of gleaming black deck. A palpable tension grows as the figure draws near. Troops almost break ranks, unsure how to act in the face of such a being. It is Doris.

The mythic figure approaches, pushing her jingling trolley with its gleaming urn. Steam rises from the urn - and from Doris. (It has been a long way from the kitchen to the Death Star and it's a warm day). BREAK! says the exasperated AD (obviously meaning Assistant Director, since Anthony Daniels never gets exasperated - ever- GOT THAT?).

PP *After my thoughts on Christmas presents(ref No 4 of TNWCINEIOFIFTMIC) I am adding another idea to my list for Santa.* A beautiful **Armchair Pooch.** Yes - never again search for that elusive TV remote control. Stuff it into this remarkably crafted armchair-arm pouchy-pooch/poochy-pouch and it stays where you always want it. This cuddly, long-eared bean-bag doggy-look-a-like is available in brown. *Perhaps I'll just throw away the remote.*

p *Did I go too far? Since mentioning that in future WCs, I wouldn't (mention him), there have been no more gifts from* **BIG H***. However,* **Jonathan Striebel** *of St Louis MO appears to have taken up the mantle. Seeing me un-gifted in Nashville and being a close follower of the WC, he generously gave me an action figure - of Threepio. Most apt in every way. Thank you again, Jonathan.*

p2 *Perhaps H won't feel quite so* **BIG** *now!*

PPPPS *Am I alone in the breathtaking panic I feel in the toiletries section of large stores. All those eager members of staff who want to squirt the latest expensive smell on you. Ugh! Or are they trying to tell me something?(See YOU WRITE)*

London, England

Um, hello

I was standing in New York. (ADNY like DKNY) (but a whole lot cheaper) Well I wasn't actually standing in New York *entier* but a representative downtown bit of it called 6th and 55th (all NY locations sound like the sort of fractions that so wrecked my childhood even to this day). I was standing next to an American friend of mine when, to his horror I became immensely excited. I gesticulated. The more animated I became the more silent he grew. Like approaching NYers, he pretended I wasn't happening. The terrified pedestrians assumed that stony or in some cases, stoned New York Look and ignored me. Honed over aeons, the NYL was developed to avoid lengthy conversations with totally mad, drunk criminals on their way home—the pedestrians' homes since most of the above don't have one. As I appeared to be completely barking I fitted at least one of the categories and that was bad enough for them (I do hope you're keeping up. If in you're feeling tired or insecure start this paragraph over again, which is what I might do if I have the energy—it's a rather muggy night here in downtown England— that is not to say that I am about to be accosted for my Rolex (I don't have one) (Not even a fake? Ed.) (OK I do have one of *those* but what's the point of being mugged for an imitation. If I do become a crime statistic, I want to be worthwhile) No—what I mean is that the weather is being a little peculiar and the air appears to have a humidity of 100 which for IQ is average but for moisture levels—muggy. (Now I'm totally lost. Where was I? Dum-di-dum-di-dum—press the arrow thing. Ah. Found it.) I gesticulated and he looked. It was big and red. It lumbered towards us. Feelings of homesickness swept over me (I had been in bits of NY for several days now). A London double-decker bus! A piece of England in this foreign land. I felt pride. *Breathes there a man with soul so dead etc* filled my mind—a poem, written by Sir Walter Scott (sadly, life member of the Dead Poets Society). (If I were honest I'd admit to having typed Dead <u>Pets</u> Society which would have been really stupid since I don't know whether or not SWS actually owned even a cat) (the '*etc*' is not actually in the poem, I just can't remember the rest of it—but it's all about patriotism.) As this mighty two-layered symbol of all that is British rolled by, I was lost for words. My chest swelled. My eyes watered and my lungs collapsed as the diesel fumes filled them, taking a Vader hold on my throat. *Breathes there a man* indeed! I was breathing my last, about to boost the otherwise falling homicide statistics for the NYPD.

And talking of vital statistics, here comes…

Wonder Column
In the Insider from the Man Inside C-3PO

Gosh!

Another time. Another street. I can't actually remember where it was. Certainly not NY. In fact not a city of any kind. Barely a town. The word *civilised* didn't exactly leap to mind. It had a huge population but since it was mostly made up of flies I don't think they count (for other things that don't count, see Ewok references WC No 4). I know we were in Tunisia and they certainly knew we'd arrived. Like an invading army we had rushed their main street. How they knew it was the main street I'm not sure. There was no TacoBellMcDonaldsKFCBurgerKingWendy's anywhere. (Come to think of it, it was quite civilised after all). We knew it was the main street because it was practically the only one they

had (so we'll move on). (At last. Ed.) The invasion force of fuming trucks and buses decamped the assorted baggage of crew and equipment required to carry the twentieth century to MedievalLand. Umbrellas to shield us from the sun. Reflectors to move the sun around. Food. Water. Styrene cups. Snickers Bars. Coke. <u>Everything</u> that is good about our time (perhaps I meant Pepsi).

Personally having nothing to unload (I normally lie on a doctor's couch for that sort of thing) I wandered off down the gritty 'street'. I was in an ancient place. I assumed that the vaporators were something the crew had made earlier but in such a bizarre land they didn't look too out-of-place on the bright blue skyline. The sun was rising fast and would soon have to be umbrella-ed into position. In the

bleaching light a strange rubber creature was trying to look real. It was failing fast. It just looked rather bored. This I knew to be a 'dewback'(first made popular by Kenner but really coming into their own in the Special Edition twenty years on—a long wait, hence the bored expression). Ever-helpful I suggested a pile of dewback-do-do underneath might add a gritty realism the scene. They ignored me. (At the SE royal premiere I looked all around the super animated dewbacks—still nothing. Has ILM no feeling for Nature? Or don't dewbacks eat? I think we should be told). The vaporators and the do-do-less dewback were ours, of course. <u>Theirs</u> was the Cantina. Or rather, <u>his</u>…

It was at the far end of the fly blown road and, in keeping with much of the local architecture, was dome-shaped. In most lands it is

Don't dewbacks do do-do?

every one's dream to have a home of your own. A dome of your own was the thing here. Igloo-like (but made of adobe gloop as opposed to snow, hence avoiding total meltdown) it was anciently bleached into the landscape as indeed was its proud owner, Ahmed. He stood proudly outside. This was the bit we were going to use—the outside. It was his family home. He was probably proud of the inside too.

We smiled at each other. Years of desert-quenching Coke had wrought its unique dental effect on him and seemingly on all his grinning friends who crowded around. This man was popular. And the rotted-tooth smiles were warm enough. The sun was well away by now and we chatted whilst we baked. Threepio may be fluent etc… but I have only a smattering of languages, naturally assuming that English is the only one necessary (though I find eating in restaurants helps a lot—my Chinese is coming on well). We did manage a passable conversation in the sort of tongues we should have had in common. I think I understood Ahmed. His

enthusiasm for and fascination with our visit from another century were evident. He was in contact with TechnoWorld. He was very happy. Even more happy with the Dinar / Deutsch-mark / goat / camel—or whatever they were swapping at the time—equivalent of the $8 a day he was receiving from the film company for the use of his personal exterior (Home? Ed.). Knowing the sort of fees paid for locations back at my home base I was shocked. He might have been happy but I had once bought a book by one of the Marx brothers. I never did read it but I knew all about the horrors of capitalism anyway. $8 a day was a rip-off. A scandal. Not fair. I told *him*.

THE PRODUCER WHO SHALL BE NAMELESS took me to one side (or the other) to explain that they were now waiting for me at the other end of the street, ready to start shooting (I misunderstood, thinking some local revolution had got out of hand). He also detailed the socio-economic effects of paying location fees above the local rate. First inflation would rise up out the land like Tyrannosaurus Wrecks and devour the nest-eggs of the pitiable peasants who had scraped together a few feeble groats for their old age and more importantly, jeopardise future film work as a source of national income. Secondly, my smiling new friend would be a wealthy man during our visit, would dramatically improve his social status, grow superior, lose the sur-

rounding group of smiling hangers-on and after our departure and the termination of such extravagant payments subside into socio-economic ruin and ultimate decay. So, far from being mean and tight-fisted, **TPWSBN** was actually being very kind in paying Ahmed only $8 a day. Of course! I should have known! I wiped the tears of understanding from my eyes and walked humbly to work.

Well, **TPWSBN** had been right about one thing. They were waiting for me. So was the

I'm waiting.

famed landspeeder. It too was baking in the sun. A fact I didn't realise until I took my seat on the back. Unprotected by the bits of gold I wasn't wearing (look closely) my seat rapidly over heated. I leapt off again. Some foam padding helped as I eventually reperched myself. Sir Alec and Mark were in first class at the front, of course. I was in economy with the baggage—Artoo strapped to the luggage rack.

C-3PO's HELPFUL HINTS FOR THE HAPPY HOST

Q. How Best To serve Ewoks?

HINT NO. 41,376

A. At room temperature!

Nevertheless I looked forward to this famed experience. To gently rise above the planet's surface. To be free. To float on air—such stuff as dreams are made of…

The carpet I noticed pinned to the rear fender looked decidedly earth-bound. I imagined that this old rug had something to do with the rather battered appearance of everything in this movie, including me. In contrast, the long, thin mirrors were retentively clean. They fringed the driver's side and duplicated the dusty terrain around us. As if there wasn't enough already. Finally everything seemed to be standing-by for a take so I removed my sun-glasses and was bolted into the ultimate sunscreen. A great silence descended on the land. The crowd artists hovered on their start marks. The camera crew watched and waited. The inhabitants of this ancient world watched and waited. Ahmed watched and smiled, anticipating the techno-miracle about to happen before his sand-hardened eyes.

ACTION! called **TMRFE.** And we swung into… well, action, I suppose.

Mark certainly swung the controls. But I had no sense of being uplifted. Rather, I had the sensation of being sealed in a London traffic jam. Funnelled by the ancient rug, exhaust

Who's got gas?

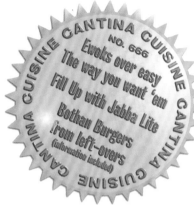

CANTINA CUISINE CANTINA CUISINE CANTINA CUISINE CANTINA CUISINE
NO. 666
Ewoks over easy
The way you want 'em
Fill Up with Jabba Lite
Bothan Burgers
from left-overs
(information included)

perched precariously over a throbbing exhaust and hovering was not at all the smooth experience I had imagined. The fumes might still be getting up my nose; the old rug trailing in the dirt might be brushing out our tracks; the tyres might be successfully hidden behind the strips of gleaming mirror but the vehicle's suspension echoed every rut and bump on the planet's mangy surface. Having regained a more or less upright position I tried, like Sir Alec, to look regal. I think we did rather a good job. Not for long.

I think Mark must have found the brakes again as we slowed in the centre of the street. But this wasn't in the script. We weren't even within smelling range of the Cantina. Mark wrestled the gently coughing vehicle to a hiccuping stop. The clear desert air filled my lungs. Another great silence descended on the land. Our landspeeder was, as they say, clean out of gas.

Of course we did it again until we got it right so the sun was falling as we packed up our umbrellas and reflectors and bits of gold. They watched us go with all our techno-trappings. We had already become a part of their folk lore history as we steamed away in our cars and coaches. Ahmed brushed aside the diesel fumes. He smiled—in his mind, clutching the $8.

And th… Oh! Mickey's clutching my wrist again.

I think… therefore I'm gone…

fumes streamed up and into my personal air conditioning system otherwise known as the small rectangular mouth in Threepio's face. I blew them out again and nearly fell off the back of the lurching speeder as Mark dramatically discovered second gear. With lightening reaction I managed to grab Obi-Wan's seat (Surely not! Ed) the back of it to be precise, bearing in mind the status of this venerable Jedi Knight. All seemed secure again when Mark accidentally hit the brakes. For an endless moment in time it looked as though I were about to be intimately united with the venerable Jedi in first class as I shot forward, heading for a soft landing. The speeder, suddenly returning to second gear unhindered, prevented this uniquely embarrassing moment in movie history. We turned the corner and swept down the street.

There they were. The camera. The crew. The crowd artists and locals. And Ahmed. All marvelling at our peculiar progress. I looked uncomfortable. Threepio does not approve of Mos Eisley. Also, I was uncomfortable. I was

ERROR ERROR ERROR ERROR*

BANTHA POODOO
The Cosmic SCOOP

should have been featured in
Keep Your Kosmos Klean No. 58 (huge special offer)

——— No. 137 ———

And not in Cantina Cuisine
BANTHA POODOO
The Cosmic SOUP

* Affected readers should seek medical attention (unless it is too late)
† We regret, no claims considered.

GOLDENROD!

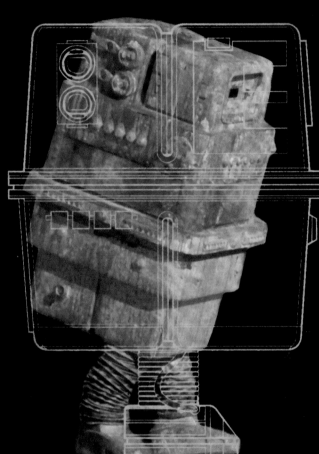

The *Star Wars* galaxy is populated with droids of all shapes· qnd sizes, but which are your favourites? The votes are in and· h'ave been counted, so we can reveal the Top 10 *Star Wars* Droids...

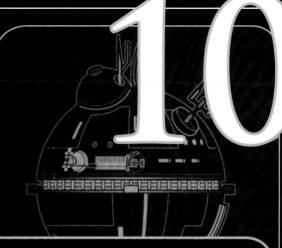

10

10. Interrogation Droid
(A New Hope)

As seen in action against Princess Leia, the IT-0 Interrogation Droid was a tool of oppression used by the Empire. Often the mere presence of this droid was enough to cause subjects to crack and give up vital information. It didn't work on Leia, and only the threatened destruction of her home planet of Alderaan was effective. Even then, she lied. Feisty girl.

9

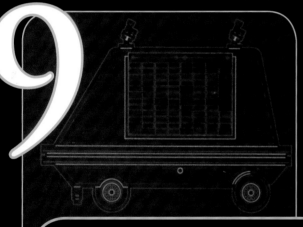

9. MSE-6 Mouse Droid
(A New Hope)

A messenger droid, often to be found around powerful people awaiting its instructions. Chewbacca takes an instant dislike to one when he's on the Death Star ... Believed in some quarters to be planning galactic domination from its base on the original Death Star. That wasn't a good choice of HQ, then.

Best fo the rest

Imperial Probe Droid/Probot
(The Empire Strikes Back)

Probe droids were originally developed for exploration, but the rise of the Empire saw them co-opted into the search and suppression of rebellious elements. It's a probe droid which locates the Rebel base on Hoth at the beginning of *The Empire Strikes Back*.

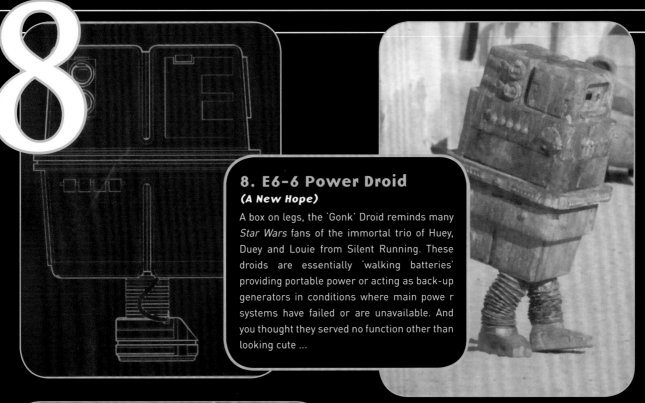

8. E6-6 Power Droid
(A New Hope)

A box on legs, the 'Gonk' Droid reminds many *Star Wars* fans of the immortal trio of Huey, Duey and Louie from Silent Running. These droids are essentially 'walking batteries' providing portable power or acting as back-up generators in conditions where main power systems have failed or are unavailable. And you thought they served no function other than looking cute ...

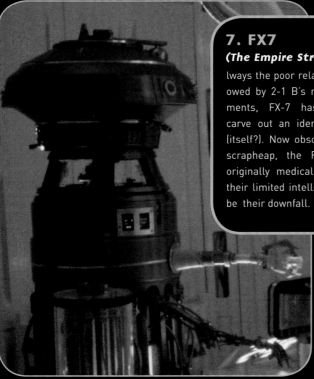

7. FX7
(The Empire Strikes Back)

lways the poor relation, over-shadowed by 2-1 B's medical achievements, FX-7 has struggled to carve out an identity for himself (itself?). Now obsolete and on the scrapheap, the FX series were originally medical assistants, but their limited intelligence proved to be their downfall.

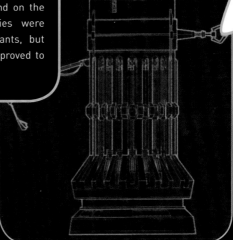

B'Omarr Brain Walker
(Return of the Jedi)

Glirnpsed in the background as C-3PO and R2-D2 enter Jabba's palace, the B'Omarr brain walkers are curious creatures/ machines. The brains of the B'Ornarr monks, the original inhabitants of Jabba's Palace. reside in these spider-like droids/vehicles.

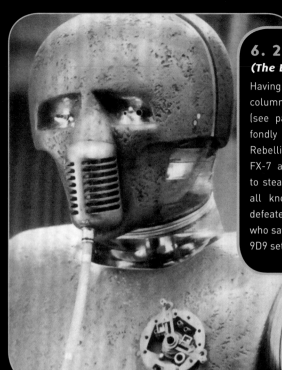

6. 2-1B
(The Empire Strikes Back)

Having found a new career as a star columnist for *Star Wars Magazine* (see page 57), 2-1 B looks back fondly on his days helping the Rebellion out, except of course for FX-7 and those others who tried to steal the glory from him. As we all know, 2-1 B single-handedly defeated the Empire, and anyone who says any different will have EV-9D9 set upon them ...

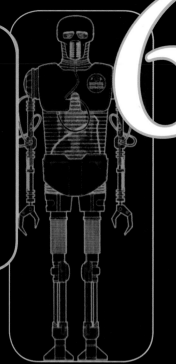

6

5

5. 8D8
(Return of the Jedi)

Strong and durable, the 8D8 droid was originally intended to operate in the high temperatures of a blast furnace. Lacking in intelligence, 8D8 was easily co-opted by that nasty piece of work, EV-9D9 who can be seen in The Empire Strikes Back torturing fellow droids ... EV-9D9 terrorised the droid population of Cloud City until the arrival of a bigger evil: the Empire. 8D8 later resurfaced in Jabba's palace, still up to his old tricks ...

Best fo the rest

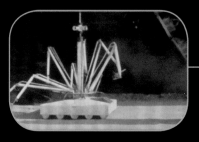

WED Treadwell
(A New Hope)

Looking like a piece of scrap, the Treadwell is a cheap and rather outdated workhorse droid, used mainly for manual labour or fiddly mechanical tasks. They come with a variety of specialist appendages for fulfilling specific tasks ... It ain't beautiful, but it gets the job done ..

4. 4-LOM and IG-88
(The Empire Strikes Back)

Ranked together are the bounty hunters and assassin droids 4-LOM and IG-88. The IG range of assassin droids were imbued with unprecedented creativity and intelligence, a mistake which came back to haunt their creators. The rogue IG droids killed their design team then embarked on a life as bounty hunters. Initially intended as a Protocol Droid range to rival the 3PO model, the LOM series gained spontaneous sentience. 4-LOM, once a ship's valet, became a master thief and bounty hunter. Both droids can be seen among the bounty hunters hired by Darth Vader in The Empire Strikes Back.

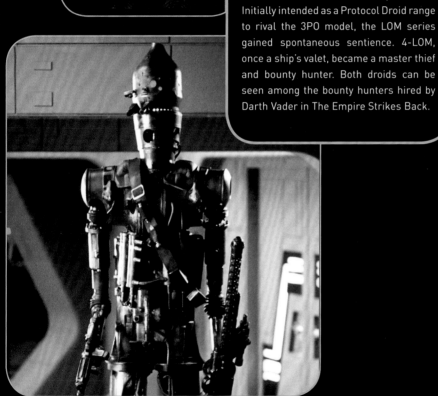

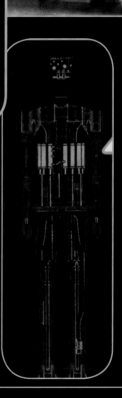

Battle Droids
(The Phantom Menace)

Adaptable and expendable, the battle droids formed the core troops of the Trade Federation army. While their sheer numbers can overwhelm, careful use of firepower (or lightsabers) can take them out. As can finding the 'off' switch on the droid control ship ..

Best fo the rest

3

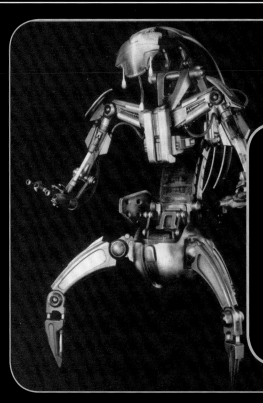

3. Droidekas
AKA Destroyer Droids
(The Phantom Menace)

They made a spectacular entrance in *The Phantom Menace*, wheeling in to threaten Obi-Wan Kenobj_and Qui-Gon Jinn. Shielded and fast-moving, the Destroyer Droids are the peak of Trade Federation-purchased technology.
However, they can still be taken out by a well-placed laser blast or lightsaber swing.

2

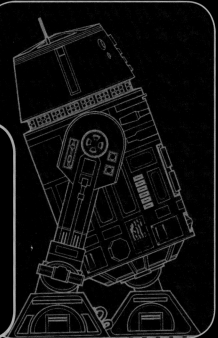

2. R5 Astromech Droid
AKA Skippy the Jedi Droid
(A New Hope)

RS -you know, the droid that exploded when the Jawa's were selling items to Uncle Owen. Luck, really, as if RS had made it all the way to the homestead unscathed, the entire history of the Rebellion may have been changed. RS's untimely end meant that (thanks to some prodding from Threepio) R2-D2 could take his place. The secret history of RS, AKA Skippy the Jedi Droid, was revealed in *Star Wars* Comic

Best fo the rest

Seeker/Lightsaber Training Droid
(A New Hope)

Hovering training remotes are used by Jedi and also by gunfighters to sharpen reflexes and develop co-ordination. They can be set to varying degrees of aggressiveness and the shock ray can be adjusted from harmless to painful. And they provide great amusement to Han Solo ...

1

1. C-3PO & R2-D2
(The *Star Wars* Saga)

Inseparable, of course, protocol droid C-3PO and astromech droid R2-D2 top our droid popularity poll. Almost everyone put either C-3PO or R2-D2 top of their lists, with the other coming second. They are at the centre of the Star Wars saga, especially after the revelation that Anakin Skywalker, AKA Darth Vader, actually constructed C-3PO in The Phantom Menace. Expect even more of both droids in Episode II. Ever popular, there remain unanswered questions about the pair ... but we've got two films yet to find out more about everyone's favourite droids.

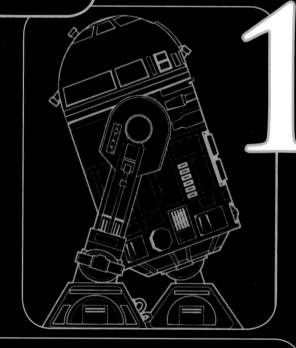

1

Pit Droids
(The Phantom Menace)

Handy little devils, the pit droids are the mechanics who keep the Pod racers running. A hit to the 'nose' folds them up for easy storage. They tend to be clumsy, easily falling over or getting caught up in equipment or machinery they are supposed to be repairing.

A state of
NELV

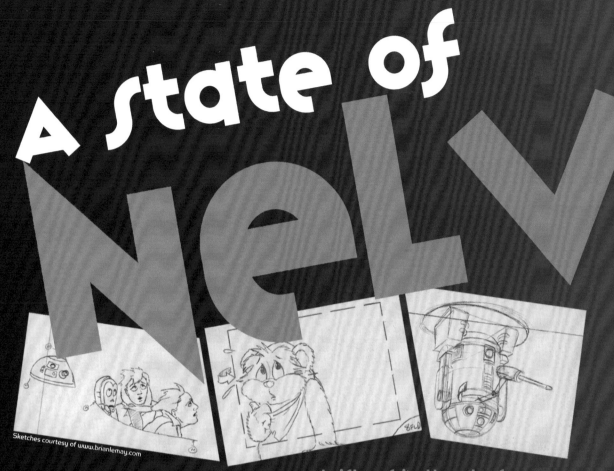

Sketches courtesy of www.brianlemay.com

In 1985, long before the *Star Wars: Clone Wars* animated micro series and the establishment of the Expanded Universe, Lucasfilm ventured into the world of animation with the *Droids* and *Ewoks Adventure Hour*, two half-hour programs that chronicled the further adventures of some of the beloved characters from the original *Star Wars* trilogy. The Canadian company Nelvana, working closely with Lucasfilm, brought these cartoons to life (as previously covered, along with a complete episode guide, in *Star Wars Insider* #27). This was not the first time, however, that Nelvana had worked with Lucasfilm on an animated *Star Wars* project.

christmas in the stars

Partners Michael Hirsh, Patrick Loubert, and Clive Smith established Nelvana in Toronto in 1971, but they never intended it to be a dedicated animation company. Instead, they hoped to establish a film company in a country that didn't really have a film industry. After a few years of producing live-action and animated films, as well as short programs for the Canadian Broadcasting Corporation (CBC), the trio soon realized that animation was becoming their specialty. In 1975, they set out to produce their first fully animated half-hour special, *A Cosmic Christmas*. Released in December 1977, *A Cosmic Christmas* achieved critical acclaim around the world. It also caught the attention

A COSMIC CHRISTMAS

and
Droids & Ewoks
Adventure Hour Revisited

By Shane Turgeon

of Lucasfilm, which had recently experienced a little success of its own.

The following year, Lucasfilm and Canadian director David Acomba were looking for a company to produce a 10-minute animated short for the now-infamous "*Star Wars* Holiday Special," which was to air on Thanksgiving. "At the time, [Lucasfilm] was determined not to work with the standard Hollywood purveyors of animation," recalls Michael Hirsh. "They wanted to be able to choose an independent company. We got a call in early 1978 from Lucasfilm asking us to send a copy of A *Cosmic Christmas* and anything else we were working on. So we did that and [were then] invited to come and meet with George himself and get a sense of the project."

Clive Smith remembers being "bloody thrilled" about the opportunity to work on *Star Wars* short. "It was a great project, and (Lucas) was really good to work with. he gave us the script, something like a 10page outline that was called *The Story of the Faithful Wookie*. Then Frank Nissen — my right-hand animator / Friend/visualizer and co-director in those days — and I worked like crazy, and, I think, in about 10 days we did entire storyboard. I don't know how many panels it would have been , but it was very a detailed board, and I took that to Lucasfil."

For the *The Story of the Faithful Wookie*, Nelvana produced a detailed and colorful cartoon that fit perfectly in the *Star Wars Universe*.

Droids and the Prequel Trilogies

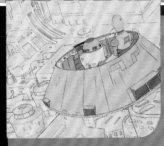

While no direct connection has ever been established between the *Droids* series and the first two installments of the Prequel Trilogy, they do share several interesting "connections." Perhaps the most significant of these comes in "A Race to the Finish," in which speeder racers Thall Joben and Jard Dusat take their speeder, the White Witch, to the Boonta Speeder Races, which is also the name of the Podrace that young Anakin wins in The Phantom Menace. Another Podrace theme is echoed in the episode "The Roon Games" when a two-man announcer team simultaneously comments on the Games in two different languages, much like the two-headed Podrace announcer does during Anakin's big race on Tatooine. From a vehicle perspective, many *Droids* characters can be seen riding in Podracers that bear a striking res emblance to those used by the Galactic Senate. Also, in the episode "The Lost Prince," Jann Tosh, who becomes the droids' second master in the series, drives a singled-wheeled speeder that is very similar in design to the hailfire droids seen in *Attack of the Clone*s.

Centered around a mystic tailsman that has adverse affects on both Luke Skywalker and Han Solo, the story delves deep into the issues of trust and friendship. It has bt'corne widely recognized not only for i11trodulinq tlw bounty hunter Bob-1 Fett, but ,ilso for perhaps being the only well-received segment of the "Holiday Special." Nelvana's, work on The Story of the Faithful Wookiee further established the company as a major player animation. Shortly thereafter, the company produced three more successful, seasonally themed specials ,and a full length picture called *Rock and Rule*. Also, for the first time in its history. Nelvana began producing several animated and live-action television series such as the *Edison Twins*, *Inspector Gadget*, , and *Strawberry Shortcake*. These projects gave Nelvana considerable experience in series production. It was a market in which it hadn't, anticipated working, but one that would prove to be its lifeblood for years to come. As a result, when Lucasfilm decided to rnake two new ,animated shows based on the Ewoks, and C3PO and R2-D2, it was Nelvana that got the call.

droid factory

The *Droids and Ewoks Adventure Hour* was, in part, intended to maintain audience interest in the *Star Wars* saga after *Return of the Jedi*, which come out in 1983. First airing on ABC in September 1985 — and coinciding with two Kenner toy lines— the initial series consisted of 13 episodes of *Ewoks*, 13 episodes of Droids, and one Droids speci.:il entitled the "The Great Heep" — which was produced concurrently with the series. The *Droids* cartoons take place 15 years before the events of *Star Wars: A New Hope* and center around the galactic travels of C- 3PO and R2 -D2 before they meet Luke Skywalker. While niost television series are fixed upon a core group of characters central location, almost every episode of *Droids* occurred on a new planet, and after every four episodes, C-3PO and R2-D2 left their current masters in search of new ones. Because of its complex nature, developing the *Droids* series proved to be quite a difficult process.

"The challenge in *Droids* was that you essentially had the *Star Wars* story to bring forward without Luke, Leia, Darth Vader, and Han Solo," recalls Michael Hirsh.

"It was a lot of work," says Patrick Loubert, "and I remember we tried to talk George out of that. We really wanted more *Star Wars* characters, because I thought we could have done really well with

> The challenge in *Droids* was that you essentially had the *Star Wars* story to bring forward without Luke, Leia, Darth Vader, and Han Solo.

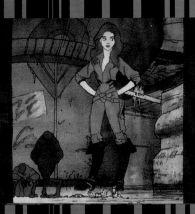

them." He adds, "George was adamant in that he didn't want to expose those characters at that time, and he wanted just the droids."

As a result, one of the first tasks that Nelvana's design team faced was creating the new characters that would serve as C-3PO and R2-D2's masters, as well as the multitude of villains they would inevitably face. While Lucasfilm supervised and approved everything, Nelvana employees had a great deal of creative control in this area and created characters such as Thall Joben, Jord Dusat, Uncle Gundy, Jan Tosh, Kez Iban, and Mungo Baobab, as well as new villains such as the Fromm Gang, Kybo Ren, Admiral Screed, and Gaff. While most of the main characters from the *Star Wars* trilogy were off-limits for the *Droids* series, there were several notable guest appearances by other characters, such as Boba Fett in "A Race to the Finish," Sy Snootles and the Max Rebo band in "The Lost Prince," and IG-88 in "The New King." With the design of the new characters complete, the next challenge facing Nelvana was to write 13 episodes and a special in a relatively short period of time. To meet this requirement, Nelvana needed several different writers, who would come from a variety of sources. Peter

Sauder, one of Nelvana's top in-house writers, and Ben Burtt, George Lucas' sound designer, wrote or co-wrote the majority of the *Droids* episodes along with Joe Johnston (another Lucasfilm employee) and Los Angeles-based writers such as Gordon Kent, Michael Reaves, and Steven Wright.

With many writers each creating episodes that took place on different worlds, a huge design department was needed to visualize their ideas. "There was a pool of designers at the studio [who became specialists]," recalls Clive Smith. "Certain people were really good at machines and believable mechanical stuff, and there were others who were really [strong with] characters, while other designers [excelled] at backgrounds and locations." Visually, the hard work of the design team and Director Ken Stephenson paid off. Every episode of the *Droids* series is bright and vibrant and truly captures the essence of the *Star Wars* universe. Unfortunately, this high degree of quality had a drawback, as well.

The amount of work that went into creating new worlds and adventures every week was staggering compared to most Saturday morning cartoons of the time and consequently, the *Droids* series became very expensive to produce. In the end, the mammoth amount of work that went into its production, and the resulting costs, proved to be unfeasible, and *Droids* was cancelled after only one season.

the ewoks strike back

Fortunately, because of the release of *Return of the Jedi* a year before, developing the Ewoks series wasn't quite so complex. Taking place before the events of Jedi, the Ewoks series follows Wicket and his friends Kneesaa, Teebo, and Latara throughout many adventures on Endor. Ray Jafelice, who directed the firsLseason of Ewoks, remembers one particular event that helped the design team to understand the moon of Endor. "One of the first things [Lucasfllm] did was send us to Skywalker Ranch near San Francisco and t3ke us ori a day trip to Muir Woods, which is this huge redwood forestin California where actual Endor footage was shot. So just walking around that park was awe-inspiring. Plus, we had the movie to look at1 aswell as the stage and set designs."

With much of the basic design work already established, the Nelvana team simply had to adapt it to work in an animated fashion. This resulted in the creation of colorful environments like the Ewok Village, the floating trees, and the swamps, which were home to the Ewoks archenemies, the Duloks. Adaptation was something that also needed to be done with many of the Ewoks who appeared in the movies. Wicket, Teebo, Chief Chirpa, Log ray, and many of the other animated Ewok characters first appeared in *Return of the Jedi*, but they needed more identifiable personas for the cartoon. Ne lvana redesigned these characters to have not only more distinguishable features but also individual personalities and character traits.

Of course, these characters needed to have adventures, and for this Lucasfilm suggested writers Paul Dini and Bob Carrau. Together they wrote all 13 episodes of the first season. Dini and Carrau weren't Nelvana employees, but by working in tandem with the Nelvana crew, an effective team was formed. As a result, after the initial 13-episode run, the *Ewoks* series was renewed for another half-season on ABC.

Sketch courtesy of www.brianlemay.com

The Story of the Faithful Wookiee has become widely recognized for introducing the bounty hunter Boba Fett.

Even Ewoks Get the Blues

Did you know that famous musicians composed the opening title themes for both Droids and Ewoks? The Droids title theme was the result of collaboration between former Police drummer Stewart Copeland and blues bassist Derek Holt. While in Hawaii, legendary blues guitarist Taj Mahal recorded the simple yet catchy opening theme for the first season of *Ewoks*. Unfortunately, neither theme has been released on CD, although Spanish versions were released on a promotional 45 by EMI in Spain in 1986. While blues icon Long John Baldry might not have contributed musically to the *Droids* and *Ewoks Adventure Hour*, his unmistakable voice can be heard as the Great Heep in the *Droids* special of the same name. He also provided additional voices for the first season of the *Ewoks*.

When the second season of *Ewoks* aired in the fall of 1986, fans noticed changes, which were implemented when a new team of designers from Lucasfilm came on board the project after completion of the first season. Twenty-two new episodes were created for Season Two, but of these, only the last episode, "Battle for the Sunstar," was full length. The rest were shortened to allow multiple stories to be told in a half-hour block. The second season also featured a new opening theme and a

Nelvana redesigned these characters to have not only more distinguishable features but also individual personalities and character traits.

substantial amount of design changes to many of the main characters. Despite the differences, Paul Dini and Bob Carrau continued to write most of the episodes, and many of the Nelvana employees who worked on the first season were on board for the second, including Dale Schott, who replaced Unit Director Ray Jafelice as director.

After the flood

While the *Droids* and *Ewoks* programs aired for a relatively short time, they attracted millions of viewers. In 1994, the series experienced a resurgence when the Sci-Fi Channel re-ran the programs, thus reintroducing them to the many Star Wars fans who grew up with the series, while also reaching an entirely new generation. This renewed popularity also sparked a new level of interest from collectors hoping to track down the remaining pre-production material Nelvana used to make not only the *Droids* and *Ewoks Adventure Hour* but also the "*Star Wars Holiday Special*."

For years, speculation has run rampant throughout the collecting community as to what ultimately happened to the material that went into the making of the Star Wars animated projects. Animation cels from the last four episodes of *Droids* (which featured the character Mungo Baobab) and cels from the second season of *Ewoks* are readily available on the secondary market. However, locating material from the "Holiday Special," the early *Droids* episodes, or the first season of *Ewoks* has been daunting for many collectors.

One rumor suggests that the material was destroyed when a fire tore through a Nelvana warehouse. In fact, there was no fire, but Patrick Loubert clearly remembers a flood that occurred one stormy Toronto evening. "I remember working over the weekend. All the material was below ground level, and the water started to leak into the basement area, and I came in and [saw that] there were actually things floating around in it. We saved what we could, but we lost a lot of stuff." Fortunately, at the time of the flood, the pre-production material from all three of the *Star Wars* projects had long since left Nelvana's

possession. Lucasfilm ultimately holds the rights to these proper-
ties, and thus most of the items were sent to the company
shortly after the projects were completed. It was there that
everything remained until the late 1980s when Lucasfilm
entered into a contract with Royal Animated Art to sell and dis-
tribute most of these items to the secondary market.

> Nelvana became a supplier
> [of animation] to ABC at a time when
> networks were quite discriminating
> about who they dealt with, and we
> became the only Canadian supplier to
> the major networks.

Images courtesy of www.nelvana.com

Joe Cesaro, owner of Sunday Funnies in Chatsworth, California,
acted as a distributor for Royal Animated Art for many years and
acquired everything that was available from the "Holiday Special" and
episodes 9–13 of Droids and the second season of Ewoks. Upon
approval from Lucasfilm, Sunday Funnies also had the right to produce limited-edition serigraph eels (seri-cels) and made four Droids
and two Ewoks seri-cels specifically for the collectors market. All of
these items are available for sale through Sunday Funnies, which has
essentially become the curator of much of the original production
material from some of Nelvana's finest productions.

The success of the Droids and Ewoks Adventure Hour was another
important turning point in Nelvana's growth as a company. "It
was a very significant time for us," says Clive Smith. "For us to
be associated with people such as George [Lucas] was good for
everybody. It made us feel like we were part of the industry. Also,
from the outside, I'm sure people looking at the company were
impressed, so I think it was very important that we made those kinds
of connections. It certainly helped us in the early days."

Michael Hirsh points out that because of their work on the two
programs, "Nelvana became a supplier [of animation] to ABC at a
time when networks were quite discriminating about who they dealt
with, and we became the only Canadian supplier to the major networks." With their newfound recognition, Nelvana went on to produce
programs such as Care Bears and Beetlejuice and soon
discovered great success in adapting classic children's stories such
as Babar, Rupert, and Franklin.

In September 2000, Canadian broadcasting conglomerate Corus
Entertainment bought Nelvana, and the studio continues to be one of
the world's top producers of animation. It recently produced cult
favorites Clone High and Undergrads, and is currently working on
popular animated programs such as Medabots, Beyblade, and Alicia
Silverstone's Braceface. Although the three original founders of
Nelvana are no longer involved with the company, the legacy they
built lives on—with both Star Wars fans and animation fans
around the world who have come to expect nothing but the best
from the name Nelvana. ☺

Related Links
http://www.nelvana.com/
http://www.sundayfunniesllc.com/

Photos courtesy of Steve Sansweet

Droids and *Ewoks*—The Collectibles

In recent years, collectibles from the Droids and Ewoks Adventure Hour have become hotter than the blade of a lightsaber. The following is just a taste of some of the most popular *Droids* and *Ewoks* collectibles from around the world.

The Artwork: As with most popular animated programs, the animation eels, sketches and pre-production material from the *Droids* and *Ewoks Adventure Hour* have become very collectible. Pencil sketches and eels without original backgrounds can be affordable entry-level collectibles, with prices ranging from $25 to $100, while full production runs that include a eel,_ original background, layouts, storyboards, and sketches can fetch between $800 and $1,500.

The Videos: J2 Communications and CBS Fox released selected episodes of *Droids* and *Ewoks* on VHS. In 1990, J2 initially released two 23-minute tapes containing one episode each. Soon after, they released two "Special Double Length Edition" volumes, which contain two episodes per tape. In 1996, Fox Home Video released one new Droids and one new Ewoks tape in a clamshell case with three re-edited episodes. Several additional episodes of *Droids* and *Ewoks* were released in the United Kingdom in PAL format, including two promotional tapes from British dairy producer Dairylea. Currently, there are no plans to release the series on DVD.

The Comics: In 1985, Marvel subsidiary Star Comics released comics based on the *Droids* and *Ewoks* adventures. The *Droids* series lasted for eight issues and furthered the adventures of C-3PO and R2-D2, but it did not feature characters from the cartoon series. The *Ewoks* series ran for 14 issues and followed Wicket, Teebo, and Kneesaa, as well as many supporting characters from the cartoons throughout their mystical adventures on Endor. Today, these comics sell for between $2 and $10 depending on the issue number and condition.

The Toys: In 1985 Kenner released two new lines of *Star Wars* toys to coincide with the *Droids* and *Ewoks* cartoons, and these are easily the most sought-after collectibles from the shows. The Droids series consists of eight new figures, redecorated versions of C-3PO and R2-D2, repackaged versions of Baba Fett and an A-Wing Pilot, and three vehicles. The *Ewoks* line included six new figures, but no new vehicles or playsets. Interest in the *Droids* and *Ewoks* has increased dramatically in recent years, and prices vary greatly between different characters, and loose and packaged items.

A second series of new figures from both Droids and Ewoks was planned for release in 1986, but was cancelled before it went into production. Today, the unproduced Droids and Ewoks prototypes are highly desired by many collectors, and comprehensive documentation of these prototypes can be found on the Star Wars Collectors Archive at http://www.toysrgus.com/images-droids.html.

International Collectibles: Some of the most intriguing *Droids* and *Ewoks* collectibles come from a variety of countries around the world. Fans in the UK were treated to several exclusive storybooks and coloring books, rolls of wallpaper, and, perhaps most interestingly, a *Droids* video game for the Commodore 64 computer system. Exclusive *Ewoks* puzzles were reieased in France, but most of the truly unique European collectibles appeared in Spain. They included trading cards, a *Droids* block puzzle, a *Droids* board game, and sticker sets.

Portions of the Droids toy line were released in Canada and Brazil with exclusive, generic-style packaging, and only the Brazilian company Glasslite released the infamous second-series Vlix figure. While the *Ewoks* line was not released in Brazil, it was in Canada, again with a unique, generic package design. Only the four Dulok figures were released in this way, while Wicket and Logray were available only as a two-pack through the 1985 Sears Canada Christmas catalogue.

ARTOO AND THREEPIO'S GREATEST HITS!

TEN MEMORABLE EXPANDED UNIVERSE ADVENTURES OF THE DYNAMIC DROID DUO!
WORDS: JASON FRY

They're *Star Wars'* odd couple—a fussy golden biped who speaks more than six million languages and specializes in etiquette and protocol, paired with a spunky, barrel-shaped astromech who communicates solely (yet quite effectively) through a complex series of beeps and whistles.

Whatever the adventure, wherever the location, you can always count on C-3PO to wish he were someplace more civilized, where he'd be less likely to be shot at by stormtroopers or battle droids, or pulverized by asteroids. Just as certain, you can count on R2-D2 to coolly save our heroes from certain death when all else has failed.

The novels of *Star Wars'* Expanded Universe have given Artoo and Threepio plenty of opportunities for heroics—and some surprising star turns along the way. Here are 10 of their greatest moments from the novels.

LOVE BUZZ

Not all of the droids' heroics came in Luke's service. In 2008's *The Clone Wars*, we see Anakin Skywalker and Ahsoka Tano escape Teth's monastery on the back of a can-cell, with Artoo using his booster rockets to follow. But how did Anakin and Ahsoka get a ride on a giant fly? Karen Traviss explains that the can-cells are attracted by the engine sounds of the Republic's gunships, which they think are mating calls. Can Artoo mimic the sound of a gunship? The little droid responds that he can mimic the full range of Republic vessels—and Separatist ones too, if he's asked nicely!

A LAST MEAL

In Aaron Allston's *Rebel Stand* (2002), Han and Leia are captured on Aphran, leaving Artoo to plan a rescue by taking advantage of the literal-mindedness of droids. Artoo discovers a loophole in the prison computers' routines for prisoner care. After a bit of messing with images in a database, Threepio is able to walk a lightsaber and blaster right through security and have them brought to Han and Leia. Thanks to Artoo, the prison computers recognize them as various Corellian foods. Leia's reaction as the weapons are delivered for breakfast? "Well, that makes this my favorite prison ever."

THREEPIO 1, BUREAUCRATS 0

In Kristine Kathryn Rusch's *The New Rebellion* (1996), Threepio and Artoo must discover who's sabotaging the New Republic's X-wings —a mystery that gets Artoo shot and Threepio buried in rubble. And that's before they tackle a receptionist droid charged with keeping petitioners away from Mon Mothma. "We are above your petty bureaucratic power gambits," Threepio warns, adding that "I will personally make certain that you are demoted to working as a translator for mechanical garbage compactors." As protocol goes, that's pretty bare-knuckled.

LICENSE REVOKED

Han Solo missed a lot while entombed in carbonite, including a mission to Coruscant, in which Luke, Lando, and Leia ran afoul of criminal kingpin Prince Xizor. As told in 1996's *Shadows of the Empire* by Steve Perry, Luke and Lando leave the droids on the *Millennium Falcon* while they infiltrate Xizor's castle. When the *Falcon*'s hiding place is discovered, Threepio has to take the wheel—and as Luke listens in horror via comlink, the protocol droid crunches through a billboard and a broadcasting tower. But he also manages to arrive just in time to save his friends—which is more than good enough, under the circumstances.

QUESTIONS OF MORTALITY

An intriguing subplot of the *New Jedi Order* series sees Threepio wrestle with the thought of his own destruction or obsolescence. Artoo doesn't think much of his counterpart's musings, telling the golden droid to face the end bravely. But in *Rebel Stand* (2002), Threepio finds an unlikely philosophical partner: the combat droid YVH 1-1A. The two watch sparks fall from Han's welding torch and wonder if sparks feel fear at knowing their end is near —an unexpectedly touching scene amidst the tale of galactic war.

TAKE THAT!

In Timothy Zahn's *Dark Force Rising* (1992), Luke falls under the spell of Joruus C'baoth, becoming judge and jury for the poor inhabitants of Jomark. Mara Jade breaks the dark side's hold, but she and Luke then face C'baoth's fury. It's a short fight. Artoo, sitting ignored in Luke's X-wing, opens up with the starfighter's cannons, knocking C'baoth out. "Artoo," an impressed Luke muses, "wasn't shooting to kill."

HOW CLUMSY OF ME!

Threepio isn't a warrior, unless you mean that skirmish with "Jedi dogs" on Geonosis (don't ask him—he doesn't remember). But he proves an effective adversary when Viqi Shesh and a squad of Yuuzhan Vong infiltrators come to kidnap baby Ben Skywalker in Troy Denning's *Star by Star* (2001). One offer of refreshments and a dropped glass ball later, the commandos are down and Shesh is running for her life. Was it something Threepio said?

OLD MEMORIES

As every *Star Wars* fan knows, Threepio has his memory wiped at the end of *Revenge of the Sith*. But Artoo's memory banks contain information of enormous interest to Luke and Leia as they wrestle with their family's legacy. In Denning's *Dark Nest* trilogy (2005), Luke stumbles across a recording of Anakin and Padmé discussing his dream that she will die in childbirth—only to have Artoo refuse to show more. When Luke finally unlocks Artoo's memory, the two trilogies are knit together by the little droid who witnessed it all.

A CORELLIAN'S CYRANO

If you needed a hint that 1994's *The Courtship of Princess Leia* would be different, you got it early in Dave Wolverton's book. After an intoxicated Han turns to Threepio for romantic advice, Threepio tries to help, and on Dathomir he breaks out a song he's written—"The Virtues of King Han Solo"—with accompanying symphonic music and even a tap-dance routine. Princess Leia is agog. You will be, too.

ARTOO ATTACK!

One of the many treats of Matthew Stover's *Luke Skywalker and the Shadows of Mindor* (2008) is seeing things from Artoo's perspective. When Han, Leia, and Chewie are dragged deep into the planet Mindor and assaulted by Melters, we watch Artoo monitor things with a computer's precision, until an old subroutine activates—and it's time for the little droid to go to war.

What does the future hold for this unlikely droid duo? If the past is any guide, lots of arguments, calculations of odds, and interfacing with computers, both helpful and malign. And, you can be sure, there will be unexpected duties and last-minute rescues. After decades of adventures, Artoo and Threepio can expect as much—as can all the readers who have grown to love them. ☉

CHOPPER ROLLS OUT!

WHEN LUCASFILM NEEDED A SPECIAL DROID, IT TURNED TO DROID-BUILDER MICHAEL MCMASTER TO CREATE A FEISTY SCREEN-ACCURATE ASTROMECH! INTERVIEW BY JONATHAN WILKINS

Star Wars Insider: How did this live-action version of Chopper come about?

Michael McMaster: I maintain the Lucasfilm R2-D2, which is used for public relations. About a year ago, [Lucasfilm senior events lead] Mary Franklin approached me with the idea of building a new droid from *Star Wars Rebels*. She said [*Star Wars Rebels'* supervising director] Dave Filoni was hoping to have one before the R2 Builders Club got wind of it and made an army of them!

How long did it take to put him together?
I spent about 87 days working on the build, start to finish.

> **"I WAS WORRIED CHOPPER MIGHT NOT WORK PROPERLY FOR THE BIG REVEAL!"**

What are the challenges in building a droid? One of the most challenging aspects of the build was simply trying to get all the details correct. Fortunately, I had plenty of reference material provided to me, and was always able to ask for more information if I was unsure about a specific detail. Also, everything had to be scratch-built, so that raised its own set of challenges. The droid is similar in many ways to other droids in the *Star Wars* universe, but there are a few things that

are unique to Chopper as well. The dome arms, which were a tribute to the original sketches by the great Ralph McQuarrie, is one example.

What did you learn from building R2 and WALL-E?
Well, Chopper is similar to R2 in his overall design, which helped as I was already very familiar with how he operated mechanically. WALL-E was

my first entirely scratch-built robot, and that certainly gave me the confidence to tackle this project.

He's 100% accurate—what was the most difficult thing to replicate?
Most of the build was relatively simple, but the design of the center wheel probably gave me the most trouble. In the animated series, the wheel sticks out at an angle, which works fine for an

Opposite page:
Michael poses with Chopper and R2-D2!

This page, clockwise from top left:
Chopper meets some of the team at Lucasfilm; a close-up look at the intricate detailing of the droid; an astromech stand-off between Chopper and R2; "Look sir, droids!" McMaster's amazing creations: WALL-E, Chopper, and R2-D2; a look at the complicated electronics that power Chopper.

Lucasfilm photos by Joel Aron; behind-the-scenes photos by Michael McMaster

animated character, but is frustrating when trying to use a castering wheel, which is what I wound up using. The wheel would loop up and bind if tipped at an angle, so I had to rework the design a tiny bit so that it would turn smoothly.

How did it feel when Chopper was unveiled to the Lucasfilm team?
I was actually a nervous wreck at that point. It was very exciting to have the team who designed the robot finally get to see it in person, but at that point it had only been tested for a very short period of time. I was worried something might not work properly for the big reveal. Fortunately, he ran perfectly, which was a great relief!

What advice would you give to anyone wanting to build droids?
I would encourage anyone interested in droid-building to seek out the R2 Builders Club. It 's a great resource and the members are very encouraging. We can be found on Yahoo Groups (R2 Builders Club), or you can visit Astromech.net. Your level of experience does not limit your ability to create a droid, as we have builders from every walk of life. Anyone can build, trust me.

Special thanks to Matt Martin and Mickey Capoferri at starwars.com for their help with this article.

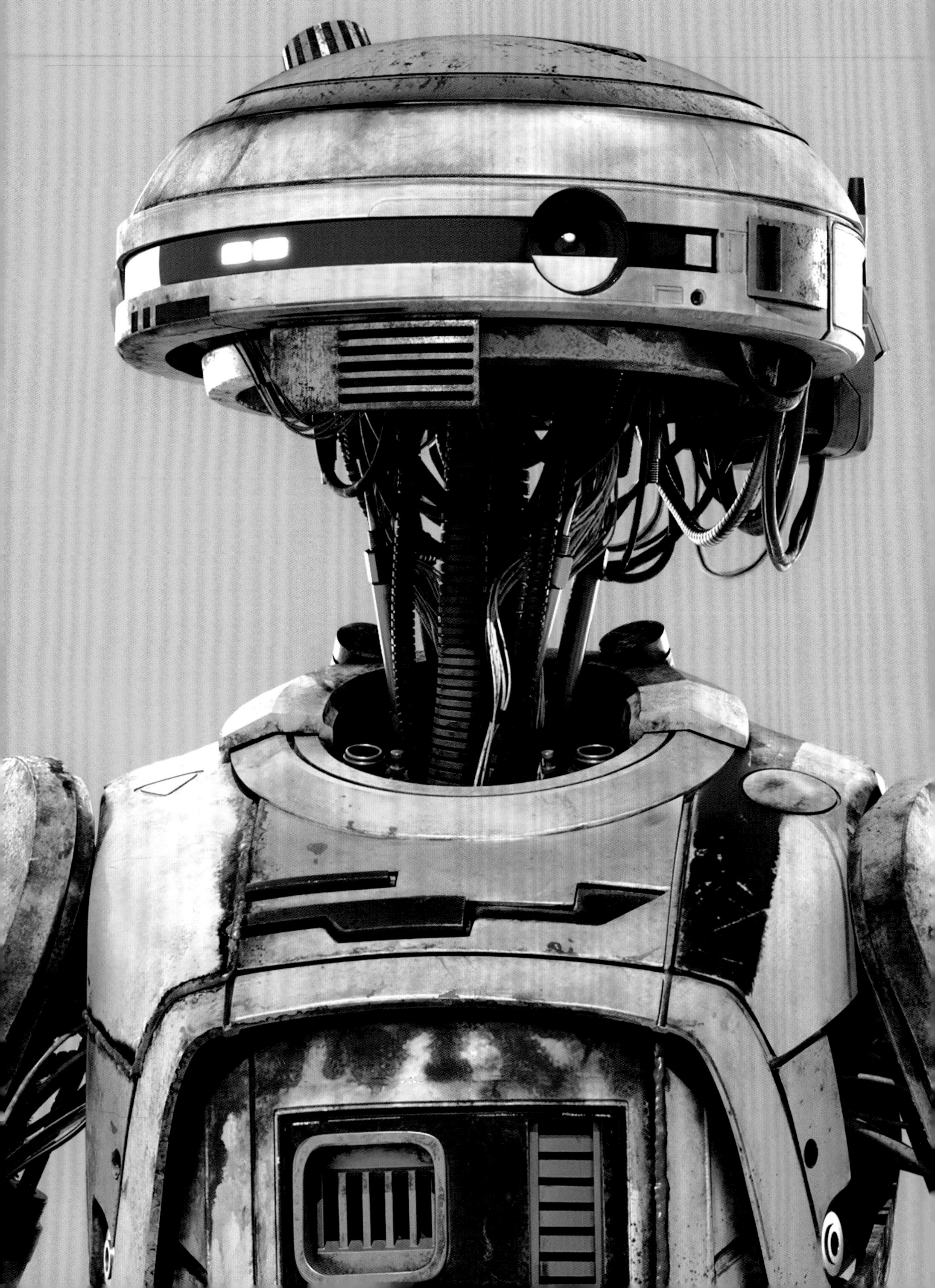

DROID RIGHTS!

In *Solo: A Star Wars Story*, breakout character L3-37 made us question our understanding of droid-kind and their place in the *Star Wars* galaxy. *Insider* examines the ideas of sentience and equal rights that the plucky droid championed.

WORDS: TRICIA BARR

01

Ubiquitous in their presence across the *Star Wars* eras for millennia, droids are such a common sight that they go about their business unnoticed, on worlds far and wide. These complex and varied utility devices, designed only to better the lives of those they serve, can be upgraded or replaced at will, and cast aside when their circuits are worn through. Taken from the perspective of mythic archetypes, when a droid 'dies' does it really matter at all?

When discussing his storytelling perspective on writing the original *Star Wars* movie, George Lucas has often cited one particular inspiration he drew from Akira Kurosawa's samurai classic, *The Hidden Fortress* (1958): a film told through the eyes of a pair of peasants who were "the two lowest characters" in the tale. From Lucas'

perspective, that is what R2-D2 and C-3PO originally represented. In terms of myth, their fates are the least important—far removed from the epic stakes fueling the journeys of Leia Organa, Luke Skywalker, and Han Solo. Droids are the lowest of the low—metal, plastic, and programming pieced together to work tirelessly until they are

obsolete or damaged beyond repair. Or at least, that's how many within that fictional universe see them.

L3-37 forces us to do a double-take on that viewpoint. The "self-made" droid is an independent being, with her own forthright opinions and beliefs; she is Lando Calrissian's partner in crime, his friend not a glorified ratchet—and she certainly doesn't see herself as his property. We shed a tear along with Lando when L3 meets her unfortunate demise, her parts scattered across the deck of the *Millennium Falcon*. As the light flickers out of her photoreceptors, she dies, and that death means something to us.

The fact is that these droid characters *do* matter; we care about them—and their fates. Is that simply because the droids feature in so many cherished fan memories, like R2's determination to deliver Leia's message to Obi-Wan Kenobi or C-3PO's comically timed interruption of Han and Leia's first kiss on the *Millennium Falcon?* Or is it because we have come to see the droids as fully realized characters who have wants and needs, just like their human counterparts? R2-D2's determination to support his friends at any cost to his personal safety is made clear on numerous occasions, while in C-3PO we recognize other attributes, such as his strong desire to continue serving his master as best he

02

All six of Lucas' *Star Wars* films rely on R2-D2 and C-3PO as their central droid characters. Though in some ways they could not be more opposite, each contains important notions about servitude and sentience for droids in a galaxy far, far away.

can and, perhaps more selfishly but understandably, to survive another day without being blown to bits. They act with free will, with forethought, and with full understanding of the impact of their actions. That's actually better than many humans manage.

No Loose Wire Jokes

Following in the footsteps of *A New Hope*, all six of Lucas' *Star Wars* films rely on R2 and C-3PO as their central droid characters. Though in some ways they could not be more opposite, each embodies important notions about servitude and sentience for droids in a galaxy far, far away.

C-3PO's origins allude back to HAL-9000 in Stanley Kubrick's 1968 masterpiece, *2001: A Space Odyssey* (see sidebar on page 72). In the original trilogy, his role as a protocol droid—a kind of interpreter and butler for a diplomat-turned-insurgent princess—leads to his eagerness to assist his human compatriots, whilst trying to avoid even the hint of mortal peril. Constructed from spare parts by Anakin Skywalker to make his mother's life easier, C-3PO goes on to serve Shmi and the Lars family for a decade until the young Jedi's fateful return to Tatooine, whereupon he assumes his familiar protocol droid functions for Leia's mother, Padmé. Throughout the Skywalker saga the movies play C-3PO's intended purpose for laughs. After all, when exactly has he ever made things easier for anyone other than the audience (for whom he delivers light relief from the unfolding drama)?

R2-D2, on the other hand, displays far more creativity and rebelliousness. For much of the original trilogy he plays the role of a trickster god for Luke, from deceiving the young farmboy into removing his restraining bolt to escaping into the Tatooine desert; from his antics on Dagobah to his covert operation to infiltrate Jabba's palace with a concealed lightsaber. But he can also be the god of luck, making

03

01 More than just a co-pilot, L3-37 is Lando's friend. (Opposite page)

02 L3-37 instigates a droid uprising on Kessel. (Opposite page)

03 R2-D2 is determined to complete his mission, even when captured by Jawas.

a fortuitously timed repair to the *Millennium Falcon* or slicing into an Imperial dataport to slam closed a blast door in the nick of time. In the prequel trilogy he plays much the same role for Anakin and Padmé—and in fact their adventure would never have begun if the brave astromech had not performed a critical repair to Queen Amidala's Royal starship during its escape through the blockade above Naboo. It wasn't until *Star Wars: Revenge of the Sith* (2005) that a long-suspected notion was confirmed: R2 possesses an elevated status among droids for not having had his memory wiped across the decades. Like HAL in *2001*, he knows more than the humans he serves.

In addition to portraying R2-D2 and C-3PO with personalities reminiscent of human characters, Lucas' films also introduced the idea of free will among droids. From the Jawa sandcrawler to the Lars homestead, the existence of restraining bolts implies that a droid can—if they wish—choose to do things they would *prefer* to do ▶

UNDERSTANDING SENTIENCE

The Merriam-Webster dictionary defines the word "sentient" in three ways: Firstly as, "responsive to or conscious of sense impressions;" secondly as, "aware;" and finally as, "finely sensitive in perception or feeling." Though there are many deeper philosophical nuances, this basic definition explains the core components of the concept. As human beings, we can understand such concepts of awareness, of our situation and surroundings. The droids of *Star Wars*, from tiny MSE-6 units to battle droids and countless protocol droids, comprehend them too, and we see this from their actions and reactions to various stimuli in scenes from every movie. While L3-37 is occasionally portrayed as oblivious (perhaps deliberately so) to the sideways glances and general incredulity of her human associates, she clearly possesses such understanding.

The question is, has such awareness merely been programmed into them, or have millennia of technological and manufacturing improvements resulted in droid processors as complex—and as capable of sentience—as biological brains?

The idea of what is and isn't sentient has changed significantly in the last half century. The generation of school kids that witnessed *A New Hope*'s initial big-screen success may remember being told that an animal is not sentient. However, in the years since then, many scientific discoveries have proven that dogs have simple but identifiable emotions and dolphins can hold a conversation. Science hasn't yet proven animals capable of complex emotions, although the sheer number of internet memes of guilty-looking dogs (guilt is a complex emotion) suggests that scientists might want to keep studying.

ANTHROPOMORPHIC AUTOMATONS

Anthropomorphic stories have attributed human traits to animals and gods for as long as there has been recorded myth. That a supernatural power who created mankind might look like a human stems from the tendency to relate to higher concepts through ideas we already understand—or, as a droid might put it, to reverse engineer a solution to a puzzle. Not all cultures imagined their creators or deities as humans, however. For the Incan gods, they were their sources of life: the sun, moon, earth, and sea; various Native American groups and ancient Egyptians worshipped divine forces in animal form; and African fables often had trickster gods appear in the shape of animals as well. Popular tales in the late 1800s and early 1900s, including *Alice in Wonderland*, *The Jungle Book*, *Winnie-the-Pooh*, and *The Chronicles of Narnia* seeded in the minds of children the idea that animals had distinct lives and even understood complex concepts like betrayal and salvation. Not remarkably, these classic childhood stories went on to become famous films.

It is little surprise, then, that the rise of science fiction brought with it the idea that anthropomorphic characteristics would exist in machines and technological devices, especially sophisticated ones. The seminal *2001: A Space Odyssey* (1968) portrays an artificial intelligence on the spacecraft *Discovery One* as malicious. HAL-9000, called "Hal" by his crew, is believed to be foolproof, but he faces an existential crisis when his programming requires him to lie to his shipmates about their true mission. Film critic Roger Ebert wrote that HAL, "behaves in the most human fashion of all of the characters." In *Terminator 2: Judgment Day* (1991), Industrial Light & Magic famously rendered a robot comprised of malleable silver metal capable of taking on human form and exercising human-like ingenuity in fulfilling its mission: to hunt down and kill humans. Fortunately, mechanical sentience can be charming, too. Pixar Animation Studio, originally a graphics group of Lucasfilm's computer division, provided proof of concept for computer-generated animation by bringing to life a desk lamp, now part of its iconic studio logo. Since then the studio has portrayed cars, planes, and childhood toys as sentient beings in a catalog of animated full-length features. *WALL-E* (2008) follows the adventures of the titular character, left on a trash-ridden Earth and continuing to work after gaining sentience that has allowed him to self-repair. He crosses paths with EVE, a robot designed to search for signs of life, and a romance ensues against the backdrop of the fate of the human race.

04

over their intended assignments. If a droid is programmed only to follow his master's bidding and cannot do otherwise, then what is there to restrain him/her (aside, perhaps, from technical malfunctions)?

When L3-37 ignites an impromptu droid uprising on Kessel, we witness the freedom and joy experienced by droids the instant their restraining bolts are removed. What's more, those droids immediately set about freeing all the other slaves trapped in the mines, suggesting empathy for their fellow prisoners that can only be a result of sentience.

Enemies and Allies

As we've noted, not only do the mechanized characters display intelligent responses to stimuli and self-awareness of their existence (and "mortality"), but also complex emotions and interpersonal empathy, just as humans do. The portrayal of droids in *Star Wars* stories has expanded far beyond the iconic duo from the original film, bringing with it the increasing notion that they are sentient beings on a par with humans and aliens.

Examples of this pepper the films. The B1 battle droids of the prequel trilogy are controlled from a central computer and display only primal emotions such as fear. Mister Bones in the *Aftermath* trilogy of novels or R0-GR in *The Freemaker Adventures* animated series (2016-2017) imply that even seemingly simple mechs are only a few sophisticated processor upgrades away from memorable personalities. In *Star Wars: The Clone Wars* (2008-2015), the super-tactical droid known as Kalani is far more competent than the Separatist

In addition to portraying R2 and C-3PO with personalities reminiscent of human characters, Lucas' films also introduced the idea of free will among droids.

05

04 BB-8 exhibits a determined streak
when his friends are in need of help.
(Opposite page)

05 On Scarif, K-2SO is willing to sacrifice
himself in aid of the rebel cause.

06 Restraining bolts crush the free will
of droid slaves in the mines of Kessel.

07 K-2SO is not short on self-awareness
or sassy comebacks.

06

07

humans he nominally serves on Onderon, ultimately killing King Rash when he is no longer of use to the Confederacy. More than a decade later on Agamar and no longer bound by allegiance to the long-defeated Separatist cause, Kalani initially deploys his battle droids against Ezra Bridger and Captain Rex (*Star Wars Rebels*, "The Last Battle"), but then agrees to ally with them after he determines that the Empire is the greater threat to his autonomously chosen objectives. The family droid of the *Ghost* crew, Chopper, acts as though he only begrudgingly participates in the activities of his organic crewmates, but by the series finale we know better, having seen him scheme, mourn, and celebrate right along with them.

In the sequel trilogy, BB-8 emotes like an actor, increasing the anthropomorphic quality of his actions. On Jakku he might well be calculating that his chances of successfully delivering the much sought-after map are greater with Rey's help than on his own, but on Takodana he chooses to leave Han Solo and Maz Kanata—two people even more likely to help complete his mission—to accompany Rey down into the bowels of the castle and then into the woods beyond. This determined streak continues in *Star Wars: The Last Jedi* (2017), where we witness BB-8 attack Canto Bight police, help DJ steal a starship, and gleefully blast stormtroopers from an AT-ST. (Deleted scenes reveal that BB-8 stows away—or in other words, tags along on the mission of his own free will.)

Then there's K-2SO of *Rogue One: A Star Wars Story* (2016), the Imperial security droid reprogrammed by Cassian Andor to serve the Rebel Alliance. K2 certainly has no shortage of self-awareness or indignation, and one could be forgiven for wondering whether his loyalty to Cassian is a result of his programming or rather by choice. In the end, however, his final act cannot be contested: K2 willingly gives his life to ensure that Cassian and Jyn Erso are successful in stealing the Death Star plans.

She's Got It Where It Counts, and Then Some

In *Star Wars: The Empire Strikes Back* (1980), C-3PO bemoans what he calls the "peculiar dialect" of the ship when asked to communicate with it to help fix the stricken vessel. Thanks to *Solo: A Star Wars Story*, we now have some insight into what the *Millennium Falcon* has to say for herself, as we've spent a decent amount of time in the company of one of the ship's most single-minded components—the prickly L3-37 herself.

Even more than K-2SO, L3-37 has autonomy in ▶

08 L3-37 revels in her victory, moments before she is shot down.

09 The fighting droids of Fort Ypso.

08

09

▶ her deeds and motivations as well as her dialogue. She sticks up not only for herself, but also for the fighting droids at Fort Ypso and the mining crew at Kessel, and exults in the liberation accomplished by the droid who goes on to free all the organic slaves bound to servitude in the Pyke Syndicate's mines—surely the fact that so many droids of all types have self-awareness and emotions lends credence to her belief that they deserve rights as well?

Moments after this powerful expression of self-purpose occurs, L3-37 is mortally wounded. Her dying words are personal, shared with Lando alone, and it's clear that they share an emotional as well as a professional bond. But for a droid, "death" isn't necessarily as terminal an end as it is for organic life. Soon after, Lando and Qi'ra upload the droid's central processor into the *Falcon*, in a desperate attempt to survive the Akkadese Maelstrom. If you subscribe to the theory that at its heart, *Solo* is a story about individuals

with varying degrees of selfish intentions (sometimes in alignment and sometimes not), then it seems no coincidence that L3's processor saves the lives of everyone on board the *Falcon* during this daring escape. Whether what remained of L3-37 was saving herself or Lando is up for debate, but the droid's single-minded determination lived on.

With a part of L3's mind at the heart of the *Falcon*, a whole new light is lent to many events taking place years later: surviving the asteroid field beyond Hoth; escaping the explosion

Even more than K-2SO, L3-37 has autonomy in her deeds and motivations as well as her dialogue.

of the second Death Star at Endor; the frantic escape through the Starship Graveyard of Jakku; and navigating the narrow caverns of crimson crystal on Crait. While the Jedi may speak of the will of the Force, perhaps these incidents, in their own way, are the will of the *Falcon*—and the self-determination of its droid brain with a mind of its own. ☸

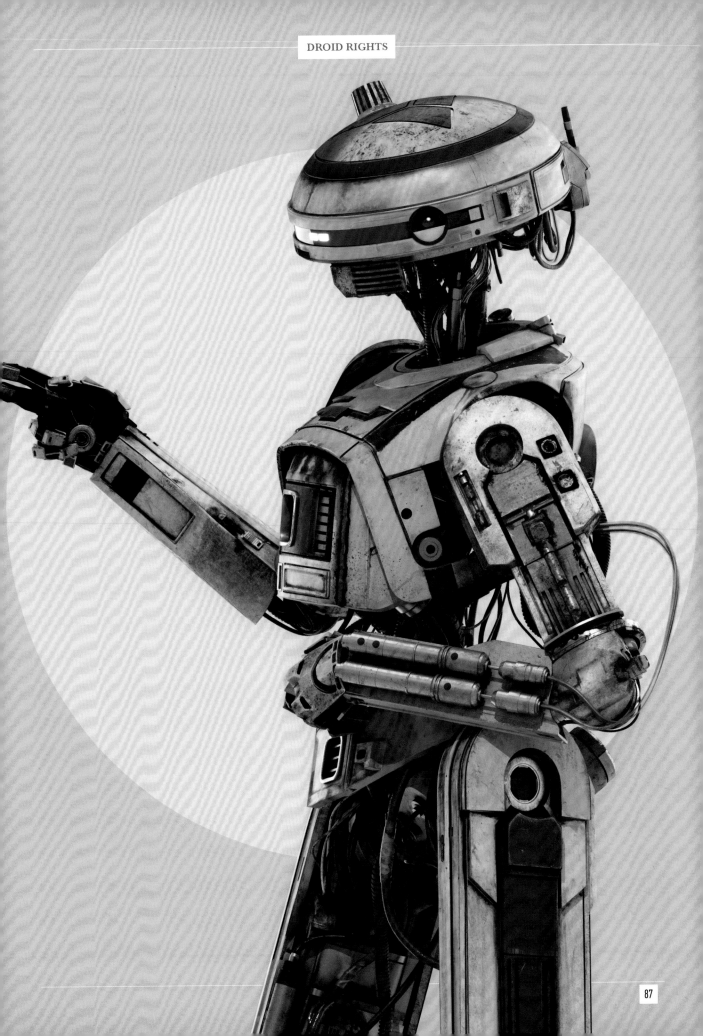

OLIVER STEEPLES' FIVE FAVORITE DROID MOMENTS IN THE STAR WARS SAGA

DROID BUILDER OLIVER STEEPLES IS PART OF THE TEAM PERSONALLY APPROACHED BY KATHLEEN KENNEDY TO CREATE DROIDS FOR *STAR WARS: THE FORCE AWAKENS*. SO, WHO BETTER TO NOMINATE FIVE GREAT MOMENTS FEATURING *STAR WARS'* MECHANICAL MARVELS?

 R2-D2 AND C-3PO ON TATOOINE (*A NEW HOPE*, 1977)

The scene with R2-D2 and C-3PO "discussing" which direction to go after landing on Tatooine—the easier, open desert route or the rocky canyon—perfectly sums up their relationship, while exemplifying R2's resolute character. R2 beeps and whistles about his mission and heads off on his own with dogged determination. Even after being captured by Jawas and sold to Owen Lars, the little droid is still dedicated to finding Obi-Wan Kenobi and delivering Princess Leia's message. As Luke says, "I've never seen such devotion in a droid before."

 THE PIT DROIDS' PERFORMANCE (*THE PHANTOM MENACE*, 1999)

I've always enjoyed seeing robots slightly deviate from their programming, which happens to perfection in *The Phantom Menace*. It occurs when all the podracers are assembling at the starting line for the Boonta Eve Classic and you see three pit droids perfectly acting out a scene that is very reminiscent of The Three Stooges. Simply a pure slice of comedy! Whether it's a protocol droid in *Star Wars* or a bending robot in *Futurama*, it's great to see them skirt the boundaries of their character to provide comic relief.

3 PROBE DROID ON PATROL
(*THE EMPIRE STRIKES BACK*, 1980)

The scene on Hoth when you first see the probe droid emerging from the crater is great. Its unique insectile head, spider-like eyes, mechanical mid-section, and long legs give it a very scary and menacing appearance. The probe droid carries on the tradition of terrifying mechanical abominations, which includes the IT-0 interrogator droid from *A New Hope* (keen observers will notice it features an R2-D2-style dome). However, the probe droid is markedly improved and a bigger threat thanks to its sensors and unknown weapons system.

4 OOM-SERIES BATTLE DROIDS (*THE PHANTOM MENACE*, 1999)

Like the pit droids, I find the battle droids fascinating and love every scene they are in. Their sole purpose is to obey instructions beamed down from the mothership; they have no intelligence whatsoever. I have two favorite scenes. The first one is the build up to the Battle of Naboo when the battle droids are offloaded from the carrier and expand in unison to form multiple ranks of soldiers. The second is when we are first introduced to the battle droids, as Qui-Gon Jinn and Obi-Wan Kenobi fight their way off the Trade Federation flagship.

5 IMPERIAL SENTRY DROIDS (*THE FORCE AWAKENS*, 2015)

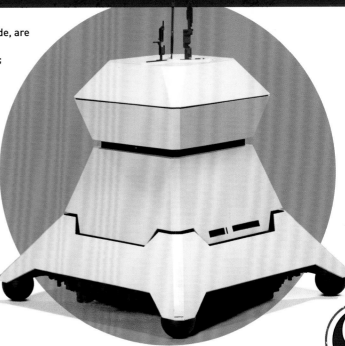

These droids, which I made, are only seen during the Star Destroyer hangar scenes; but it was very fulfilling to see them in the final film, especially as they reflect off the Imperial flight desk with all the explosions going off! I created a prototype first, which was based off concept sketches from Luke Fisher. After it was approved, I made the other two. They were originally supposed to be a mottled gray color, similar to a Star Destroyer, but this was changed to a high gloss to match the stormtroopers.

Interview by Mark Newbold

MY STAR WARS

LEE TOWERSEY WENT FROM A MEMBER OF THE R2 BUILDER'S CLUB TO CREATING ACTUAL DROIDS FOR *STAR WARS: THE FORCE AWAKENS* INCLUDING THE ALL-NEW DROID, BB-8! INTERVIEW: MARK NEWBOLD

When did you become involved in *Star Wars* fandom and build your first R2 unit?
My serious interest in all things *Star Wars* started in 2007. Before then I had built a few remote-control cars, planes, and boats. I decided I needed a new challenge, so I built a working R2-D2. I had originally started to build a Dalek (from *Doctor Who*) but it was just too big. To justify to my wife the reason for doing so, I discovered the Rebel Legion and started going to the same events they did.

When did you see *The Force Awakens* for the first time?
At the last minute I was fortunate enough to be asked to the London Premiere to help the Creature Effects Team operate BB-8. I was not supposed to be seeing the film that night, but one of our crew kindly asked if I could get in.

How does it feel to be a *Star Wars* celebrity?
I really don't see myself as a celebrity. I'm happy to be referred to as such—I'm not shy—but I feel no differently now than before working on *Star Wars*. Many talented people worked on this film, and all are worthy of being recognized for their contributions.

When did you sign your first *Star Wars* autograph?
I believe it was in 2015 when I was at *Star Wars Celebration* in Anaheim. At first, Oliver Steeples and I had planned to attend as fans, just like everybody else. Little did we know what was going to happen! [Director] J.J. Abrams and [executive producer] Kathleen

Kennedy asked us to join them on stage at the opening of Celebration, which was an honor. I was also invited to the Rebel Legion dinner where Oliver and I were made honorary members! The award they gave me is proudly displayed at home in a small area where my wife lets me show off my limited collection of *Star Wars*-related items.

What stands out most for you in *The Force Awakens*?
The humor throughout the film, because it wasn't overdone. I felt like everyone had an onscreen comedic moment, and no one person stood out as the "comedian."

What is the best gift you've received by being involved with *Star Wars*?
Firstly, it has to be the friends I have made in the industry. I was running my own business from home before all of this happened; as much as I enjoyed it, I spent a lot of time on my own while the rest of the family was at work or school. To be with a group of talented people working as a team was a welcome change to being home alone!

Secondly, I love that I have been able to travel. Since November 2015 I've attended events in New York and Japan, to name a couple of places, to operate BB-8 and promote *The Force Awakens*.

How many people from your Builder's Club attend these events?
We have two teams of two who attend events to operate what we call the "Red Carpet" version of BB-8, which was first seen at Celebration in Anaheim during April of last year. The main team includes BB-8 builders Matt Denton and Josh Lee; and if they can't attend events, Adam Wright and I will go.

What is your favorite *Star Wars* film and why?
A New Hope, hands down. It was one of the first films I saw, and I really think it has withstood the test of time. If time travel existed I would go back and tell my seven-year-old self what I'm doing now! I'm certain I would blow my own mind! ✤

THE ART SIDE OF THE FORCE

FROM HOWARD CHAYKIN'S PRE-RELEASE *STAR WARS* POSTER IN 1976 TO THE PRESENT DAY, ARTISTIC INTERPRETATIONS OF GEORGE LUCAS' SAGA HAVE ALWAYS BEEN WITH US. THREE SUCH ARTISTS ARE ROY GRINNELL, KRYSTII MELAINE, AND ANN HANSON, WHO WERE CHOSEN TO CONTRIBUTE TO THE RECENT *STAR WARS ART: VISIONS* BOOK, AND WHOSE ART ALSO GRACED THE BLU-RAY BOOKLET.

Roy Grinnell

ROY GRINNELL
"Wait...the Droid Just Wants to Say Hello"

Roy Grinnell was born in Santa Barbara, California. As a child, he enjoyed drawing airplanes: a passion that he has never lost. After serving time in the Navy, he attended the Art Center School of Design in Los Angeles, graduating with honors. He is currently the official artist for the American Fighter Aces, and the Commemorative Airpower Heritage Museum.

As the official artist of the American Fighter Aces, it's a surprise that you haven't contributed an image of an X-wing or a dogfight. Were you tempted to take that route?
My main theory in all my paintings is remembering "Imagination is the key to success." Being an artist for the Fighter Aces does help my brain to flow in that vein, but I do like to deviate to my other interests as well.
I did, however, paint a combat scene that appeared in the *Star Wars Art: Visions* Limited Edition version (available from Abrams Books).

It shows Anakin Skywalker in a Naboo N-1 starfighter firing laser cannons at droid starfighters. There's a lot of action in that one (above, right)!

Was it important to get personality into the giant droid?
I tried to give the droid some human feelings. I wanted to show the droid was lost and lonely on a barren planet. Having found Artoo-Detoo and Threepio, he is offering his hand in friendship. The accompanying "Space Cowboy" is having a hard time controlling the CRILOC Horse's reaction to seeing the droid. I wanted the viewer to feel friendliness as well as the desperation of the encounter.

What were the challenges of painting things that don't exist in our world?
The situation opens up total imagination of what could exist and could happen. The challenge is only limited by the level of one's imagination. In my work for the Fighter Aces, I have to portray what it was like to be

in that situation of combat as the fighter pilot explains his vivid scene of life or death to me. I try to visualize his desperation and to put on canvas a factual account of his aerial combat and victory.

Do you have any plans to do any more *Star Wars* art?
I would deeply love to have an opportunity to paint more *Star Wars* art. George Lucas has set a high standard of excellence in whatever venture he undertakes. In the *Star Wars Art: Visions* book project, magnificent and creative artists were chosen from around the world to illustrate his creations. It exemplifies his taste and ability to achieve greatness in fantasy. The project was a joy to work on from start to finish.

EXPANDED

You can enjoy more of Roy's work here at www.roygrinnell.com/

UNIVERSE

KRYSTII MELAINE
"Fur Balls"

Classically trained in the realist tradition of the old masters, Australian-born artist Krystii Melaine's art explores themes of the American West. Her work incorporates wildlife, cowboys, and Native Americans, and has won numerous accolades, including many Best of Show awards.

How did you come to be commissioned for the *Star Wars Art: Visions* book?
I first heard of the project through Big Horn Galleries in Cody, Wyoming, which represents me and a number of the other artists in the book. The gallery owner hesitantly said he had heard of a project that I might not be interested in, as it wasn't within my normal painting subject range. When he told me it was to paint an image from *Star Wars*, I immediately said I'd love to do it! I still remember the night I saw the first *Star Wars* movie in Adelaide, South Australia. It had a big impact on me. I loved painting monsters, dragons, and imaginary characters as a teenager, but the opportunity to paint such things as a professional artist doesn't come along very often. Once I had completed the painting, George Lucas decided to purchase it for his personal collection. (In the book, my painting appears much darker and redder than the original, which has a greenish background to indicate the forest setting.) I painted Han Solo with more natural skin tones, reflecting how he looked in the cool filtered light of the forest.

How different was this project from what you usually do?
I'm a portrait and wildlife artist, so a portrait of Han Solo with a bunch of Ewoks was actually quite close to what I normally paint. Han Solo was my favorite human character from the first moment he appeared on the screen. I loved the Ewoks as soon as I saw them in *Return of the Jedi*, so the decision of what to paint for the book was easily made. Apart from the clothes and weapons, and a higher level of intelligence and activity, Ewoks are pretty similar to the Koalas that I have painted. I approached them in the same way I do for any new species I want to paint —studying their appearance, anatomy, habitat, history, and personalities. I wanted to show them defiant and ready to face anything, to honor their essential role in the destruction of the second Death Star and the Rebel victory over the Empire!

Do you have a favorite Ewok?
I like them all, but there's a little guy in a reddish hood who was very busy getting into

the background of nearly every shot when the Ewoks catch Han, Luke, and the others in the forest. (He appears in at least 21 shots throughout that scene.) With that much determination, I just had to include him and placed him in the back left of my painting!

What are the challenges of capturing Harrison Ford's likeness?
Harrison Ford is so famous that capturing his likeness accurately was a huge challenge. His face is not perfectly symmetrical, and I resisted the urge to straighten his features. I spent a lot of time studying every image of

Harrison that I could find, in order to portray him as he really looked at the time and to capture his personality. *Star Wars* is a galactic Western in many ways, and Han Solo is very like the cowboys I know and have painted, both visually and in attitude. He was always armed and ready for any eventuality. I think he even wore the same clothes every day!

Have you any plans to do any more *Star Wars* art and if so, which character would you like to do?
I'd really enjoy painting more *Star Wars* art and when I first saw the book, it

inspired a whole bunch of new ideas for paintings. There are so many interesting characters and I'd love to paint their portraits. Imagine having some of those beautifully strange personalities sitting in my studio for a portrait painted from life. What amazing conversations we could have as I painted them!

EXPANDED

Visit Krystii's site at http://krystiimelaine.com/

UNIVERSE

A rough, premilinary sketch of the finished piece (above).

A premilinary sketch of
the finished piece (above).

ANN HANSON
"On the Hunt"

Ann Hanson paints with oils and pastels, and is noted for her very realistic and highly detailed work. Although she did a lot of science fiction and fantasy artwork in her youth, she now specializes in artwork in the Western genre. Her paintings have been exhibited across America and have been featured on numerous magazine covers.

Where there any other ideas that you toyed with before going for the Boba Fett image?
Yes, there were. The first sketch I submitted was a scene which included George Lucas reading to some children. They already had a few pieces with Mr. Lucas in them, so I went on to "plan B." I do a lot of Western art featuring cowboys. I really liked the idea of Boba Fett as the misunderstood bad guy with a cowboy-like attitude.

What were the challenges of painting a creature that doesn't exist?
That was the really cool part—Boba Fett and Boga [the varactyl that Obi-Wan rides on Utapau] do exist, even if it is only on the big screen. I was able to use some of the original concept art as reference. Also, I had a great excuse to watch all the *Star Wars* movies over and over again!

How does illustrating fantasy differ from Western art?
I actually did a lot of fantasy work when I was younger. Of course, the subject matter is different, but my method is the same—extensive drawings, work out the design and composition, and make sure I know my subject well before I start painting.

What makes Boba Fett so popular?
As a bounty hunter, there is something innately romantic about him. I had a blast drawing him! He was a perfect choice with his guns in the air, galloping at full speed after his latest bounty; totally Western.

How long did the piece take to complete?
Because of the preliminary work taking a little longer than usual, I worked on this piece for a couple of months.

Have you any plans to do any more *Star Wars* art and, if so, which character would you like to do?
It is always fun to get back to your roots. I would love to revisit fantasy art again! I've been working on a series of cowgirls recently—there are lots of *Star Wars* women who would qualify! ☻

An early idea, in which Boba Fett rode a strange, exotic horse-like creature.

GUIDE TO THE GALAXY

STAR WARS
THE COMPLETE SAGA

EXPANDED
To see more of Ann's art, visit
http://annhanson.com
UNIVERSE

"THANK THE MAKER"

WORDS: NEIL EDWARDS

WHY IT'S A CLASSIC

"Thank the Maker" gives us a rare glimpse into the mind of Darth Vader during the events of the classic trilogy, after he has learned of the existence of the rebel known as Luke Skywalker. By this time, Vader has realized that Luke is his son, and has surely also realized that the Emperor lied to him when he told him that Anakin had killed Padmé before she gave birth. As he cradles the head of C-3PO in a Cloud City room after the droid has been blasted by stormtroopers, Vader remembers how he was once the Tatooine slave boy who saved the droid from the junkyard and promised his mother that he would be responsible for him.

Remembering that promise, and hearing of Chewbacca's similar actions in rescuing C-3PO from a junk pile, Vader changes his mind about having the droid smelted and has the droid's parts returned to the rebel prisoners. Vader's moment of reflection over his past is surely one of the first steps in the redemption that will lead to him throwing the Emperor into the Death Star reactor in order to save his son. As we see at the end of the story, however, when he leaves for his "appointment" with Han Solo in the interrogation chamber, Vader hasn't reached that point yet. The balance of the Force, however, is shifting.

WHAT THEY SAID

I'd always wondered about how C-3PO's parts wound up in Chewbacca's cell on Cloud City. It wasn't until after I read the screenplay for Episode I that I considered the possibility that Darth Vader was responsible. I thought the story would be more effective if it had flashbacks of young Anakin, revealing his optimistic reasons for building C-3PO, as that contrasted well with Vader's subsequent actions. I'm not sure, but "Thank the Maker" may have been the first story set during the Original Trilogy with a flashback to the Prequels.

Here is my thumbnail sketch for the ninth page. As you can see, the artist, Killian Plunket improved on it quite a bit!
—Ryder Windham, 2012

ESSENTIAL TRIVIA

The image from the comic of Darth Vader holding C-3PO's severed head in his hand, Hamlet-style, has become so iconic, it inspired a Deluxe Mini Bust by Gentle Giant Studios in 2011.

Blood-Feud: WARRIOR OF

THE TENUOUS RELATIONSHIP BETWEEN THE MON CALAMARI AND THE QUARREN WAS CENTRAL TO THE OPENING STORY ARC OF SEASON FOUR OF *STAR WARS: THE CLONE WARS*. LELAND Y. CHEE TAKES A LOOK BENEATH THE SURFACE OF THE CONFLICT.

S THE DEEP!

Squid Head and Mon Calamari. *Star Wars: Episode VI Return of the Jedi* (1983) introduced a pair of alien species to the *Star Wars* galaxy that bore squid-like facial features: one had tentacles drooping in place of a chin and the other, represented by the honorable Admiral Ackbar, had bulbous eyes and a large cranium. It was only a matter of time before the Expanded Universe would explore the relationship between these two species. In *Star Wars Insider* #124, we explored the ongoing development of the rivalry between Wookiees and Trandoshans, culminating in the portrayal of this rivalry in *The Clone Wars* Season Three finale. The fourth season of *The Clone Wars* kicked off with a story arc delving into relations between the Mon Calamari and the Quarren, the eventual name given to the Squid Head species. Let's explore the evolution of this inter-species rivalry that has raged throughout the EU.

Return of the Jedi introduced two species at war although we didn't know it at the time: The Quarren (this image and right) and Mon Calamari (below).

INTRODUCING THE MON CALAMARI

Admiral Ackbar's introduction to *Star Wars* fans came well in advance of his appearance in *Return of the Jedi*. He appeared in the Official *Star Wars* Fan Club newsletter *Bantha Tracks* #17 (1982) and made an appearance in the Archie Goodwin and Al Williamson *Star Wars* weekly comic strip. By early 1983, Ackbar was made available as an action figure through a free mail-away TV-advertised offer from Kenner in packaging that still referred to the film as *Revenge of the Jedi*. As the leader of the Rebel fleet in the attack on the second Death Star, Admiral Ackbar, performed by puppeteer Tim Rose and voiced by Eric Bauersfeld, and his fellow officers (called out as "Calamari Men" during production) expressed the urgency, concern, and commitment to the Rebel Alliance of the entire Mon Calamari species. Also significant to the Alliance cause was identifying the new, large ships of the Rebel fleet as Mon Calamari cruisers that were capable of going toe-to-toe with Imperial Star Destroyers.

FROM SQUID HEAD TO QUARREN

While the Mon Calamari had a distinct species name, and, in Ackbar, a prominent named character, the tentacle-faced background character seen in Jabba's palace dubbed by production as Squid Head, went uncredited and had no audible dialogue. Squid Head only gained recognition by being a part of the first wave of *Return of the Jedi* action figures from Kenner. But aside from his production name, little backstory of this character was known. Being the only representative of this species, it was unclear if "Squid Head" was supposed to be a species name or the individual's name. The species eventually was named "Quarren" in *The Star Wars Sourcebook* (1987), though the individual in Jabba's palace would not be identified until *Galaxy Guide: 5* (1990), where he was given the name Tessek. *The Star Wars Sourcebook* established the official in-universe link between the Quarren and the Mon Calamari species.

Squid Head, in the days before his species were named 'Quarren'.

No. 70770   Ages 4 and up

STAR WARS
RETURN OF THE
JEDI

Squid Head.

Kenner.

WATERWORLD

The Star Wars Sourcebook revealed that both the Mon Calamari and the Quarren came from a water planet then known simply as Calamari (later, the planet would be more widely referred to as Mon Calamari, and sometimes Dac, the name of the planet in the Mon Calamari and Quarren native tongue.) As described in the *Sourcebook*, the Mon Calamari lived on the planet's surface in floating cities while the Quarren inhabited the same cities, in levels deep below the surface. While the Mon Calamari embraced progress and dreams for the future, the Quarren held fast to tradition. It should be noted that according to the *Sourcebook*, the first Mon Calamari starship that ventured into space encountered Imperials and that Mon Calamari was a world with no history of war. Both of these themes would be abandoned in later EU stories.

The beautiful but war-torn water planet, Mon Calamari.

IMPERIAL ENCOUNTER

The encounter with the Empire drastically altered the course of Mon Calamari history. The anti-alien doctrine of the Empire made the Mon Calamari and Quarren prime targets for use as slaves who would be used to serve the Imperial war machine. When the population of Mon Calamari peacefully resisted, the Emperor struck at the planet without mercy. A Quarren named Seggor Tels, who harbored hatred and jealously towards the Mon Calamari, abetted the Imperial devastation of Mon Calamari by lowering the planetary shields that defended the water world. Intending to send a message to others who would resist the Empire, the Imperial fleet destroyed many of the planet's cities. With Mon Calamari and Quarren blood on his hands resulting from the betrayal of his homeworld, Seggor Tels hoped to make amends by rallying the Quarren in uniting with the Mon Calamari to resist the Empire. They quickly joined the Rebel Alliance and converted their unarmed passenger liners into warships that became the backbone of the Rebel fleet at the Battle of Endor.

The Empire targets Mon Calamari in a brutal assualt.

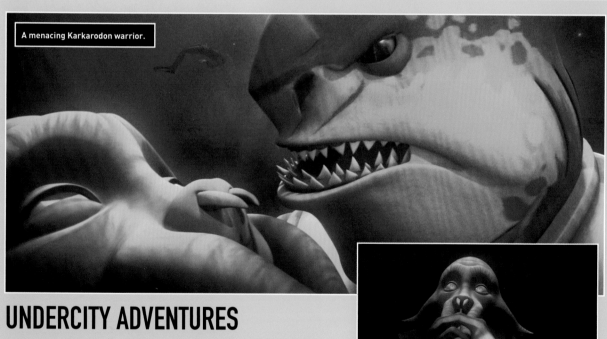

A menacing Karkarodon warrior.

UNDERCITY ADVENTURES

In *The Clone Wars* series, sinister forces from off-world conspired to subvert Mon Calamari affairs, resulting in the assassination of the Mon Calamari King, Yos Kolina. His death created a dispute over the line of succession that sparked civil war. Treacherous forces from off-world attempting to spark tensions between the Mon Calamari and the Quarren were a major component of the roleplaying game supplement *Death in the Undercity* (1990).

A team of Rebels went to Mon Calamari to investigate the disruption of mining operations in the city of Morjanssik, one of the major suppliers of farium, a metal used in starship hull construction. As the title implies, death became the catalyst for the adventure as the chief manager of the mining city of Morjanssik was murdered and the Rebels became the prime suspects. The culprits were proven to be agents of the Imperial Intelligence Destabilization branch whose "Calamari Project" involved human Imperials disguised as Mon Calamari determined to incite violence between the Mon Calamari and the Quarren.

War beneath the waves! Mon Calamari vs Quarren.

AT WAR...

Death in the Undercity also further developed the violent history of the relationship between the Mon Calamari and the Quarren. Rather than being characterized as a planet that did not know war, armed conflict between the Quarren and the Mon Calamari had raged on for generations. Though the Mon Calamari were by nature pacifistic, their efforts to ignore the primitive, but warlike and proud tendencies of their deep-water neighbors proved fruitless. The Quarren attacked the technologically superior Mon Calamari time after time. And time after time, they were defeated. After the last war between the Quarren and Mon Calamari ended, the Mon Calamari found themselves with over a million Quarren prisoners. In an effort to prevent future war, the Mon Calamari began a social experiment to civilize the Quarren people. Young Quarren

were isolated from their parents and sent to be educated in literacy, science, mathematics, and other foundations of civilization. As a result, a rift between the elder, more traditional Quarren and the educated younger generation emerged. Eventually, the younger generations of Quarren were integrated into Mon Calamari society, but despite these efforts, the Quarren continued to view themselves as second-class citizens. These perceived inequalities manifested themselves in *The Clone Wars* series as a major point of contention about Quarren sovereignty and the divine right of the Mon Calamari king.

....AND AT PEACE!

Quarren and Mon Calamari relations have not always been adversarial. In the *X-Wing Rogue Squadron* comics (1996-1998), Rogue Squadron found itself with two pilots from Mon Calamari—Nrin Vakil, a male Quarren, and Ibtisam, a female Mon Calamari. Like most Quarren, Nrin Vakil clung to the past, unwilling to embrace change. Ibtisam started off somewhat haughty and arrogant. At first, Vakil and Ibtisam's interactions conjured up the age-old rivalries of their homeworld. But after fighting alongside one another as Rogues, they formed a mutual respect and friendship that grew into something greater. They spoke of using the bond they shared between each other as a shining example of how love could breach the rift between their people. Sadly, Ibtisam's life was cut short before their dreams could be realized.

The Quarren feature in the Galactic Senate in the prequels while the Mon Calamari take arms in the *Clone Wars* micro-series (below).

THE CLONE WARS ERA

With Quarren and Mon Calamari appearing in the prequel trilogy and having representation in the Republic Senate, the previous notion of the planet Mon Calamari being isolated until they were discovered by the Empire was abandoned. As a result, they became increasingly prevalent in the EU of that era. The Mon Calamari even found themselves in the ranks of the Jedi, most notably with the recurring character Bant Eerin from the *Jedi Apprentice* junior novels. When it came time to explore the Clone Wars in the EU, the Mon Calamari and the Quarren often took center-stage. In an interesting twist, and to further support the crawl of Episode III indicating that there were heroes on both sides, *Republic* #50: "The Defense of Kamino" (2003) introduced a legendary and honorable Mon Calamari Commander named Merai who led a faction of Mon Calamari supporting the Confederacy. Genndy Tartakovsky's *Clone Wars* micro-series (2003) highlighted the Mon Calamari/Quarren conflict with the Republic-backed Mon Calamari against the Dooku-allied Quarren Isolation League. In this conflict, the Mon Calamari Knights, led by a shirtless Kit Fisto, used the more primitive weapons of war as they fought while mounted on eel creatures called keelkana. The Quarren, on the other hand, employed an enormous,

advanced, prawn-shaped superweapon powerful enough to destroy a Republic assault ship with a single blast. The similarly themed and illustrated "Fierce Currents" from *Clone Wars Adventures* vol. 1 (2004) also featured Kit Fisto on Mon Calamari in the aftermath of the events of the micro-series. In this story, it was revealed that a group consciousness organism known as the Moappa had been giving the Quarren orders.

Millennia-old rivalries. Racial inequality.

Off-world interference. Betrayal. Murder. *The Clone Wars* animated series continues to integrate and expand upon these themes on Mon Calamari and Quarren relations whose seeds were planted in the EU—themes that have been continuously evolving for nearly 25 years. And now, the series has added the coronation of a new Mon Calamari king, the Karkarodon species, bio-mechanical jellyfish, and most surprisingly of all, Gungans to this ever-growing canon. ☪

EWOKS: CUTE, CUDDLY, AND COLLECTIBLE!

"YUB NUB!" WE ROUND UP ALL THE EWOK COLLECTIBLES WORTH HAVING (AND SOME NOT)!

WORDS AND PICTURES: GUS LOPEZ

While *Star Wars* fans are divided about their love for Ewoks, there's a huge volume of Ewok-related collectibles, some of which are in extremely high demand with collectors. Ewok merchandise was introduced for the release of *Return of the Jedi*, followed by the *Ewoks* cartoon series, two made-for-television Ewok films, Ewoks in Ice Capades, the Wicket the Ewok preschool line, and many other promotions in the past 27 years.

1] As characters that already look like teddy bears, an obvious product introduced by Kenner for *Return of the Jedi* was a series of plush Ewoks in teddy bear form.

For an even larger dose of fur-inspired saccharin, Kenner also released half a dozen "Woklings," smaller plush toys based on the adorable baby Ewoks. Over the years other plush Ewok toys were introduced, and recent examples include a plush Wicket toy and a magnet sold in the Star Tours shops at Disney parks.

2] Two years after *Return of the Jedi*, Lucasfilm created the *Ewoks* cartoon series with a range of product for the show. Kenner produced six action figures in the same scale as the *Star Wars* action figure line from the movies, and only one wave of *Ewoks* figures made it to market. The actual *Ewoks* characters were scarce from this line, consisting only of Logray and

Wicket. Although the show lasted two seasons, subsequent releases of *Ewoks* action figures never made it to market. Prototypes from this series, including unproduced characters and artwork for the toys, remain popular today with collectors.

3] Ewoks were also represented extensively in costume, mask, and apparel form. Ben Cooper, the one-time producer of kids Halloween costumes in the U.S., expanded its *Star Wars* line to include a Wicket costume for *Return of the Jedi*. Kids could also wear Ewok underwear to accessorize their costumes. Wicket joined the line-up of Underoos characters for the *Return of the Jedi* line. This popular character appeared in both

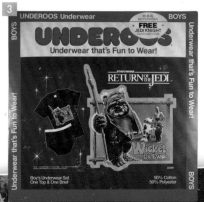

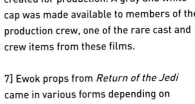

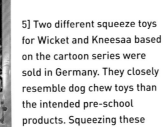

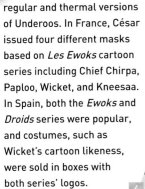

regular and thermal versions of Underoos. In France, César issued four different masks based on *Les Ewoks* cartoon series including Chief Chirpa, Paploo, Wicket, and Kneesaa. In Spain, both the *Ewoks* and *Droids* series were popular, and costumes, such as Wicket's cartoon likeness, were sold in boxes with both series' logos.

4] Ewoks were used extensively on food promotions throughout the world. One of the three Jedi Läsk sodas from

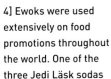

Sweden featured Paploo the Ewok. For the *Ewoks* cartoon series, Dairylea produced several different styles of cheese boxes with wedge strips of characters from the *Ewoks* and *Droids* cartoon series. Although the promotion was intended for both shows, the wedges were dominated by Ewok characters. In Spain, Panrico's pastries came bundled with small plastic figurines

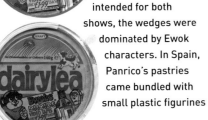

from the *Ewoks* cartoon in a variety of colors.

5] Two different squeeze toys for Wicket and Kneesaa based on the cartoon series were sold in Germany. They closely resemble dog chew toys than the intended pre-school products. Squeezing these

items produces squeak sounds that are only decipherable by babies and canines. In the U.S., Ewoks were featured in the Ice Capades show in the mid-1980s. A limited amount of memorabilia from that show was created including various Ewok pennants.

6] Only a handful of items were made for the *Ewoks* television movies, although

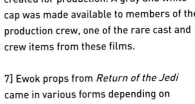

some of the more unique pieces were created for production. A gray and white cap was made available to members of the production crew, one of the rare cast and crew items from these films.

7] Ewok props from *Return of the Jedi* came in various forms depending on their use in the film. Many of the stunt spears, bows, and arrows were carved out of wood. Each Ewok mask was unique, using different shapes and colors of artificial fur made by Stuart Freeborn's shop in the United Kingdom. There are precious few Ewok costume and wardrobe pieces in private collections, but there are no other Ewok collectibles that better exhibit the detail and craftsmanship that went into creating the on-screen characters. ☾

MY STAR WARS

VERSATILE PERFORMER SIMON J. WILLIAMSON PLAYED THREE PARTS IN *RETURN OF THE JEDI*, INCLUDING A MON CALAMARI AND A GAMORREAN GUARD, BUT IT'S HIS PERFORMANCE AS BANDLEADER MAX REBO THAT WON HIM A PLACE IN FANS' HEARTS. INTERVIEW BY MARK NEWBOLD

When did you first become aware of *Star Wars*?
I was at University in Cardiff when it was released in 1977. I was aware of some word of mouth, but was not in a great hurry to see it, thinking it to be a movie more geared toward kids. Gradually the positive reviews and abundance of arresting imagery of the iconic Darth Vader, in particular, compelled me to check it out.

What was your reaction to seeing *Star Wars* for the first time?
I suppose I most remember the highly impressive opening sequence with John Williams' music over the scrolling prologue and the Cantina sequence, which was both fun and menacing. Little did I know that years later I would be part of an attempt to re-create that kind of scene via the creatures in Jabba's palace. I was studying zoology at the time, so was well aware of squid issues surrounding the Mon Calamari and my performance was therefore total Method acting!

Where did you sign your first *Star Wars* autograph?
By mail around 2002/3, I had already signed several, when even more requests started to come in, once the Internet Movie Database featured my full *Star Wars* credit. (When the movie was released, I was merely credited as a puppeteer.)

What was the most challenging aspect of being in *Return of the Jedi*?
The lack of vision and hearing within Max Rebo. Never mind whether it was hot in the costume (it was), the lack of vision and only being able to have one-way communication via an earpiece was difficult. This earpiece got pushed so far in that it made me deaf for several days and I had to have my ears syringed over two days. The Gamorrean guards, although heavy and bulky were much easier. For real difficulty, it was the mystic (urSol) in *The Dark Crystal*, where we had to spend hours in a crouch, with one side of the body stretching forward and then had to move in a really slow, controlled manner while the bodily tension was extreme.

Why has Max Rebo become such a fan favorite?
He's anarchic, silly, and blue. He's a musician and therefore automatically cool (even though his musical taste veers more toward Beethoven, Handel, and Bach). He's also easy to describe: "The blue elephant thing!" And everyone secretly aspires to be "a blue elephant thing." Now, come on, admit it...

Can you reveal something about yourself that will surprise *Star Wars* fans?
I generally like to keep things private, but—continuing the creature theme—I was once a reindeer in a Christmas Brut commercial with boxer Henry Cooper and motorcyclist Barry Sheene. I also narrated the unabridged biography of Archbishop Desmond Tutu (*Voice of the Voiceless*) even attempting to imitate his voice.

I have in my home a blue fiberglass bodycast taken of me when I was going to be one (of two) actors playing the Lion in Disney's *Return to Oz*. Bizarrely, it is minus head, hands, and feet. So whoever has them, can they contact me please?

Where is the strangest place you've been recognized?
The Cannes Film Festival 2006. Despite what you might think, unless one of the *Star Wars* films is being shown or seeking partners, Cannes is mostly unimpressed with the *Star Wars* phenomenon. As I walked along the Croissette, I heard someone say "That's Simon Williamson!" It was a member of the 501st Legion who had met me at a convention and was working for a Film Sales/Distribution company!

Do you have a favorite character?
Apart from Max Rebo, it would have to be Darth Maul. I did several years training in Wado Ryu karate, so like to see good martial arts portrayed on film. Ray Park's ability and application is pretty damn good. The red makeup and lenses make for a pretty awesome villain, too.☮

EXPANDED
Read more about Simon J. Williamson's career at www.simonjwilliamson.co.uk
UNIVERSE

ALIENS OF

Star Wars Magazine examines the Utapauns, the Mustafarians, and the Polis Massans, with insight from the creators who brought these extraterrestrials to life: concept artists Iain McCaig, Derek Thompson and Sang Jun Lee, and sculptors Robert Barnes and Mike Murnane.

Words: Daniel Wallace

Star Wars: Episode III *Revenge of the Sith* is many things – a war epic, a morality play, a tragedy. But one thing it isn't is a monster mash. Unlike the riotous zoos of *A New Hope*'s cantina and *Return of the Jedi*'s gangster palace, *Revenge of the Sith* focuses on the lean, linear journey of Anakin Skywalker from hero to horror with little time for stopovers in the bizarre.

Things could have been different. During the earliest stages of conceptual development, Episode III opened with a Clone Wars montage of battlefields across the galaxy. Explains concept artist Derek Thompson, "We batted around using the cantina scene from the original *Star Wars* as a starting point, saying, 'What if all the guys in the cantina scene were veterans of the Clone Wars?' Using them as a springboard, I did a bunch of conceptual art imagining the Hammerhead planet and other planets."

Ultimately, George Lucas dropped the montage. But in the realm of *Star Wars*, exoticism can't help but bleed into every frame. Several all-new alien species make their debut in Episode III, although they appear in such a low-key fashion, you might have to slow down to appreciate them.

EPISODE III

UTAPAUNS

In *Star Wars* lore, the Utapauns are known as "the Ancients," a consequence of life spans that can be measured in centuries. The proper name of their species is the Pau'ans, and they are masters at harvesting wind power to energize their lonely, vertical cities. Utapaun resistance fighters joined the struggle to chase General Grievous' forces from their world but were caught flat-footed when the Republic's triumphant clone troopers turned hostile and seized Utapau in the name of the Emperor.

Utapauns are an intimidating people. With their towering frames, leathery skin, and carnivorous teeth, they seem well suited for their sinkhole cities of stone and bone. Yet the irony of the Utapauns is that they weren't intended to live on Utapau at all.

In fact, the original Utapaun concept was of a furry, cuddly species akin to lemurs. "One day, George Lucas saw an advertisement for lemurs near the San Francisco Zoo," explains Sang Jun Lee. "It was our first [piece of] design information, and I spent a couple of months on all kinds of lemur designs for the Utapauns." Adds Thompson, "[Utapau] was originally a very frail world, and the creatures themselves were very fleet-footed and delicate. One of the first drawings I did was a variation on the lemur that was more like a flying squirrel."

Ultimately, however, the inhabitants of Utapau would be anything but cute. For inspiration, George Lucas needed to look no farther than version 1.0 of the lava-loving Mustafarians.

For Mustafar, Sang Jun Lee had sketched mystic-robed humanoids to inhabit the smoky planet's glowing crevasses. "I started designing a human-type character who lived in a secret society, closer to a religious type of character than [those of] other planets," he says. "Also, it created interesting ideas for the costumes. It became George's favourite character for Episode III. He loved the dry skin [of] the dark, magic-looking characters." At Lucas's request, Sang Jun Lee's Mustafar design transplanted itself to the other side of the galaxy, displacing the lemurs and becoming the basis for the new Utapauns. Says Lee, "[Lucas] told me that he loved the characters so much [that] he wanted to find a more important place for them."

In the film, Port Administrator Tion Medon greets Obi-Wan Kenobi upon the Jedi's arrival on Utapau. Medon has a long face lined by deep facial grooves, a characteristic inspired by ritualistic tribal scarring. "At first, I think [Lucas] may have been thinking lines of colour, like a tattoo, but at some point, they became three-dimensional," says Robert Barnes, who also started the design process with his mind firmly set in Mustafar. "We all liked the idea of them looking prematurely aged with the skin stretched in striated wrinkles over their faces, almost like healed burns; it sort of fit for the lava planet. Little did we know that they would end up in the Utapau sinkhole."

Bruce Spence as Tion Medon

Lemur concept by Sang Jun Lee

After approval of the art concepts, Barnes and Mike Murnane sculpted several Utapaun faces. Barnes experimented with skin differentiation between the genders, shaping a female face with raised lines and more curvilinear elements than the male version. "I saw it as a challenge to make what might be taken as a deformity and try to give it beauty," he says. "I think George liked it, but in the end, only the [male] inset-line version was used for the practical make-up effects." Murnane compares the bald Utapauns to a certain pinheaded movie villain, describing them as "very *Hellraiser*."

Bruce Spence portrayed Tion Medon in *Revenge of the Sith*. A veteran of films including *The Road Warrior* and *The Matrix Revolutions*, Spence underwent hours of smothering make-up application to achieve the striated gray of Medon's skin. Eventually, Spence reached a tipping point at which the thick make-up and heavy prosthetics felt like extensions of his own body. "On the day of the shoot, I just forgot I had this on," he says. "I just forgot that all this was there. And it's funny because there I am, walking around looking like nothing on Earth, feeling completely normal."

For his role, Spence treated Tion Medon as a revered elder statesman. "Obi-Wan Kenobi still hasn't reached that moment in time where he can be one of the great nobles," he says. "And I think Tion Medon really feels a teensy weensy bit superior."

When he watches the scene now, Thompson can't shake his memories of Mustafar development. "There's a lot of thought and attention that goes into a concept, but George is always pulling, mixing, and matching things and locations. You just get used to that idea because things have been changing in *Star Wars* since the beginning."

Almost forgotten on desolate Utapau are the Utai, a squat species of bulging-eyed labourers common to the dark depths of the sinkhole grottos. The Utai, realized as CG creations, would have been much more prominent in Episode III had a scene where Obi-Wan Kenobi visited a lizard corral remained in the final script.

Mustafar/ Utapau female sculpture by Robert E. Barnes

Lemur concepts by Erik Tiemens

MUSTAFARIANS

If Mustafar is an analog for hell, then the Mustafarians are its demons. The eerie aliens can be seen scooping molten melt from magma flows and marching in sinister procession on the backs of beetles. With no speaking roles and no clear shots on screen, the Mustafarians maintain a ghostly presence on the fringes of the fiery landscape.

The official Mustafarian backstory divides them into two distinct subspecies: the tall northern Mustafarians keep their distance from erupting volcanoes, while their squat, southern cousins often surf above the lava flows as ore miners. Being sentient arthropods, they possess tough, shell-like exoskeletons that are so resistant to heat damage they can withstand a direct hit from a blaster pistol.

As soon as the original Mustafarian concepts had been uprooted and moved to Utapau, Sang Jun Lee began sketching their replacements. In his mind, the Mustafarians were representatives of the dark side of the Force. "I started sketching abstract shapes, then human proportions," he says. "In the end, they were closer to insect-looking aliens. They have small skulls, long mouths, and air filters on their backs, and they ride giant insects as horses."

Thompson remembers some of the intriguing, but ultimately rejected, concepts for Mustafar and its inhabitants. "[Concept artist] Iain McCaig had the notion that it was a droid hell. [Later] we tooled around with the idea that if this was an industrial ore planet, that maybe because of Anakin's partial machine arm he would be perceived as a quasi-deity [to] feed his delusions of grandeur." Thompson even experimented with costume designs inspired by Darth Vader's padded armour on the assumption that the Mustafarians would be the ones responsible for Anakin Skywalker's cyborg reconstruction.

The finished Mustafarian design is of a spindly biped with two dark eyes and a flexible facial proboscis. The climate-controlling units on their backs only partially alleviate the liquefying temperatures of Mustafar's undying inferno.

Says Thompson, "You never really know who the Mustafarian citizens are in the final movie. We tried to fit in guards and sentries, but when the final film came together, there weren't any locals showcased. Maybe that was a missed opportunity, or maybe they'll come back to that when they do the TV show."

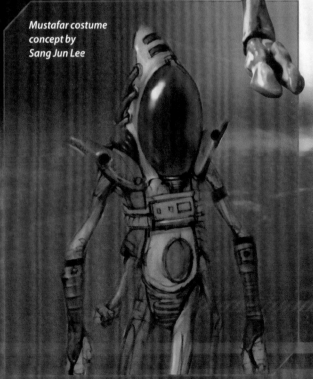

Mustafar concept by Sang Jun Lee

Mustafar costume concept by Sang Jun Lee

*Mustafar alien concept
by Derek Thompson*

*Mustafar concept
by Derek Thompson*

POLIS MASSANS

According to the Expanded Universe, the Polis Massans seen in *Revenge of the Sith* are members of an archaeological excavation team. They are scouring the asteroids on the hunt for clues to the long-vanished Eellayin species, which may or may not be related to the Polis Massans themselves. They communicate through hand gestures and have little contact with the outside galaxy.

Keepers of the asteroid hideaway where Padmé gives birth to the twins, the Polis Massans are maddeningly enigmatic. Their faces reveal nothing but two eyes swimming in a featureless expanse of skin, giving the Polis Massans the appearance of spooky spectres. With that blank-faced biology, the questions are fundamental and numerous: Do they talk? What do they eat? How do they breathe?

Not even the basics have yet emerged in the Polis Massan back-story. From the start, the concept artist crew knew that this species was a strange one. "For a while, we weren't sure if the face design was supposed to be a mask," says Barnes, "but George eventually made it clear that it *was* the face and that there were no markings or other features than the eyes. It would be skin."

Doug Chiang sketched the earliest Polis Massan during development of *Attack of the Clones*. As Barnes remembers, George Lucas had originally given Chiang a black-and-white photo of "a very simple mask that was sort of a wide heart shape with two circles cut out for eyes and no other features." Chiang's design, passed over for Episode II, saw renewed attention during work on *Sith*. Sang Jun Lee sketched heads and costumes, while Murnane sculpted busts. "They reminded us of [Japanese director Hayao] Miyazaki's stuff, like the little head-shaker beings in the trees of *Princess Mononoke*," says Murnane.

Early Polis Massan concepts by Stian Dahlslett

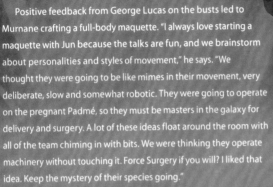

Positive feedback from George Lucas on the busts led to Murnane crafting a full-body maquette. "I always love starting a maquette with Jun because the talks are fun, and we brainstorm about personalities and styles of movement," he says. "We thought they were going to be like mimes in their movement, very deliberate, slow and somewhat robotic. They were going to operate on the pregnant Padmé, so they must be masters in the galaxy for delivery and surgery. A lot of these ideas float around the room with all of the team chiming in with bits. We were thinking they operate machinery without touching it. Force Surgery if you will? I liked that idea. Keep the mystery of their species going."

In the finished film, the Polis Massans came to life as computer-generated creations, but it was their medical droid that wound up with the most screen time. In their reduced role, they seem to be steeped even deeper in secrets. Says Barnes, "I think that placid face is perfectly suited to the somber setting on Polis Massa, and the medical environment surrounding the birth of the twins." ☻

Polis Massan concepts by Stian Dahlslett

Polis Massan concepts by Sang Jun Lee

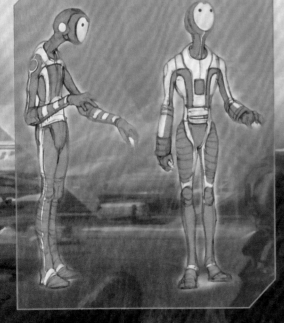

INTO THE ARENA!

Dan Wallace braves the Petranaki arena on Geonosis to catalogue the deadly creatures pitted against our heroes in *Attack of the Clones*!

The arena beasts from *Attack of the Clones* are wildly imaginative and genuinely frightening. They also exhibit a rock-paper-scissors balance of strengths and weaknesses: The reek can crush the nexu, the nexu can gut the acklay, and the acklay can spear the reek.

ACKLAY

dangling under its chin (an organ known as the silphum), to detect its prey's body electricity. When it finds a nest of the sleepers, it punctures their leathery armor with swift jabs of its foreclaws and devours the soft flesh within. During the arena fight, the acklay uses these scimitar-like claws in an attempt to toothpick Obi-Wan like an hors d'oeuvre. Every time it misses, it stabs the dirt floor with a satisfying *thunk*.

Acklays spread from Vendaxa to Geonosis generations before the Clone Wars, thanks to offworld business executives who learned that the Geonosian archduke would readily accept payment for droids in the form of exotic predators. Acklays became favorite attractions in the arena, and escaped breeding specimens quickly went feral and slashed their way to the top of the violent Geonosian food chain. Most wild acklays live near the planet's stagnant Ebon Sea and creep into the lower tunnels of Geonosian hives to feast on worker drones.

The acklay is arguably the most memorable, sporting all the most unpleasant qualities of a lobster, a scorpion, and a crocodile. "I pictured the acklay as the embodiment of chaos," says Robert Barnes, the creature's chief designer. The acklay is an ever-moving riot of claws, legs, and spines, conceived out of George Lucas' request for the conceptual spawn of a praying mantis and a velociraptor. At one point during development the crew nicknamed the beast "dinolobster."

The acklay's eyes are piggish and tiny, a result of the caustic sunlight that engulfs its lush homeworld of Vendaxa. On the Vendaxan plains the acklay hunts for dozing forms of nocturnal lemnai, using the wattle

REEK

The reek is a big *Star Wars* bull, right down to the ring in its nose and the way it paws the earth before charging. Found on Ylesia and the Codian Moon, the reek possesses a brown leathery hide that turns red when the animal is fed a meat-heavy diet. Although Anakin calmed the arena reek and even used it as a ride, the beast proved no match for a single shot from Jango Fett's blaster pistol.

Bullish influences aside, the first inspiration for the reek was *Placerias*, a hippo-like reptile belonging to the dicynodont family that lived during the time of the dinosaurs. Concept sculptor Michael Patrick Murnane shepherded the reek through several iterations and into

its final Episode II design. The animal's three horns are perfect for goring enemies and head-locking rival males during dominance displays. The reek's howl has a weird stutter effect, as if it's roaring through the rotating blades of a ceiling fan.

The reeks evolved on Ylesia, then spread offworld to breeding ranches including some on the Codian Moon. Ranchers happily fattened up their reeks for slaughter by feeding them wood-moss, but when the bottom dropped out of the reek market, bankrupt ranchers discovered that their animals became carnivorous when faced with starvation. The sale of such specimens to battle arenas helped ease the sting of financial ruin.

MIKE MURNANE
REEK COLOR
SWII 8·1·00
0015M

ReBARNES
NEXN COLOR STUDY #2
9.7.00

NEXU

Vicious but fragile, the nexu is a tiger-like jungle predator with a face only its mother could love. Found mostly in the dense forests of Cholganna, nexus are often the target of big-game hunters who kill them for sport or capture them for sale on the galactic black market as watch-beasts.

Nexus come from the Indona continent in the northern latitudes of Cholganna. Other breeds exist on the planet, but only the forest nexu has four eyes. This extra pair of peepers allows it to see in the infrared wavelengths, making it easy to hunt warm-blooded prey such as bark rats and tree-climbing octopi. Once a nexu hooks its prey with its claws, it bites down and savagely shakes its lunch to death.

"Bad Kitty" was the nickname it carried during production, courtesy of the ILM crew. But in truth it's hard to blame the nexu for its poor temperament. You'd be irritable too if Geonosian picadors kept shocking you with electric spears.

The nexu wins a bit of revenge early in the film, knocking a Geonosian from his orray mount to the delight of the crowd. Its moves are gracefully supple and contrast nicely with the straight-line charge of the reek and the unconfined frenzy of the acklay's scamper. But it's the nexu's mix-and-match body that leaves a lasting impression: the lithe muscles of a panther, the quills of a porcupine, and the hairless tail of a rat.

Though early designs for the nexu closely resembled an Earth-bound lion, the final version is downright hallucinatory. Says concept sculptor Robert Barnes, "I was thinking of a mutated hybrid of human and feline energy, which was a very disturbing image in my mind."

who was called Richard Glass, funnily enough – because I was wearing red contact lenses over my eyeballs. I would then sit in a dentist's chair and Nick Dudman, my make-up man, would start to apply the make-up. We would time it, and by the last day of filming, we had managed to get it down to 59 minutes!

"There was definitely a learning curve with the make-up, and it was all very dependent on the quality of the rubber pieces that had been moulded the night before. Sometimes they'd come out very well, with good fine edges, so you could get them on very easily and very quickly. But other times, the edges would be slightly curled and that caused all manner of problems – it could add two hours onto the make-up time."

Despite the lengthy trials and tribulations surrounding the make-up process, Carter feels that the end result more than justified the means. "Bib was quite a striking character. Ironically, I had no idea what he was going to look like until I put all the make-up on the first time. I'd seen a maquette of him, but the design of the model couldn't really fit on a human being's head. So although it was based on the model, I knew it was going to be a little bit different. During the three months prior to the start of filming, I regularly went up to Borehamwood [the home of Elstree Studios, where the original *Star Wars* trilogy was shot] to try various things on, and gradually Bib's appearance took shape."

Carter, a distinguished RADA graduate, landed the role of Bib Fortuna whilst he was starring in a play, *The Streets of London*, back in 1981. "Mary Selway, who was *Return of the Jedi*'s casting director, saw me in *The Streets of London*. They were looking for someone who was tall and a good mover to play Bib. I played a kind of creepy character, a bad guy who turns good, and I apparently moved very quickly in the play. In fact, a lot of people kept asking me if I used to be a boxer; I hadn't been, but everyone thought I had because I moved so well. Anyway, that was why I was called in to meet [director] Richard Marquand, to talk about a film called *Blue Harvest*."

During his meeting with Marquand, Carter learned that *Blue Harvest* was a big-budget horror film and provisionally agreed to play a supporting role. Much to his surprise, the actor was then told that there was no such film as *Blue Harvest*, and that he actually just won a place in the third *Star Wars* film, then titled *Revenge of the Jedi*.

"When Richard told me that, I thought it was great," says Carter. "I had seen the first two films and enjoyed them enormously, so I thought it would be great to do one. Plus, the kids

With his bright red eyes, bulging forehead and tentacle-like skull appendages, Bib Fortuna was the kind of guy that really stood out in a crowd. Even amidst the bizarre creatures that inhabited Jabba the Hutt's court palace in Tatooine, the demonic-looking Twi'lek was unmissable.

Given Bib Fortuna's distinctive appearance, it comes as no surprise to learn that Michael Carter faced a series of lengthy sessions in the make-up chair to play the ominous alien in *Return of the Jedi*. "On the Friday before I started filming, I put the make-up on for the first time and it took about eight hours," he recalls. "I was in every day for five weeks and we had a kind of routine in the morning: I would go in, have a cup of coffee, and would have my eyes examined by the resident optician –

Above: Actor Michael Carter, free from the prosthetics that transformed him into Jabba's henchman Bib Fortuna.

British actor Michael Carter made a striking impression as Bib Fortuna, Jabba's tentacle-headed major-

domo, in Return of the Jedi. *"It was great fun and a bit like being a kid again,"* he tells David Bassom...

Below: Carter had to undergo a tortuous make-up process for the Bib Fortuna transformation.

DAYS

LETTING GO

Carter is quick to point out that the film's leading cast-members did their utmost to ensure that everybody around them was enjoying themselves. "Mark Hamill was very nice indeed, extremely pleasant and very down to earth. He used to come in to my make-up room quite a bit and just rabbit away about anything under the sun – not necessarily *Star Wars*. Anthony Daniels [C-3PO] also used to visit me a lot, because I knew Anthony from the theatre. I found Carrie [Fisher, Princess Leia] charming. Billy Dee Williams [Lando Calrissian] was extremely nice as well, I liked him a lot. The only member of the cast I didn't see much of was Harrison Ford [Han Solo], simply because he came late to the filming.

"There was a kind of family feeling around them; they all knew each other and this was the second or third time they'd worked together. And they obviously got on very well. They were all pleased to get on with the job and they were great ambassadors for the film in the sense that they were very easy to work with, and always tried to have fun.

"I've been on film sets, TV sets and even done things with the National Theatre where everything was a real bloody chore. *Return of the Jedi* wasn't. Basically, it was great fun and a bit like being a big kid again – a disciplined big kid... You're not standing there, thinking in purist acting terms. You have to let go and get into the fantasy of it." ■

would have killed me if I didn't do it... At the time, Martin was four, Hannah was five and Daddy was in *Star Wars* – it was amazing! It meant so much to them."

It wasn't just *Return of the Jedi*'s casting that took place in rather mysterious circumstances. To ensure that the film's storyline remained a secret before its release, every element of the production was cloaked in secrecy.

"It was a given that you didn't tell people anything about *Return of the Jedi*, or that you were even in the film; you avoided journalists in particular. You were only given the section of the script your character appeared in, and each page was stamped with a code, so that if the press got hold of part of the script, it could be traced back to you.

"I did tell my kids I was doing the film, but I also told them not to discuss it with anyone. I remember one day, my daughter came back from school crying. I was worried so I asked her what was wrong, and she replied, 'I told two of my friends at school you were in the new *Star Wars* film.' She was afraid that someone would get hold of the story, and was very upset about it! I reassured her, and told her that everything was going to be alright."

Carter himself learned just how desperate everyone was to maintain the secrecy surrounding *Return of the Jedi* before he had even started working on the film. "On the Friday before I started filming, I had to do a lighting test with full make-up," he recalls. "I was prepared in a make-up room near the front of Borehamwood, and I then had to get up to Stage 9 on the other side of the lot. They brought a car to take me there, but I couldn't get in it because Bib's head was too big!

"I then said that I'd just walk across the lot – it was only couple hundreds of yards – but everyone was terrified of publicity, and they didn't want anyone to see my character before the film was released. So someone asked me, 'Just in case there's a journalist on Borehamwood High Street with a 400mm lens, do you mind if we disguise you?' I said I didn't mind, and they put a dustbin bag over my head! I was then led to the studio by [make-up artist] Nick Dudman and someone else, and later guided back to the make-up room."

Three days later, Carter began his five-week stint on *Return of the Jedi*. The first thing he filmed was the scene in which Luke

Left: *Bib Fortuna meets C-3PO and R2-D2 in this pre-production illustration by conceptual artist Ralph McQuarrie.*

Skywalker (Mark Hamill) uses a Jedi mind trick on Bib Fortuna to gain an audience with his master, Jabba the Hutt. Besides the obvious problems of acting under heavy prosthetics, Carter's debut as the Twi'lek was made doubly difficult by the fact that the scene's dialogue was in Huttese.

"Mark and I had both learned our lines," he explains, "and I had to walk into the frame, hit my mark and say my first line. Unfortunately, I couldn't see my mark – I could hardly see anything at all through the contacts, I had tunnel vision – so they had to nail a baton down on the floor, and when I hit the baton, I knew that was my mark. During the first take, however, my foot hit the baton and I fell over!

"As soon as we got that sorted out, Mark and I had to have a long conversation in Huttese, this invented language which was sort of Mongolian backwards or something. It was a very interesting language, and I always remember my first line in the film

"He's a bit stupid and a bit dense, and I think that's appealing to the audience."

– the classic line, 'Die wanna Wanga'! Now, when you're talking nonsense, you just memorise your own lines, but how does the other guy know when he's supposed to say his line? I'd be talking Huttese, and I'd be looking at Mark and seeing him thinking, 'Has he finished speaking yet?' Then there'd be a pause and he'd speak... It was very funny."

Carter also holds the film's late director, Richard Marquand, and *Star Wars* creator George Lucas in similarly high regard. In particular, the actor was impressed by their willingness to listen to and try out new ideas.

"I was larking about with [first assistant director] David Tomblin one day, and we worked out a joke on set," he recalls. "We showed it to George, and he decided to film it. Basically, Bib was drunk at the party and getting very worked up about this woman, while Salacious Crumb was nicking his drink... It was very erotic, but in the end George said, 'Look it's all very funny, but this is a kids' film.' and he cut it out. Still, the nice thing was that you could suggest things to George and Richard, and they would think about it and perhaps even film it."

Whilst playing Bib Fortuna, Carter gave little thought to the prestige that accompanied playing a part in *Return of the Jedi*. Over the years, however, the actor has learned that having a *Star Wars* film on one's CV never fails to impress people. "There's a bit of kudos attached to the *Star Wars* films, simply because they were such great fun and everybody saw them," he explains. "And, of course, everybody's kids had seen them, and wanted the X-wing fighters and everything else.

"I went for an interview for an episode of some television series, and the director stood there looking at my CV, with all my credits – the National Theatre and all that stuff – and he just said, 'God you were in *Return of the Jedi*!' It's quite a big thing

COVER STARS

1. ELOMIN – A native of the planet Elom, a planet enslaved by Imperial forces. Under martial law, its population mined Iommite. Following the Battle of Endor, the Elomin people joined the New Republic. (Elom, incidentally, is 'mole' spelled backwards!)

2. WHIPHID – Also known as 'Toothface'. From the cold planet Toola in the Kaelta system, whiphids are ferocious predators sometimes known to taken on bounty hunting contracts from law-enforcement agencies, criminal organisations and the Empire.

3. GRAN – A slobbering, drunkard gran named Ree-Yees was one of the more obnoxious members of Jabba's court.

4. SAURIN – A Saurin was most prominently seen in the cantina bar on Tatooine. The creature in question was Saitorr Kal Fas – a bodyguard to the droid trader Hrchek. Saurins hail from the planet Durkteel.

5. TWI'LEK – Both Bib Fortuna and dancing girl Oola belong to this species from the planet Ryloth in the Outer Rim. The Twi'Lek are an omnivorous people who can supplement verbal communication with subtle movement of their head-tails.

6. UGNAUGHT – Humanoid-porcine beings who may be found in the Cloud City on Bespin. They are employed in the in the depths of the floating city, or in the Tibanna gas-processing plants.

7. ISHI TIB – The Ishi Tib species hail from the planet Tibrin, where they live in cities constructed atop carefully cultivated coral reefs. They are noted for their prowess as managers and technicians.

8. SNIVVIAN – Another creature most prominently seen in the cantina bar at Mos Eisley. The Snivvian seen at Mos Eisley was called Takeel; other Snivvians were subsequently glimpsed in other locations.

9. QUARREN – Also known as Squid Heads, these amphibious beings co-habit the planet Calamari with the Mon Calamari species. The Quarren generally prefer the depths of the floating cities to the upper reaches inhabited by the Mon Cals.

10. GAMORREAN – A violent species with a good understanding of many alien tongues, but a limited capacity to reproduce intelligible conversation themselves, Gamorreans are often employed as labourers and mercenaries.

11. YAK FACE – The unofficial name of this distinctive-looking creature seen, alongside many of the other creatures seen here, in the court of Jabba the Hutt on Tatooine. Yak Face is a member of an unknown species. ■

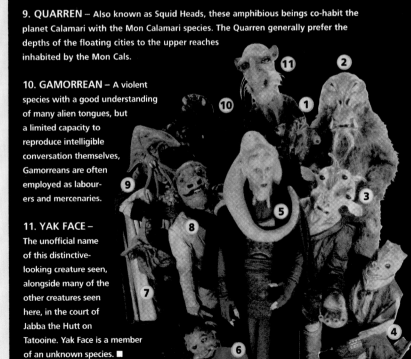

to have been in... So it gives you a little boost in interviews, because a lot of people in the profession are actually quite impressed that I've been in a *Star Wars* film.

"I remember two years ago, I did a Chekhov play and we were on tour in Hull or somewhere. When I told one of the young guys in the company, Michael Sheen, that I was Bib Fortuna, he was completely knocked out! He used to have posters on his wall and everything. In the end, I had to get signed pictures for three youngsters in the company!"

Things like that tend to happen to Carter even more in United States, where the *Star Wars* saga is firmly embedded in popular culture. "My second wife is American, and I got married in Hawaii on 23 December last year. My wife's American family were there and when they found out I'd been in *Return of the Jedi*, they just looked at me in a completely different way! I was just a nice bloke before that, but then, suddenly, I became something else – I was Bib Fortuna in *Return of the Jedi*! They all talked about it, told me how they had models of me and asked if I had any photographs. This was at my wedding!

"I worked on Broadway in 1990 with Dustin Hoffman [in *Merchant of Venice*], and people would turn up at the stage door and ask me for my autograph. I would naively believe it was because of my superb performance as the Prince of Aragon, only to discover that it was because the programme said I was in *Return of the Jedi*!"

Bib Fortuna didn't have a great deal of screen time in *Return of the Jedi*, yet, like a certain bounty hunter called Boba Fett, he has become an immensely popular character in the *Star Wars* saga. During the past 14 years he has featured in various books and comic

Above: "I'd seen a maquette of him," says Michael Carter, "but the design of the model couldn't really fit on a human being's head."

Below left: Bib Fortuna incurs his master's wrath by admitting Luke Skywalker to the Tatooine palace.

Below right: A pre-production sketch of Bib Fortuna from Return of the Jedi.

strips and gained something of a cult status amongst *Star Wars* fans.

"I didn't realise Bib was as popular as he is until recently," revealed Carter. "He's a pretty weird looking creature – with the red eyes, the domed head and the tentacles – and he's nasty, yet he's quite sweet in a way. He's quite a funny, humorous character. He's also a bit stupid and a bit dense, and I think that's appealing to the audience."

The Twi'lek has also been immortalised as various pieces of merchandise, including as a *Star Wars* figure. Naturally, the actor has his own Bib Fortuna figure at home. "A mate of mine bought one at a stall down at an antiques fair in Hampshire somewhere," he laughs. "The guy dropped the price from a tenner to a fiver on the condition that he got him my autograph!"

Unsurprisingly, Carter has never been recognised on the street as the man behind Bib Fortuna. "What usually happens is, when people discover I played Bib, they look at me and say, 'Yeah, I can see it'. When my second wife saw a videotape of *Return of the Jedi* recently, she looked at it and said, 'Yeah I can recognise you'. Funnily enough, Dermot Crowley, who played one of the Rebel leaders [General Madine], recognised me on set when I had the full gear on. He said, 'Is that you, Mike?' and we had a good chat."

Carter's depiction of Bib Fortuna proved so successful that he was offered a series of roles as monstrous villains and aliens following the release of *Return of the Jedi*. After playing two such characters in *The Keep* and *The Ghosts of Christmas Past*, he decided not to star in any more creature features, to avoid being typecast.

"Word had gone around the special effects and animatronics grapevine that I could handle prosthetics, so I was offered those kinds of roles," he explains. "But you rapidly become categorised as someone who can use prosthetics. I suppose I could have gone on and made a few more monster pictures, but I really didn't want to. I decided I'd had enough of aliens. I'd done my bit – I'd done my Bib, and *The Keep* and *The Ghosts of Christmas Past* – and that was it."

Today, Michael Carter divides his time between acting and writing. He is currently working on his second screenplay which, appropriately, is a science fiction story. Even if his latest ventures proves to be a stellar success, however, Carter accepts that it's unlikely to eclipse people's memories of his portrayal of Bib Fortuna.

"I'm very pleased to be associated with *Return of the Jedi*" he says. "When young people find out I've been in *Return of the Jedi*, their lights go on. They ask you about it and it kind of means something in a way. That makes you realise that you've brought five minutes of sunshine into people's lives. So being in a film like *Return of the Jedi*, which is obviously universally enjoyed by people, is just great." ■

FROM PUPPETS TO PAO

THE INSIDE STORY OF A REBEL COMMANDO

From the London stage to *The Force Awakens'* luggabeast, actor, and puppeteer Derek Arnold has quite literally had a hand in bringing numerous aliens to life. But it was as rebel commando Pao in *Rogue One* that Arnold realized a childhood dream: to be the model for a *Star Wars* action figure!

WORDS: AMY RATCLIFFE

01

Derek Arnold's first step into a larger world began with *The Force Awakens,* but his career up to that point had already seen him make his mark in some major live productions.

"I was a puppeteer in the stage version *War Horse* in London's West End," says the English performer. "Then I did the opening ceremony for the London 2012 Olympic Games. I operated a 90-foot Voldemort puppet [from *Harry Potter*]!

"One of the puppeteers I met during the Olympics was Brian Herring. We stayed friends, and he called me up about a year later. He said, 'I'm working on a project and I think you might be good for it.'"

Arnold made his way to Pinewood Studios near London, England, unaware of what he would soon be working on.

"I went, signed a non-disclosure agreement, and then walked up through the offices," Arnold smiles. "Even though it was a different title on the paperwork [*The Force Awakens* went by the codename "AVCO" during production], I realized that it must be *Star Wars,* because everything in the offices was *Star Wars*! I walked past a bunch of young women sewing together a Chewie costume! So I became part of the creature and droid team quite early on, about eight months before principal photography started. The first time I ever stepped onto a set was in Abu Dhabi, and it was mind blowing."

The first creature that Arnold worked on was the lumbering luggabeast, the operation of which drew on his previous experience.

"It's a practical puppet, and they loosely based it on the *War Horse* design," Arnold explains. "It needed two guys inside it: one controlling the front legs and one controlling the back legs. For seven months I went in on a weekly basis as they were building it. We brought in a puppeteer named Tom Wilton, who I'd worked with on *War Horse.*

01 Paodok'Draba'Takat, the Drabatan rebel commando played by Derek Arnold.

"I REALIZED IT MUST BE *STAR WARS*, BECAUSE EVERYTHING IN THE OFFICES WAS *STAR WARS*! I WALKED PAST A GROUP OF YOUNG WOMEN SEWING TOGETHER A CHEWIE COSTUME!"

He ended up moving the front legs of the luggabeast, and I ended up moving the back."

Over the course of developing the luggabeast, Arnold got to know Neal Scanlan and the staff in the creature department well, which in turn led to further opportunities.

"They said, 'You guys are physical performers and we have a lot of other creatures in this movie, so if you want to stick around...' They kept bringing us back and

asking us to do a little bit more, and a little bit more. I guess it helped that they already had our body molds!"

Joining the Rebellion

After production wrapped on *The Force Awakens*, Arnold was invited back to lend his talents to the next *Star Wars* movie. Only this wasn't *The Last Jedi*, but the standalone *Rogue One: A Star Wars Story*, about the Rebellion's attempt to ▶

02

steal the Death Star plans. He didn't have to think for very long before saying yes.

"You just want to keep working for Neal Scanlan, the guy who created the special creature effects," Arnold enthuses about the man who won an Oscar for his work on *Babe* (1995). "He's a legend. He's done anything and everything, and his teams are the best in the business, hands down. They're the loveliest people and incredibly loyal. Everybody goes above and beyond because they care about each other as well as the project. I really like that. Neal employs the best and the kindest people to do the job."

An especially exciting prospect for Arnold on *Rogue One* was the opportunity to focus on a single

character: the lizard-like rebel commando Pao.

"It was exciting because when you do the luggabeast or, say, the puppets in Maz's castle, you film for a week, maybe two, then you move on to the next character. With Pao, he was all I did from the very first fitting to my last day on set. That and a two-week stint doing [Saw Gerrera's mind-reading monster] Bor Gullet, which took 15 puppeteers to operate.

"It was just amazing to spend a couple of months on Pao. There were a lot of different challenges. With the animatronic head on, I couldn't see or hear anything. If you're on the outside, the animatronic motors sound like a little buzzing, but inside it's like being in a cave, and it is really loud!"

"THAT'S THE HARDEST THING TO DO, CONNECTING THE EYE LINE. THE LAST THING YOU WANT TO DO IS MAKE PAO SEEM LIKE HE'S LOOKING PAST SOMEONE."

The claustrophobic headgear made life as Pao far from easy, especially when running around during battle scenes. So Arnold was very appreciative of the support he got from his fellow Pao performers.

"I had an earpiece that went to our movement director Paul Kasey,

03

02 Arnold operated the rear legs of the luggabeast, in *The Force Awakens*.

03 Pao (Derek Arnold) comes under heavy fire during the Battle of Scarif.

and to our external puppeteer, Phill Woodfine, who controlled Pao's facial features remotely," Arnold explains. "He's done everything, so it was nice to know I was in safe hands. Phill was a really calming, soothing voice in my ear when I had the head on!"

Eyeline of Duty

Arnold and Pao's support team planned each day's performance meticulously, which meant an early start on set.

"We would get there before everybody else," says Arnold. "Because we knew what scenes we were filming ahead of time, we would get the lay of the land and physically map out where I needed to go.

"For instance, on one particular shot, I knew I would have to walk 10 steps, and that there would be an actor over my left shoulder and I would be looking that way. I also knew that other rebels would be over my right shoulder, just in front

of me. Paul, Phill, and I spent a lot of time mapping out everything so that when we filmed my actions would look as natural as possible."

Once the cameras rolled, the challenges continued, as Arnold interacted with the other performers in real time. He is keen to stress it was a real group effort.

"It definitely takes a team," he says. "It'd be incredibly selfish if I said, 'Oh, I was Pao,' because I couldn't have done it without Phill. He didn't just create the facial expressions, he guided me as well. He let me know what was happening; where Felicity [Jones] was, where Diego [Luna] was. That way I knew what angle I needed to have my head at to make sure Pao's eyeline was there.

"That's the hardest thing to do, connecting the eyeline. The last thing you want to do is make Pao seem like he's looking past someone instead of at them. Phill or Paul would be telling me in my ear: 'Left, left, left. Straight, straight, straight. Right, right, right. STOP!'"

Another vital part of Team Pao was lead fabricator Morna MacPherson, for whom Arnold has nothing but praise.

"Morna was the one who took care of Pao," he says.

"She would be there an hour before everyone else, prepping him, and she would be there at the end of the day to fix him if there was anything wrong. Between every take she would run in with an umbrella, or with water, or air. She made sure I got what I needed. There was always a group of people constantly around each alien and creature."

Living the Dream

For a lifelong *Star Wars* fan (he regularly tweets

PLASTIC PAO

While numerous toys have been made of the *Star Wars* creatures Derek Arnold has portrayed, it's his Pao action figure that takes pride of place. So what was his reaction to becoming an action figure?

"It was, 'Tick that one off the bucket list,'" laughs Arnold. "The figures are all based on digital scans, so that's an actual, accurate representation of me, scaled down to 3.75 inches!

"It's incredibly surreal, but you can't help but smile. The important part is to remind yourself, constantly, what a privileged position you're in. Because, if you don't, you can lose your perspective really fast."

about his games of *Star Wars: Imperial Assault*), Arnold sees his adventures in a galaxy far, far away as a dream come true. For that reason, he finds it hard to pin down a favorite moment or experience during filming.

"It's really hard," he says, "because you're surrounded by what you grew up with. To indulge your eight-year-old self by getting caught up in all this action… It's like playing in the schoolyard. But then to be able to touch a real X-wing… It's what we all dreamed of as kids. It sounds amazing when I hear myself telling my friends about it, but I can't quite process it when I'm actually doing it. To be doing that for Disney, for *Star Wars*, is really cool!" ☮

JAR JAR GENESIS

» Your step-by-step, inside story of how the visual artists at ILM rose to their greatest challenge yet—the creation of computer generated hero Jar Jar Binks

by Mark Cotta Vaz

THERE HAVE BEEN, OVER THE COURSE OF FILM HISTORY, a few seismic shifts—events and arrivals that changed the course of the medium, such as when silent reelers gave way to the "Talkies" in the late Twenties. Yet despite all the advances, the movies have basically always been a medium of cameras and celluloid, chemical processing and light projection. Film.

But now, a new motion picture era is dawning, a time of breakthrough three-dimensional computer graphics (CG), and digital cameras, and data—the end of "film" itself. And like the fulfillment of a prophecy, the shape of things to come can be seen in every aspect of *Star Wars*: Episode I *The Phantom Menace*. From the model shop miniatures digitally fused with CG structures to create the vast alien cityscapes of Coruscant and Naboo, to the insertion of live, flesh-and-blood actors into synthetic, electronic environments, the long awaited "digital backlot" is here.

The face of the future is also embodied in the gangling, goggle-eyed Gungan Jar Jar Binks, the star performer of a new generation of digital actors. More than the animated characters of *Toy Story* (the first all-CG feature), this new wave of virtual creations must inhabit live-action worlds and perform alongside real, living performers.

The marriage of live actors with animation goes back to the Twenties and the hand-drawn *Out of the Inkwell* series produced by the fabled Fleischer Studios. The peak of that style of fusion of live action and traditional animation was Disney's *Who Framed Roger Rabbit?* (1988), when actor Bob Hoskins got into the toon zone with a host of classic cartoon characters.

But it was the effects artists at Lucasfilm's Industrial Light & Magic who pioneered something new for feature films: the integration of photorealistic 3-D animation with live action. Way back in 1985, for *Young Sherlock Holmes*, ILM produced a computer generated knight who magically burst from a stained glass window. The next evolution took the amoeboid form of the watery pseudopod creature of *The Abyss* (1989) and the shape-changing, liquid-metal cyborg of *Terminator 2* (1991). The breakthrough into the illusion of organic creatures came two years later with the digital dinosaurs of *Jurassic Park*.

One of those awestruck by the sights of a ruthless cyborg and a rampaging T-rex seemingly invading reality was Rob Coleman, a traditional cel animator and future Episode I animation director. "Seeing these creatures living in our real world, I just had to come to ILM," smiled Coleman, whose pre-*Phantom* ILM work included supervising the menagerie of CG aliens on *Men in Black*.

"After I arrived," he continued, "we started moving into thinking, acting characters. A lot of us came from traditional animation, so we were used to making line drawings move, breathing life into something that doesn't exist. The next step was to take that understanding and create a three-dimensional character which interacts with something every audience member understands—a real human being."

That select company of ILM's "thinking, acting" CG characters includes the ghosts of *Casper* (1995) and the talking dragon Draco in *Dragonheart* (1996). But the digital actors of Episode I are a quantum leap on the evolutionary scale. The troupe of phenomenal *Phantom Menace* CG performers includes Watto, the cantankerous space junk dealer on Tatooine, and Sebulba, the ruthless Podrace pilot.

But Jar Jar Binks was a movie unto himself: almost 400 shots. Jar Jar would follow Jedi Knights Qui-Gon Jinn (Liam Neeson) and Obi-Wan Kenobi (Ewan McGregor) on a journey from the underwater city of Otoh Gunga to the exotic capital of Theed, from the desert wastes of Tatooine back to the battlefields of Naboo.

"Jar Jar is just as important to the plot as Qui-Gon, Obi-Wan, or the Queen," noted computer graphics supervisor Doug Smythe. "He interacts with the live action characters—he's really on a par with them. After a while you forget he's a computer generated character!"

Added Kevin Martel, one of the lead Jar Jar animators, "I think this is the first time there's ever been a fully CG character who's just one of the guys."

WHAT DOES A GUNGAN LOOK LIKE?

THE COMPLICATED CREATION OF JAR JAR (and all the CG characters) began with building a three-dimensional model form in the computer, and then animating it with believable performances. Next came the details: adding digital clothing; utilising virtual lighting to integrate the character into his surrounding environment; completing the all-important "rendering" (the process of calculating the images of a CG character based on the model, animation, colour and lighting) of the CG image; and, finally, compositing the character into the final scene.

But while Jar Jar's destiny was to be a breakthrough CG creation, the character's image was first developed with low-tech tools: pencil and marker on paper. Jar Jar started on the drawing boards, an idea that evolved out of Doug Chiang's concept design department, that creative font of the *Star Wars* universe located on the third floor of the Main House at Skywalker Ranch. Concept artist Terryl Whitlatch, an expert in animal anatomy who handled the lion's share of creature designs, began working on the character in January, 1995.

In the concept phase, imagination rules. A proposed design can go through many iterations, but Jar Jar (who would also be the prototypal figure for the entire Gungan species), was one of the toughest *Phantom* characters to conjure. It would take a year and a half before Lucas approved a final design.

While Lucas described some characters to the smallest physical detail, Jar Jar began as an idea stripped to its basics: the male of the species, tall, amphibious, lead digital character. Fleshed out from the start was Lucas'

» Concept art for Jar Jar Binks, by Terryl Whitlatch

concept of Jar Jar's personality: earnest but bumbling, a social misfit, a character with the physical grace—and penchant for slapstick pratfalls—of Charlie Chaplin, Buster Keaton, and other classic comics of the cinema.

Whitlatch would later confess she sometimes despaired of ever coming up with a design Lucas would approve. The creative breakthrough came when the director saw an old doodle Whitlatch had pinned to her bulletin board. She'd sketched out three views of a frog-like critter on its hind legs, eyes on stalks, a worried expression on its face. Lucas loved the look and from that image, which Whitlatch dubbed "proto-Jar Jar," a strange creature began to take form, a figure with the gait of a flightless emu; a muscular, swan-like neck; the head and duck-billed face of a Hadrosaur dinosaur; and long, fish-finned puppy dog ears.

HOW WOULD A GUNGAN MOVE?

BUT WHILE A CONCEPT HAD TAKEN FORM on paper, that wasn't the end of the design—in some ways it was the beginning. As CG modellers and others began to enter the picture, Lucas toyed with the possibilities of his emerging creation, from giving Jar Jar the power to physically expand and contract (discarded as making things too complex) to possibly realising the character with a CG head composited onto the body of a live performer wearing a Jar Jar costume (with Lucas concluding the Gungan was best realised as a full CG figure).

The transition from two-dimensional drawings to a 3-D performer required the concept department to take Jar Jar line art, have it blown up to life-size, and then put it over a cardboard cut-out figure to begin appreciating the real scale of the eventual CG creation.

Another step was to sculpt and paint a detailed foot-tall physical reference model. Although such sculptures can then be scanned into a computer to form the basis for the CG figure, the Jar Jar animation model was built cold in the computer by model supervisor Geoff Campbell and his team. "For us the challenge and fun of Jar Jar was taking a drawing and translating that into a three-dimensional sculpture in the computer," Campbell said.

Lucas was eager to get going on the creation of his digital actor, so Campbell and modeler Stephen Aplin brought their computers from ILM and plugged them in at the Main House. A rough 3-D Jar Jar model allowed Lucas, Chiang's concept team, and Campbell's modellers to experiment with and finalize the physical characteristics and facial expressions that would define the character.

"It's basically like working with clay, where we take a roughed-out model and are actually sculpting in the computer," Campbell explained. "ILM has a software team that provides software packages that allow us to sculpt quickly and in real time. [Concept artist] Iain McCaig was doing terrific sketches of Jar Jar expressions and we'd take those drawings and sculpt furiously. We'd just keep going over the model with changes. We sculpturally defined how far the character could go before it went 'off-model' and became something uncharacteristic of what the character was supposed to be."

Case in point were concept drawings featuring a long, crocodile shaped mouth, which was deemed too unwieldy and made smaller in the computer model. "There was a phase of figuring out how happy-go-lucky or goofy he was going to be," Campbell recalled. "We also tried things such as having the structure

of his teeth and gums change when he smiled, but that proved too unrealistic. All these alien type ideas would be proposed, then thrown out, as slowly the character was brought back to reality."

Although the lighting, compositing, and other concerns would come later in the production timeline, the pre-production phase was vital for making sure the model could withstand the creative rigours ahead. "Pre-production is important because we want to make sure the character can be put into various environments," explained CG supervisor Smythe. "In pre-production we work out all the physical characteristics for every inch of his body. What's his colour and [skin] reflectivity? Is his body smooth or bumpy? There are a bunch of these nitty-gritty issues which we test in different lighting environments to make sure they'll work."

» Sculpting the Jar Jar head

A CG character takes shape when geometric points in the computer are moved and fused into "patches"—solid shapes that are the building blocks of a form. A CG character's figure is also given "armature," literally a skeleton complete with joint placements that allow animators to bend an arm, swivel a head, and generally replicate mechanics of motion.

"During the modeling phase a TD [technical director] will take the model as it's nearing completion and run it through a process we call 'turntable,'" Smythe added. "On our end a digital painter would match the painted sculpture, we'd add basic lighting, and then rotate the model to judge the paint work and evaluate what would be needed to take it from a physical sculpture to something that looks like a living, breathing character."

Ultimately, the potential range and quality of the performance an animator can get out of a CG model is based on the physical characteristics pre-set by the modellers. Key to giving Jar Jar a jolt of life force were libraries of facial shapes and expressions, everything from eye blinks to the phonemic lip-syncs that would make it look like Jar Jar was pronouncing every word of his dialogue.

"We'd sculpt and set up hundreds of shapes, so the possibilities for the animators were pretty endless," Campbell noted. "The idea is these animation shapes could overlap, that animators could mix from a palette of facial expressions. For example, instead of a straight smile pose, you could have eyes blink on frame 50, and two frames later start going into his smile."

» Computer wireframe of Jar Jar Binks.

JAR JAR BINKS, MEET AHMED BEST

WHILE THE CONCEPT ARTISTS AND CG MODELLERS were setting the stage for the animators, Lucas' live-action photography was already accounting for the eventual integration of the synthetic creation. Interacting on set and location with Liam Neeson, Ewan McGregor, and the other actors was Jar Jar's other half, the very live Ahmed Best, an acclaimed theatrical performer who also contributed the Gungan's voice.

For Jar Jar shots, Lucas shot two versions of the same scene—the first with Best dressed in a rough Gungan costume and interacting with the actors, the second repeated with the live performers acting to an invisible character. In most final takes, Best was only a reference for determining size relations and key poses, with the CG animation added to the "clean" footage.

Sometimes Lucas liked the dynamics when Best was performing alongside the other actors, so animators created final animation for that footage, which required digitally removing Best from the scene and replacing him with the final animation.

"George understood the necessity of having actors on set who were going to be replaced later," Coleman noted. "If you're acting to nothing your eyes tend to wander, but with Ahmed on set, Liam and Ewan had someone to act to, so eyelines could match [with the digital actor added later] and the timing would be there during exchanges of dialogue."

Although Lucas directed Best as if he were Jar Jar, no human, even in a creature suit, could move with ease and match the unusual Gungan body type. "Ahmed is a very physical guy and can do amazing things with his body, but we wanted to stretch Jar Jar even more," Coleman noted. "George told me to think of Jar Jar as not having bones but cartilage, and talked at length about the need to make Jar Jar magical, other-worldly."

» LEFT: Ahmed Best in the motion-capture suit.

GET TO THE ESSENCE OF THE GUNGAN

EVERY DIGITAL CHARACTER IN THE MOVIE had its own animation team—and Jar Jar, with the most shots, had the biggest team: 15 animators. Within the character team, CG artists were assigned according to their strengths, such as those skilled in physical action handling Jar Jar's slapstick moments, while animators with a talent for lip sync were given the character's heavy dialogue scenes.

"You've got 15 different personalities and styles that have to bring one character to life—it's like running with a team of horses," Coleman observed. "And any digital actor you're putting into a live set is a challenge, because you have the immediate reference of a real person. With Jar Jar, you've got this goofy, amphibian digital character that doesn't really exist yet must hold a scene with great actors."

For Lucas, the logistics of dealing with a digital actor meant every nuance of acting in any given scene was communicated to the animation team through Coleman and lead Jar Jar animator Lou Dellarosa. Twice a week and throughout the production, Coleman met with Lucas for an ongoing dialogue on the digital characters. "In Jar Jar's case we discussed the arc of his action in the movie, what Jar Jar learns, what he's doing, and where he's going—all the questions you'd explore with 'real' actors," Coleman explained.

One of the realities of a freshly minted model is the inevitable learning curve animators must ride out before coming to a complete understanding of a character. Through the mechanics of motion and libraries of expression pre-set by the modellers, the animation team had to manipulate every gesture, every eye-blink, and make it all "read" as distinctly Jar Jar. With the large Jar Jar animation team it took almost three months of daily meetings before everyone found "common ground," according to Coleman.

"You get to that moment where everybody understands the essence of Jar Jar," Coleman recalled, "where it's obvious if some animation isn't right. One of the distinctive things about Jar Jar is his physicality. As a starting point, George told me to look at the great Buster Keaton, who did physical comedy with a deadpan look on his face. There's this happy-clown thing to Buster, that he takes whatever the world gives him. Jar Jar is a mixture of Buster, Chaplin, Jerry Lewis, and all the comic icons of our culture.

"But he's different from them, too. He bumbles along, helping the Jedi because he has the world experience of Naboo that they need, but he doesn't really connect the dots. He always wants to know what's going on but never really does."

GET INTO THE GUNGAN'S HEAD

ALTHOUGH THE FINAL COMPUTER ANIMATION would be scanned out to film at the "high-resolution" image detail needed for the big screen, the animators worked with a "low-resolution" Jar Jar model. When assigned a scene, animators received a video of the live action sequence which included Ahmed Best's reference performance. For completely computer generated environments into which Jar Jar animation would be placed, such as the climactic ground battle, the animators had online panels of drawn storyboard art for inspiration. (For totally CG scenes, the animators could still call up Best footage from other live action scenes for reference.)

Before animation, each animator mentally prepared for their virtual performance. A classic way of getting into the mood of a scene was to sketch out on paper the possible key poses. Kevin Martel, whose animation of Jar Jar getting zapped by a Podracer energy bolt appeared in the film's first theatrical trailer, also favoured videotaping himself acting out a scene and then studying the result.

Some animators found inspiration in Keaton, Chaplin, and company, but Jar Jar lead Dellarosa detected a kindred spirit in another gangly cartoon character. "There's some Buster Keaton in Jar Jar but, I have to say that there's a little bit of Goofy also," Dellarosa laughed. "Jar Jar's got the same kind of goofy walk—but without looking ridiculous. We can't push things the way you would in traditional cartoon animation, otherwise the movements would be out of the context of live action."

Still, Dellarosa, like others, came to the 3-D world from traditional animation. Before arriving at ILM, Dellarosa worked at Disney's Orlando animation studio on such characters as the villainous Jafar of *Aladdin* and the cackling hyenas in *The Lion King*.

"I'd learned all the traditional animation techniques, so 3-D animation seemed like the logical next step," Dellarosa smiled. "But it was when I was

»Jar Jar Binks encounters the Jedi Knights

working on Draco in *Dragonheart* that I realised computer animation is a different medium altogether! In traditional animation you can draw to what looks good, but in a 3-D world, we all have to work with an existing model. In traditional animation you can cheat things like scale, but in the 3-D world the digital actor has to always be kept in scale with the live actors."

Martel, who graduated to *Phantom Menace* from Sheridan College, a famed animation school in Toronto, agreed. "Animating a CG figure is kind of like being a puppeteer, but it's also unlike anything else," he said. "Sometimes you feel like you're in there with the character, and sometimes you *wish* you could just reach in, grab him, and move him into position!"

A typical, painstaking animation sequence would begin with "blocking" the rough movements that Lucas could then comment on or approve. From there, the animators continually refined and developed the key poses. Although the computer could automatically do the "in-between" movements of each key pose, even those interpolations required hands-on animation.

"It's not a matter of going from pose to pose," noted Dellarosa. "We'd go into the interpolations and further refine and place secondary actions so the final movement had more believability. Anyone can move things around—it's *how* you do it. It's the timing and composition. You have to know how Jar Jar fits into a shot."

THE GUNGAN GETS INTO *YOUR* HEAD

AS THE CREATIVE JOURNEY PROGRESSED, and the animators began to understand the creature's alien nature, the Gungan got under their skin and into their subconscious. "I found myself walking around my apartment swinging my arms all loosey-goosey like Jar Jar," Martel chuckled. "Sometimes he even got into my dreams—which is when you know you've been sitting at the computer a little too long! But he definitely became a part of me. Understanding a character is a big part of animating him.

"I guess animation is like being an actor without the glamour," Martel continued. "We'd get a scene from Rob and he'd communicate what needed to be done. We'd learn our lines, because there's a lot of dialogue to deal with, then try to give our best performance. Each scene became its own challenge. But ultimately he [Lucas] knew what he wanted and continually communicated that to us."

Martel said he found that one of his biggest challenges was making Jar Jar move believably. "The hardest part of animating Jar Jar was making it look like he's thinking and not just moving around," he said. "A lot can be communicated through the eyes. The goal throughout was to make it look like there was a connection between his brain and his limbs, that he was a living, breathing thing."

And just as real actors get into the persona of their characters, and sometimes improvise a scene, so too were the *Phantom* animators able to play off the digital actors and sometimes go beyond the original concept

for specific scenes. Such was the case with the scene when Liam Neeson's Qui-Gon and Jar Jar encounter Watto in the Podrace hangar. When a storypoint called for the winged Watto to fly past Qui-Gon, Coleman considered having the junk dealer buzz behind the Jedi—but then had another inspiration.

"Watto, who doesn't care for Jar Jar, flies around Qui-Gon and pushes Jar Jar in the chest to get him out of the way," Coleman explained. "This little bit of business was never in the storyboards, but became natural because I had the Jar Jar and Watto teams in my head and understood the personality of the two characters. Here you have Jar Jar, who's from a water planet, and now he's on a desert planet in the middle of a noisy room and, once again, he doesn't know what's going on and is tucked behind this Jedi Master, scared out of his head. And there's this other, curmudgeonly character who has to fly around Qui-Gon and what's he going to do if Jar Jar is in the way? Knock the guy in the head! I remember suggesting the moment to George and he said, 'Yeah, go for it!' It was real—the moment was believable."

» A computer-generated study of Jar Jar Binks

THE FINISHING TOUCHES

ANY ANIMATED FILM IS A LONG, LABORIOUS PROCESS. Jar Jar alone required nearly two years of animation—indeed, it began way back in November 1997 when the digital actor was first added to scenes (although it wasn't until the end of April 1998 that Lucas "finalled" the first Jar Jar shot). The reality of such a long creative timeline is that animation inevitably gets better as time goes by.

One of the unwritten rules is to never begin animation with what will be the character's first appearance, as that introductory scene is vital to "selling" a character and merits the peak animation performance. Thus, the Jar Jar animation process began with the Gungan in Watto's shop on Tatooine, a sequence slated to appear toward the middle of the movie.

The Jar Jar team thought they'd nailed the complex character that first time, but later in the production timeline, Coleman took another look at those first shots in Watto's shop and tagged a few as "CBB"—"Could Be Better." It was with pride that Coleman said he got some of those first shots back, with animators able to return to the seminal scenes and bring the animation up to the high standard of the subsequent Jar Jar shots.

As animation was completed, other functions vital to finaling a shot

» Jar Jar Binks in a moment of panic.

were begun, sometimes concurrently if the animation work was far enough along. One of the final acts in the animation stage was adding digital clothing, an ILM breakthrough given that the company's previous CG characters included a dragon, ghosts, dinosaurs, and other creations that didn't need clothes.

ILM's in-house "cloth simulation" software allowed the computer to automatically conform the outer clothing to Jar Jar's movements. To save time, a library of painted wrinkle elements was created and textured onto the cloth. The simulation package also automatically generated the subtle movements of Jar Jar's floppy ears, a time saver for animators who could concentrate on creating the overall performance and not worry about keeping the ears active in each shot.

Technical directors handled the virtual lighting for the digital actor, a process with all the tools, and none of the physical constraints, of a real cinematographer. "Every CG light source has a position and direction in [virtual] space, so we place them around the animation model to mimic the direction of the light sources—whatever it takes to fit Jar Jar into the scene," CG supervisor Smythe explained. "You can set the colour and brightness of the lights, even do things impossible in the real world, like control which objects cast shadows."

Then comes the final computing, or rendering, of the digital image and its compositing into a scene. "There's usually an overlap, because before we're finished getting the lighting exactly right we'll start putting the character into the scene," Smythe noted. "You want to see the character within the context of the shot to judge the lighting."

» Jar Jar shows off his amazing sense of balance.

RELEASE THE GUNGAN

AS THE PRODUCTION WOUND DOWN, the Jar Jar team realised they'd soon be letting go of a character that had become their creative obsession. Kevin Martel, for one, left Jar Jar back on the battlefield of Naboo. "My final Jar Jar shot was of him in the ground battle, flailing his arms and afraid as always," Martel smiled. "For me there was a sense of loss at the end, but it was also a fantastic feeling that this character we'd been hanging out with for years was going to be introduced to the world."

"It's almost a shame to stop working on a character, particularly one you've been working with for a while," said Smythe. "I don't know if Jar

Jar's going to make an appearance in any future movies—that's up to George to decide. But if he does, it'll be like saying 'hi' to an old friend."

Concluded Coleman, "ILM has become a specialist in combining [CG] animation and live action—we're in this new realm—and in my mind Jar Jar is at the next level of sophistication, light-years away from Draco. What makes Jar Jar the next generation of digital actor is the subtlety of control in his facial features, the experience of the animators, and the ability to do the simulation of clothing and ear movements. We were able to get the life force into that body." ☻

ADDED MUSCLE

STAR WARS FROM PAUL DINI'S POINT OF VIEW

Author Paul Dini gets inside the helmet of Boba Fett for the short-story anthology *From a Certain Point of View*. It's the latest in a series of contributions to the *Star Wars* universe that dates back to the 1980s.

WORDS: JOSEPH MCCABE

Just in case anyone still needed proof that *A New Hope* is the gift that keeps on giving, 2017 saw the release of the short-story collection *From a Certain Point of View*. A 40th-anniversary anthology, it comprises 40 tales by 40 authors, each of whom has taken a scene from the movie and presented it anew as from the perspective of a background character. Some of the writers are new to *Star Wars*, while others are much-loved veterans. Few, however, have a track record—within *Star Wars* and without—as impressive as Paul Dini's.

Today, Dini is probably best known as the man who created Harley Quinn and Mark Hamill's unique incarnation of the Joker for *Batman: The Animated Series* (1992-95). But he is also the Emmy Award-winning story editor behind *Tiny Toon Adventures* (1992-95), and the Eisner Award-winning writer of comic books such as *Superman: Peace on Earth* (1998), and the *Batman: Arkham* series of videogames. Most notably for *Star Wars* fans, however, Dini was story editor for the animated TV series *Droids* and *Ewoks* in the 1980s, and returned to the galaxy far, far away to write for *Star Wars: The Clone Wars* in 2007.

For his contribution to *From a Certain Point of View*, Dini has taken a slightly different path from his fellow authors, drawing story inspiration not from the original 1977 version of *Star Wars*, but the Special Edition of *A New Hope* released in 1997. His story, "Added Muscle," is based on the new scene in which Jabba the Hutt confronts Han Solo—with the one and only Boba Fett in tow. ▶

PROFILE
PAUL DINI

New York City native Paul Dini began working as an animator at Filmation while he was still at college. He made his name writing for cartoon series like *He-Man*, and *G.I.Joe*, and the renowned *Batman: The Animated Series*. Well known for his work in comics and animation, Dini has been awarded 5 Emmys and created the popular DC Comics character Harley Quinn.

Dini recalls, "When I was asked to contribute, I thought: Everyone's sort of forgotten that Boba Fett has been retconned into the film. He's a colorful character and he's part of the universe, so why not write about him?

"All he really does in the movie is stand there and back-up Jabba. My story is kind of loopy because it's about what he's thinking while he's holding a gun on Han and Chewie. It's mostly: Am I getting paid for this? When do we drink? What a hassle! I even borrowed a little smidge from Kevin Smith's *Clerks* (1984), where I have him say, 'I'm not even supposed to be here today!' The title, 'Added Muscle,' is a wink to the fact that Boba Fett was added in later and now he's part of the official story."

A Long Time Ago... In College

It's clear that Dini's irreverence is born out of love for the saga, and a great familiarity with its quirks. Like so many others, his passion for *Star Wars* began in 1977, when Dini himself was a college student.

"I grew up in the [San Francisco] Bay Area," Dini explains, "and I heard they were making a space movie over in Marin County. At that point—we're talking 1976 or something—all space movies were really lame and science fiction was in the doldrums. I thought that the best they could hope for would be something like the movie *Silent Running* (1972).

"When I eventually saw the first trailer for *Star Wars*, I wasn't very

01 Paul Dini finds out what is on Fett's mind in short story "Added Muscle"

02 Fett's guest appearance in *A New Hope: The Special Edition.*

03 Vile bounty hunter Boba Fett. (Right)

impressed at all. It was described as 'the story of a boy, a girl, and a galaxy.' I mean, it was really cornball stuff.

"Soon after, I heard that Marvel Comics was doing a comic-book adaptation, and I saw a couple of pieces of artwork that looked kind of good," Dini recalls. "And then I heard they were having a sneak preview in Boston, where I was going to school at the time. So I walked down to the movie theater, where a good-sized crowd stood waiting in line. So I thought: 'I'm gonna see it. I'm not doing anything tonight.' I went in, and it was a knockout experience. It was the last thing I expected, and I was sucked into it completely. I was an instant fan.

"It was fun, because I saw the movie about two weeks before it actually opened," Dini remembers. "For a while I got to have this fun little secret, going around telling

all my friends, 'Yeah, I saw this movie. You're gonna really like it...' Of course, before long there were legions and legions of fans. It was great to see it all evolve."

Adventure Time

Not long after the film's release, Dini started his career as a writer on animated shows such as Filmation's Tarzan (1976-79), Flash Gordon (1979-82), and He-Man and the Masters of the Universe (1983-85). By the time Lucasfilm decided to make its own cartoon adventures, he was already a well-known and respected name in the industry.

"It would have been 1984, and Lucasfilm was looking to do The Ewoks and Droids Adventure Hour," says D. "They put out feelers in Los Angeles for writers and producers to do the show. They were being kind of selective in who they were talking to, but I thought it would be a really good

> "I LOBBIED TO USE BOBA FETT IN THE *DROIDS* SERIES AS I THOUGHT HE WOULD BE A GOOD RECURRING VILLAIN."

03

"THE TITLE, 'ADDED MUSCLE,' IS A WINK TO THE FACT THAT BOBA FETT WAS ADDED IN LATER AND NOW HE'S PART OF THE OFFICIAL STORY."

opportunity, so I sent a couple of scripts and an episode of *Dungeons & Dragons* that I had written, and they loved it. They could tell that I knew about *Star Wars* and had a real affection for it, and that's what got me hired."

As a story editor on both halves of the Nelvana-produced *Ewoks* and *Droids* show, Dini worked with George Lucas and his team on the first ever weekly *Star Wars* animated series.

"I really enjoyed being in the Lucasfilm environment," he says. "We had great creative resources in luminaries like Joe Johnston, *Ewoks* movie writer Bob Carrau, sound designer Ben Burtt, and of course,

George himself.

Debuting on the ABC network in September 1985, *The Ewoks and Droids Adventure Hour* comprised two half-hour shows: *Ewoks* and *Star Wars: Droids: The Adventures of R2-D2 and C-3PO*, known more simply as *Droids*.

"I was story-editing both shows, but writing more for *Ewoks*," Dini explains. "*Droids* had a few writers at that point, and I think it was the more difficult to work on: it was the show that really wanted to be *Star Wars*. Each week, R2-D2 and C-3PO would go from action scenario to action scenario, meeting a different master and then having to say goodbye to them.

"Early on, we were thinking that sometimes the master would be killed, or the droids would have to abandon their masters because that was the only way to save them," says Dini. "When we discussed the series with George, he really wanted to have a heart-tugging element to it: The droids really had no home until they met Luke and Leia, as they were always on the run and always looking for a place to fit in," he adds

"I thought that was a really good idea, because that way you have a lot of humanity in these basically inhuman characters. Threepio is sympathetic and comical up to a point, and Artoo is basically a puppy," he explains. "So it would get to be like *Lassie*, with Lassie having a different home and then having to leave and always stay on the road. I lobbied to use Boba Fett in the *Droids* series, as I thought he would be a good recurring villain. We only got him in once, though."

Pushing the Boundaries

Among the many scripts Dini wrote for *Ewoks* were the few in which the Empire encroached upon the Forest Moon.

"At first we didn't want to have any Imperial elements on *Ewoks*," he says. "We just wanted adventures on the self-contained, little world of Endor. But as we got into the second season, we thought: Let's bring in the Empire and go for as many interesting and diverse elements as we can. If we'd done a third season, we might have done more of that Dini reveals.

"I remember one of the very first stories I pitched was a story I really wanted to do. It was about a TIE fighter pilot who crashes on the Ewoks' home planet, and they take care of him and nurse him back to health. At first he treats them like vermin: 'Nasty little creatures. Get away from me!' But they make a sacrifice to help him get off of the planet. And then when they're in trouble he goes back to help them.

"Nelvana generated some new conceptual artwork for that story that I thought was really nice," he ▶

continues, "showing the contrast between this pilot, who's basically a drone of the Empire, and how his involvement with the Ewoks opens him up as a person and he's able to care for them. I wanted to do more stories like that, because that was the tone of what they were doing in the live-action Ewok movies that George Lucas was producing for television."

Unfortunately, however, the network was not so keen on such a considered storytelling approach on either *Droids* or *Ewoks*.

"Both series were produced for a very restrictive time on Saturday morning TV," says Dini. "The execs at the network and the Broadcast Standards people controlled all of the content. We wanted to make our series with all the emotion and action that propelled the movies, but they really wanted *Care Bears*.

04

05

"I WAS VERY HAPPY TO BE GIVEN THE CHANCE TO WRITE FOR *THE CLONE WARS*."

06 *The Clone Wars* reunited Dini with two familiar droids.

"So we constantly had to rein in our ideas, based on the network's fear that the show might scare or confuse kids," he continues. "I still think the work we did was pretty good for the time, even if we didn't get to push the boundaries as much as we wanted to."

In order to make the best shows possible within the network's strict guidelines, Dini turned to humor to capture the *Star Wars* spirit.

"We tried to play up the more humorous elements," he recalls, "with the Ewoks' interpersonal relationships, and the Duloks [another species indigenous to Endor] as their recurring foils. We looked to add fun wherever we could, as another way to include some real emotion and heart.

"That's what we wanted to go for, and I think that we achieved

those goals on a few occasions. There were a couple of funny episodes that I thought were genuinely good, and the episode about finding Princess Kneesaa's sister had an emotional core to it.

"It helped that Nelvana totally knocked it out of the park with the artwork," Dini adds, "especially in the first season. They really threw a lot into the animation and the design."

Back at the Ranch

Dini returned to *Star Wars* writing 20 years later, with two second season episodes of *The Clone Wars*: "Holocron Heist" and "Voyage of Temptation." At long last, this gave him the opportunity to pen *Star Wars* stories with a harder edge than he was ever allowed to on the *Droids* or *Ewoks* cartoons.

07

04 Wicket with Princess Kneesaa in *Ewoks*. (Left)

05 The Duloks of Endor were no friends of the Ewoks. (Left)

07 Bounty hunter Cad Bane gets his hands on a holocron, in "Holocron Heist."

08 Trouble for Anakin in Paul Dini's *The Clone Wars* episode "Voyage of Temptation".

08

"I was very happy to be given the chance to write for *The Clone Wars*, as I finally got to do some intense *Star Wars* action," he says. "I had very fond memories of my time working at Skywalker Ranch in the 1980s, so when my friend Henry Gilroy went up there as head writer on *The Clone Wars*, he and I got to talking about it. That led to general *Star Wars* talk, and my love for it was obvious. Before long he said, 'Do you want to write a few?'

"It was a lot of fun to work in a 'grown-up' *Star Wars* universe and craft stories that were more complex,"reflects Dini. "It provided an opportunity for actual humor, rather than just slapstick goofiness, as well as some real life-or-death situations."

Today, Dini is busy with a raft of exciting new projects, including the animated DC Comics series *Justice League Action*, and a new monthly *Joker Loves Harley* comic book. He's also launched a Kickstarter campaign for *BOO & HISS*—a new graphic novel concept about a ghost mouse haunting the cat that killed him. He hasn't ruled out a return to *Star Wars*, either, since he still has lots of story ideas…

"Oh yeah," Dini laughs with glee. "I've got tons! Like Batman and Gotham City, the *Star Wars* universe and the characters within it are very easy for me to visualize and to step into now. Mostly I'm working on my own stuff, but as with *From a Certain Point of View*, if something comes my way, I'll always jump at the chance to do it. It's always fun to play with those characters again." ☙

THE GRIEVOUS GROWL

Matthew Wood reveals his incredible double life as supervising sound editor and sound designer at Skywalker Sound—and the Separatist droid army's fiendish cyborg leader with a hacking cough.

WORDS: AMY RATCLIFFE

I t's fall 2002. George Lucas, producer Rick McCallum, concept artists, and other key production members are meeting each Friday to review the latest designs for *Star Wars: Revenge of the Sith* (2005). On November 22, Lucas tells the assembly that the Episode III villain could be a Separatist droid general. "I won't limit it at this point to a droid. It could be an alien of some kind. I'm not sure if I want him to be human. It's the Darth Maul. It's the Jango Fett. Darth Vader..." he's recorded explaining in *The Making of Return of the Sith*. He tells the artists the villain is not a Sith, that it has to be able to do dialogue scenes, and that it has to be iconic.

And so General Grievous, the Supreme Commander of the Separatist droid army, was born. Two weeks after Lucas' instruction to design the foe, concept artist Warren Fu presented illustrations for the character that caught the director's eye. Fellow concept artist Ian McCaig had advised them to think of their worst nightmares, and Fu imagined a scary masked enemy. His designs became the foundation for the fearsome cyborg who would stalk across the big screen in the final *Star Wars* prequel.

Bela Lugosi

A combination of robotic technology with an organic base, General Grievous' voice is grating and loud, part mechanical and part biological. That voice is provided by Matthew Wood, supervising sound editor and sound designer at Skywalker Sound, and it came to be rather late in the process. "My ▶

▶ first look at what fully rendered Grievous was going to look like was actually in *Star Wars Insider*," Wood tells us. "It was on the cover, and I remember thinking, 'Whoa, that's cool. Who's gonna voice that?' Because the character has no mouth, we could wait a certain amount of time before Industrial Light & Magic (ILM) needed our final voice-overs."

Busy working on audio effects for *Revenge of the Sith*, Wood knew that Lucas wanted the voice to sound as if it was synthesized through the circuitry of a voice box, with computerized, cybernetic qualities, and he and co-sound editor Christopher Scarabosio developed a distinctive resonance for Grievous. "We ran it through some processing, including ring modulation, to give it that synthesized timbre. We put every audition we got through that same process, as an egalitarian method for every actor's performance. I would play those for George to get his feedback on what things he did or didn't like. And I had the ability to sit in on all those auditions and also process them," Wood explains.

Having that perspective put Wood in a very unique position. McCallum was getting nervous because they needed to cast the role of Grievous and time was running out, so Scarabosio encouraged Wood to audition. Wood, a trained actor, had performed voices for *Star Wars* before, so he anonymously submitted his file to Lucas with the other auditions. He approached Grievous with a gruff, harsh voice, something to convey the character's militaristic sense. And he also added a little old-school villain style, in the vein of 1930s horror movie actor Bela Lugosi. Wood recalls, "I'd coincidentally come back from

visiting a friend in Prague, so it was fresh in my mind, and that's what I went with: yelling in a classic villain voice with an Eastern European accent. As that hit the processor, I could hear there was this nice gravelly quality. Then I got the surprising call that George had picked my audition."

Wood's performance of General Grievous' biting metallic voice cuts through the Battle of Coruscant in Episode III's opening scenes, as Anakin Skywalker (Hayden Christensen) and Obi-Wan Kenobi (Ewan McGregor) confront the metal general after his kidnapping of Chancellor Palpatine, but McGregor never knew who voiced Grievous until some years after the movie's release. Grievous battled with Kenobi more than once in *Revenge of the Sith*, and during filming McGregor was most often sparring with stunt double Kyle Rowling, who stood in for the CG cyborg, with Grievous' lines being read in from off-camera. "I worked with Ewan in my sound capacity on all the prequels," Wood says. "I'd record him all the time for the post-production dialogue recording we had to do. It wasn't until I worked with him years later, when I brought him in to do a whispery voice for *The Force Awakens*, that I actually got to tell him, 'Hey, did you know what ended up happening with that voice? It was me.' And he was like, 'No way!'"

Catching Breath

After Dooku's death, Grievous took over his position and moved the Separatist Council from Utapau to Mustafar at Darth Sidious' behest. The over-confident cyborg engaged with Kenobi for what would be the final time, as the duel ended with Grievous' demise. To his last, Grievous barked out orders and taunts punctuated by a phlegmy cough. Lucas wanted Grievous to have breathing troubles because he was essentially a testing ground for the technology that would

01 The fearsome Grievous, as voiced by Matthew Wood.

02 Wood again played the general in *Star Wars: The Clone Wars* (2008).

03 Grievous played a big part in *The Clone Wars* animated series.

04 General Grievous in *Revenge of the Sith*.

05 Matthew Wood in a recording booth at Skywalker Sound.

06 Grievous versus Obi-Wan.

> "I remember thinking, 'Whoa, that's cool. Who's gonna voice that?'"

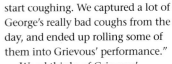

> **"We captured a lot of George's really bad coughs from the day, and ended up rolling some of them into Grievous' performance."**

start coughing. We captured a lot of George's really bad coughs from the day, and ended up rolling some of them into Grievous' performance."

Wood thinks of Grievous' voice as comprising of two-parts: the dramatic element and the processing layer. "I pitch him down about a semi-tone to give him that lower pitch register, and in a way that his voice has an artifacting quality to it where it doesn't sound perfect," he explains. "I'm going for imperfection, so when he's yelling, I want to make it almost like he's so angry that his vocal processor is unable to translate his emotion into voice perfectly."

Wood had to perform with a hyper-enunciated yell in order to get Grievous' words and emotion across through the gravelly, scratchy qualities in his voice. The delay ▶

eventually create Darth Vader. By luck, both Wood and Lucas were in a state to provide the required rattles and hacks.

"For a lot of those lines, you really have to use the diaphragm big time and yell this guttural performance," Wood recalls. "I would run out of breath and cough, and George himself had a really bad cough that day. I remember telling Chris Scarabosio to keep the tape rolling, because George would come up to direct me and he would

▶ and ring-modulation Wood applied is not unlike the standard procedure he uses for droid processing, but Grievous got a little something extra. "It's a mix and match of a few different things, because George wanted to communicate that Grievous had a biological component to illustrate that he had a weakness," says Wood. "The cough was to illustrate that, too. It's such an odd and creepy character. It's a part I've really loved and respected all these years."

The Grievous Gig

Wood had the opportunity to reprise the role in *Star Wars: The Clone Wars*. Set in the years between *Star Wars: Attack of the Clones* (2002) and *Revenge of the Sith*, the animated series takes an on-the-ground look at the galactic conflict between the Republic and the Separatists, with Grievous and his droid army at the center of numerous key struggles. *The Art of Star Wars: The Clone Wars* explains how they adjusted General Grievous' grim countenance to match the style of the show. Designer Atsushi Takeuchi used simpler shapes for Grievous' complex head and limbs to maintain the look of the character, while exaggerating the chest and shoulders to make him more menacing. Grievous strode

into battle with an intimidating lumber, while attempting to pair his excellent planning with commanding an army of inept battle droids.

"My main performance goals were frustration," Wood says. "I think the guy was always frustrated. He was trying to be something more than he was, and making a name for himself by going up against the Jedi is the ultimate thing he could do. Feeling like he technically knew the ways of the Force and knew how to wield the lightsaber was just enough for him to try and take on the Jedi. Of course, it wasn't. Ultimately, the combination of his cowardice and going up against the Force is never going to work. And then his battle droids really are quite dumb, and their processors are not very high-end because the factory stamps out thousands of these things."

So this clever, nearly indestructible, and bold-yet-craven leader was stuck with commanding an endless supply of incompetent soldiers. Grievous found a way to work with the battle droids, even if it meant using them as fodder while seeking a Jedi to fight, or taking a risky move, such as abducting Senator Amidala in the episode, "Destroy Malevolence." Dooku found Grievous to be

07 Grievous' sharp golden eyes are some of his few remaining organic parts.

08 Woods reprised his Grievous role for the video game *Star Wars: Battlefront II*.

GENERAL GRIEVOUS

A sharp military strategist and dangerous fighter trained by Count Dooku in the ways of Jedi combat, Grievous is all the more formidable because of his cybernetic enhancements. He's not Force-sensitive, but with his multiple claw-like limbs and graceful articulation, he's more than agile enough to wield lightsabers with precision. A Kaleesh warrior who was critically wounded, Grievous voluntarily gave himself over to mechanical modifications; his brain, heart, lungs, spinal cord, and haunting golden eyes are the only organic remnants of his body.

> ## "I try to look for the empathy in the character that way, and perform him as a lesson as to what you don't want to be."

a successful leader because the cyborg looked at the big picture; the general executed high-handed plans like using hidden listening posts to ambush Republic fleets and attempting to invade Kamino to stop clone production. As Wood said, he was always trying to make a name for himself and his every appearance during *The Clone Wars* certainly emphasizes that.

The Allure of Grievous
General Grievous has also gone on to appear elsewhere in the *Star Wars* galaxy. Notably, he appeared in Dark Horse Comics' *Darth Maul: Son of Dathomir* (in which he killed Mother Talzin), and two Marvel Comics series, *Jedi of the Republic: Mace Windu* and *Kanan*. Most recently, Wood voiced the villain again in downloadable content for the video game *Star Wars: Battlefront II*. He had to break his recording sessions up over multiple days so that he didn't destroy his voice. "You can't really be subtle. Grievous having a fireside chat with somebody is not something we've seen before or are likely to," Wood jokes. "Most of his lines have to be super-projected. In order to hit the plug-in processor that I use, the way that I want it to, the voice definitely has to be pushed."

In performing a character that presents such physical and technical obstacles, what is it that keeps Wood coming back to the role? "I like his struggle," he answers. "It's nice to have a character as a juxtaposition to the heroes. Grievous is somebody in whom you can see all his bad points. He's cowardly, and he doesn't really have many friends—in *The Clone Wars* we went to his lair, and there's a droid that's his bickering friend, but it's pretty stark. He lives alone, he's always boastful about all the things he's going to do to you or how he's going to rule you, and it's obvious his ego gets the best of him. So, I try to look for the empathy in the character that way, and perform him as a lesson as to what you don't want to be. That's how it is for me, showcasing that you can't have light without dark; my performance in this dark world exists to give the light something to shine on." ☺

TIM ROSE
LOOKING FOR MR. ACKBAR

by Scott Chernoff

For most performers, playing just one great character in a *Star Wars* film would be enough to pretty much build a career around.

It's probably safe to say that at the moment Tim Rose won the job of playing Sy Snootles, the sultry and spindly singer at Jabba's palace in *Return of the Jedi*, he had pretty much, as they say in Hollywood, made it. But Tim Rose wanted more.

Hired to finish building the Sy Snootles puppet and perform the character when it was done, Rose, then 26, went on to play no less than three key roles in *Jedi*, adding Jabba's cackling sidekick Salacious Crumb *and* Admiral Ackbar, the brilliant and ultra-suave Mon Calamari Rebel hero, to his call sheet.

"I was very young and inexperienced at the time," Rose remembers. "Admiral Ackbar was sitting on a stand in a corner. I liked the sculpt. The whole film was a complete mystery, because we would build things but didn't know how they'd fit into the film. So I said to Phil [Tippett, the original

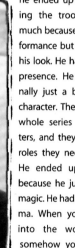

PULLING STRINGS: Puppeteer Tim Rose.

trilogy's stop-motion guru], 'So who's that then?' And he said, 'Oh, that's another background character that appears later in the film.' And I said, 'Oh, can I do him, too? Please, please, please!' I begged him to let me do this other background character, thinking he was going to be in the third row in a new cantina sequence or something."

Instead, the eager young performer signed on to play Admiral Ackbar, whose fish-like salmon-colored head, big warm eyes, and wide-mouthed white military uniform combined to make him one of the most visually striking and memorable new characters introduced in the final instalment of the saga. But what made Admiral Ackbar really stand out

wasn't just his looks but the fact that this unusual character was smack-dab in the middle of the Rebel leadership, lecturing Luke Skywalker, commanding Lando and the rest of the fleet, and exclaiming, "It's a trap!"

But despite the obvious strength of his work, Rose modestly offers that Ackbar's superstardom in the *Star Wars* universe was simply a matter of destiny. "To be honest," he says, "I think he ended up commanding the troops not so much because of my performance but because of his look. He had a screen presence. He was originally just a background character. They created a whole series of characters, and they had these roles they needed filled. He ended up filling it because he just had the magic. He had the charisma. When you came into the workshop, somehow you looked at him instead of the four other creatures. There was the one next to him with the three eyes on the end of stalks [Ree-Yees] – it might just as easily have been him. But Ackbar became a character in the process of building him."

Says Rose, "I was just excited I was rubbing elbows with all these famous people, and I went for it and tried to do my best at it."

His best turned out to be more than good enough. Ackbar made such an impression in his one scene that he not only spawned a popular Kenner action figure but also ended up enduring as one of the most popular characters in the original trilogy and ensuing novels and comics.

In fact, Rose has also been, by far, one of the most-requested interview subjects for this column. There was only one problem: nobody seemed to know where he was. Finally, reader Jamey Hornsby in Deatsville, Alabama, came to our aid, supplying us with Rose's address in England. (Rose quickly agreed to an interview as long as we could mention how grateful he is to all the people who wrote him fan letters after *Jedi* – and how sorry he is that he was never able to keep up with it all.)

Most readers who were interested in Rose didn't realise that he also played Sy Snootles and Salacious Crumb, or that Ackbar was, like the other two, a puppet. "He had cables for the eyes, but he was a hand puppet," Rose says. "Mike Quinn operated the eyes while I did the mouth. Then Mike did the mouth [by remote] for me when I was walking around in the full-body suit as Admiral Ackbar. For the close-ups, I'm actually inside the chest of it and

THE MANY PERSONALITIES OF TIM ROSE: *Return of the Jedi* creatures Salacious Crumb (top), Sy Snootles (below) and Admiral Ackbar (left).

operating the head like a hand puppet."

As for Ackbar's trademark gravelly and authoritative voice, Rose says "It was synthesised, but whether they synthesised my voice or dubbed in someone else, I don't know. I *think* it's my voice as Salacious."

Crumb, the Kowakian monkey-lizard, was Richard Marquand. "He used to talk to the puppet all the time," Rose recalls. "When you're doing a good job with a puppet, people treat the puppet as if he's the actor, as though he's alive – and Richard used to love to talk to Salacious Crumb. He found it totally fascinating that this silly little rubber monster could comment on camera angles and things like that. He'd come and sit down next to the puppet and say, 'What do you think, Salacious?' and I'd go, 'Yeah, I bet if you lift the camera a little bit and shoot down that way, you'll see a few more of these background characters!'"

It should be no surprise that Rose's work

"I ORIGINALLY SET OUT TO BE A MASTER PUPPETEER. WITH THE OLD STUFF—MARIONETTE SHOWS AND HAND PUPPETS."

Rose's other signature character, and he worked hard to give the character a personality that would make him stand out amid the gaggle of creatures in Jabba's crowded palace. "When I'd finish in the workshop late at night," Rose remembers, "I used to go off into the back room and set up the video and sort of play with Salacious Crumb. There's a funny bit in the 'making-of' video with Salacious in a poorly-lit room coming up to the camera and knocking on the lens – that was one of those tapes I'd done late night when I was trying to work out what sort of character to give this guy so he could become important in the film."

The taunting wise-guy of a character that emerged found an early fan in the late *Jedi* director

ABOVE: The authoritative Admiral Ackbar in *Return of the Jedi*. The distinctive character was essentially a hand puppet.

was successful in *Jedi*, since he'd spent his whole life puppeteering. "I originally set out to be a master puppeteer," says Rose, who was born in Illinois but grew up in New York. "I was in love with the old stuff – marionette shows and hand puppets. In my teens, *The Muppet Show* was very popular, and I used to sit there in front of the television set and try to spot the rods and work out how they did it all."

Before *The Muppet Show* went off the air, Rose got a chance to have all his questions answered up close when he landed a job in the Muppet workshop, where he became right-hand man to animatronics pioneer Faz Fazakas. "Animatronics was the new cutting-edge technology at the time – George Lucas kept coming around to visit just to see what they were up to," Rose said. "My dad had always done radio-controlled airplanes, so I knew how to plug a servo into a receiver and make a transmitter move it, and I became very valuable to Faz. We built all the remote puppets in *The Great Muppet Caper* and I got to perform a lot of background puppets."

Rose got even closer to his goal of moving from building to performing when Henson gave him the part of the Treasurer Skeksis, and some background characters, in *The Dark Crystal*. But when Rose didn't get a major part on Henson's new series *Fraggle Rock*, he quit. "I was sitting around going, 'I can't believe I just

quit working for the biggest puppet company – what am I going to do? I must be a complete fool', when I got a call from my friend Mike McCormick. Mike had been working on pre-production for *Return of the Jedi*, and he was on an overhead rig trying to do a prototype for Sy Snootles, and he tripped and fell off the rig and broke his arm – which for a puppeteer renders one not very puppeteerable. So he asked if I was interested in taking his place in the movie.

"It was extremely exciting," Rose continues, "because I was young enough that when *Star Wars* came out, I was still quite young, and by the time the third movie came out, I was actually sitting in one of the ships."

One of the first things he did was to change the Snootles set-up so that the singer of the classic dance hit 'Lapti Nek' could be operated from below (and no, that's not his voice doing the singing). Another change: Rose reveals that Salacious Crumb, who became famous as Jabba's psycho yes-man, wasn't originally slated to be teamed up with Jabba at all.

Instead, the character was going to be partnered with Ephant Mon, an obscure elephant-ish palace dweller (a photo of the two together can be seen in the powerhouse book *Star Wars Chronicles*). "Mike's idea was to do them as a double-act," Rose says. "He was going to wear the one [Ephant Mon] as a full-body costume and Salacious Crumb sat on his

arm. But the big guy's head ended up being about 50 pounds, so it was all you could do just to do the one on his own, let alone puppeteer a hand puppet on his arm at the same time. So Salacious Crumb got separated from him at that point."

The separation was more like a liberation for the brazen Salacious – and Rose. Since bursting into the *Star Wars* saga with three characters (presumably the extra two were to make up for the two prior movies he had missed), Rose has continued to work as both a puppeteer and puppet builder for film and television, primarily in a series of successful television commercials.

After *Jedi*, Rose worked on such films as *Return to Oz*, *Teenage Mutant Ninja Turtles*, *High Spirits*, *Fierce Creatures*, and *The Muppet Christmas Carol*, as well as the landmark puppet satire *Spitting Image*, and two 1986 films for Lucasfilm: *Labyrinth* and *Howard the Duck*, for which he was the principal performer of the title character. More recently, Rose made the heads for the kiddies' television phenomenon *Teletubbies* and helped create a dragon for the upcoming *Dragonheart 2*.

All we can say to the producers of *Dragonheart 2*, or any other film Tim Rose works on, is this: you'd better have at least three characters for him to play – that is, if you want your movie to be any good. ☻

PHANTOM MENACES

Actor Alan Ruscoe is familiar to fans of science fiction thanks to roles in Luc Besson's *The Fifth Element* and *Doctor Who*. A consummate theatrical performer, he joined the cast of *The Phantom Menace* to create a trio of memorable characters. Words: Jonathan Wilkins

This picture: Lott Dod (right) witnesses the *Attack of the Clones*! Left: Daultay Dofine from *The Phantom Menace*.

Star Wars Insider: How did you come to have three parts in *The Phantom Menace*.

Alan Ruscoe: I was originally contracted to play Plo Koon. Then I was asked to play Daultay Dofine and Bib Fortuna. When you wear a mask you are recyclable! It's a lot easier to make a rig for one actor than making three or four for different actors. From the actor's point of view, you get to do more bits and pieces, which is a win-win situation, though you don't always think that at 6 a.m. when you're having appliances stuck on to your face!

Bib Fortuna as seen in *The Phantom Menace*.

Prosthetics are comfortable; it's not like wearing an animatronic head. Plo Koon looked stunning, but was really uncomfortable; a bit like wearing a trainer on my head! I couldn't take it off, because it was a pull-on mask that was molded to me and had a hook-and-eye system with a sealer on the back. Once I was in, I was in for the day.

How was working with Frank Oz?

He's a genius. Not just as a puppeteer, but as an actor! At one point I sat and watched him while we had downtime between takes. He was on the floor with his monitor, and he was messing around as Yoda. He was using Yoda's speech patterns while improvising and messing about and calling for his dresser. One of the female runners would go past, and Yoda would ask her back to his trailer!

You also appeared in Episode II. Can you confirm which character you played?

There seems to be an awful lot of conjecture about the character I played. Silas Carson played Lott Dod in *The Phantom Menace*. He was unable to play Lott Dod the second time around, and so I took over. I hope that puts it to rest! ♟

I had the easy part, because I turned up and they stuck something on me. The real stars are the guys who create the makeup. As part of my contract, I had to sign a statement to say that I wasn't claustrophobic. If the person in front of the camera panics and starts suddenly trying to tear the makeup off their face, that's a lot of money lost and a whole day's shoot gone.

How long were you in makeup for?

For Bib Fortuna, it was four hours, because that was a major three-piece prosthetic. Four hours to get in, two hours to get out, which is still nothing to what Mike Carter [Bib Fortuna in *Return of the Jedi*] went through. I think he was eight hours to get in, four hours to get out!

Alan Ruscoe: The man beneath the mask! Below: Plo Koon takes his place in the Jedi Temple.

When Femi Taylor reprised the role of Oola – Jabba's agile plaything – for the **Return of the Jedi Special Edition,** *she proved she had lost none of her old prowess. Iain Lowson discover's the unique circumstances behind Taylor's original casting – and her comeback.*

"I see myself now as an actress who can sing and dance," says Femi Taylor, who portrayed Oola the hapless dancing girl in *Return of the Jedi*. When this interview was conducted, she was appearing in *Jesus Christ Superstar* at the Lyceum Theatre, London, where she was able to use all three talents to good effect.

"It's interesting: some people see the part of Oola as a dancing role, some people see it as an acting role. An actress dancing *and* playing the role of Oola – I much prefer that."

In *Return of the Jedi*, Oola dances for Jabba, before she is dropped into the rancor pit for her master's amusement.

"Originally, there was going to be a lot more for the character to do," she recalls. "I was setting up the scene for Princess Leia; the director, Richard Marquand, showed me the storyboards. I was going to escape, run away and then meet my destiny. The budget didn't allow me to do that, but as things turned out it was wonderful, and a nice surprise, to be asked back 15 years later to add a bit more. More of what George Lucas originally wanted."

15 years ago, Femi Taylor (then in her very early twenties) was part of the original cast of the musical *Cats*. The show was going very well when she got a call from her agent saying that a company was casting for a new film, and was looking for a girl who could dance and who might have to do some acting. The company would not, however, reveal the name of the film.

"I said, 'Well as long as it's not a blue movie, fine. My parents wouldn't appreciate me doing that kind of stuff after they've put so much money into my training'. My agent said, 'You have to wear your bikini'. I thought this was rather odd, but my agent said, 'Go along and see what happens,' so I went."

Director Richard Marquand was in attendance at the audition, and he asked all of the usual questions: what have you done?, what are you doing now?, and so on. Femi asked what the film was, but was again told that he couldn't say. Marquand went to great lengths to reassure Taylor that the whole thing wasn't as bad as it sounded.

"He said they were doing a film for which they needed someone who could move really well, and he said that the character was green. Richard asked if I would take my coat off and walk up and down. I was a little apprehensive, but he was very understanding, agreeing that it did all sound a little strange. He said 'Trust me,' so I did."

Marquand agreed that Taylor moved very well, and said that they might call her back to dance. A week later, Femi found herself in a gruelling audition with 25 to 30 other girls. After the audition, the girls all asked what the film was. When told it was the next *Star Wars* film, their reaction was a heady mixture of relief and excitement.

On the way back from this audition, Taylor

The

gave a lift to the original choreographer for the dance number. Anthony Van Last confirmed during the journey that the strong audition performance had won her the role of Oola.

"The funny thing was that, when I went for the audition, I was looking at Richard Marquand thinking, 'I know this face from somewhere.' My father is a film director too, and when I got parts [in films] he would often ask who was directing because he might know them. I said, 'Oh, this guy called Richard Marquand, or something,' and he told me that Richard Marquand used to come for Sunday lunch when I was about five or six.

"It was nice to get the part on talent, rather than because I knew him. He [Marquand] had to call me up for something, and I told him that he knew me. It turns out that he had been thinking [during the audition] 'I know this face from somewhere...'"

She was contracted for one week's rehearsal and one (hard) week's shooting. When not on set, she had to stay in her dressing room because of the green body make-up. The character was never really explained, leaving Femi to glean what she could from the few pages of script she had. The character didn't have a name until the third day of the shooting, with Marquand pushing for a stronger identity for Oola despite having to sacrifice so many of the character's scenes.

Although by that time in her life Taylor had been around films, she found that *Revenge of the*

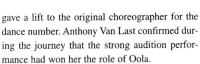

"When they called me up and said they were doing the Special Edition, they asked 'Have you put on weight? We'd like to get you back.'"

Jedi (as it was then known) was different: a film on a much grander scale. As well as all of the creatures, the other-worldly dialogue, and the total environment set, there was also the presence of a cast of big-name actors.

"Mark Hamill was a darling. He was lovely, very relaxed. Harrison Ford was very focused. He used to just pace up and down between shots, focused. Billy Dee Williams was a real charmer."

Femi opted to perform the fall into the five-foot deep pit, though she had been told that a double could do it. The scene was shot in various stages. From the front, she just had to slip backwards, as if falling. From the back, she had to jump off a box placed in the pit and then duck right down as Jabba's throne was drawn over the opening.

"The tentacles were so hard to work with. I wasn't expecting that. That and [Jabba's] leash, which was about 20 feet long. Gillian Gregory was the choreographer, and she explained in

Top: Femi Taylor recreates Oola's struggle with Jabba for the Return of the Jedi Special Edition *(left) for sequences that were intercut with the original scene in* Return of the Jedi *(right).*

Dancer's Tails

Above: The tentacles attached to the back of Taylor's head caused great discomfort.

Below: The raised platform beneath Jabba disguised the numerous operators controlling the giant puppet - and gave Taylor the chance for a rest.

"The tentacles were so heavy... they kept on slapping me in the face when I did turns."

rehearsals that I was attached to a leash. A lot of stuff that I rehearsed was a little bit lost because I had to compensate for my costuming.

"The tentacles were so heavy that your body weight kept on going back. It was hard. They were on an actual helmet with the foam tentacles coming out. But they kept on slapping me in the face when I did turns. There was so much else to deal with. There was the sand on the floor and in my sandals, Jabba pulling me. There were three men working Jabba, and the guy doing his hands had to know where I was going... It was hard!"

From that, one begins to understand why it took a week to shoot a relatively short scene. How did Taylor feel about the results?

"I was expecting to see more. I thought, 'My gosh, I've done all that work and half of it is on the cutting room floor.' But that happens, that's inevitable. I would have used different bits of the dance scene, but that's out of my control."

When the opportunity arose to go back to Jabba's palace, Taylor saw it as a chance to do more with both the character and the scene. In that respect, she was thinking along the same lines as the producers of the *Return of the Jedi Special Edition*.

"When they called me up and said they were doing the Special Edition, they asked 'Have you put on weight? We'd like to get you back.' I

asked if I would have to recreate the dance routine, which would have been difficult after all that time. They said 'We'll just send you a video of the bits we want you to re-do.' They'd kept all of the [old] footage and added all the original bits in. I think it's a much stronger scene now."

During the six day shoot, she was reunited with her old costume, the same one used in the original film, but this time she was ready for it. As it was, things were a little different.

"I didn't have to dance," she explains. "They blue-screened me struggling and my death scene, and used original footage for the dancing."

Taylor performed her own roll down the chute and into the rancor pit. The death scene adds a lot more personality to the scene, making Jabba appear even more evil, and Oola's reaction to the approaching monster is a chilling set-up for when we finally see it as Luke and the Gamorrean follow the unfortunate dancer. The reaction from those she was working with, especially on the death scene, was very positive.

"My brother, Benedict Taylor, is an actor and he was doing a *Young Indy* television film and got quite friendly with [producer] Rick McCallum, and they've kept in touch. Ben asked Rick what he was doing, and Rick said he was doing the next *Star Wars* movie. Ben said, 'Oh, my sister did that.' Rick didn't click that I was the one who played Oola; he just thought I'd been one of the extras.

"When I was going to leave, Ben caught up with me, wished me all the best with it, and said 'If you bump into Rick McCallum – I'm not sure he's involved with it, I'm sure he's not – but if you bump into him, please say hello.' When I had a few minutes between scenes on the first day, I asked if a person named Rick McCallum was possibly one of the producers on the Special Edition. They said he was due on set the next day, because he was working with George Lucas.

"I was given his number, so I called him. I said, 'Hey listen, you know my brother, Benedict Taylor!', and he said 'Oh my God, are you the one?' He hadn't clicked."

On set, during the filming of the new dancers and the space the CGI band members would fill, Femi empathised with the hard time the three women had in comparison with her "easy gig" this time around. She remembered the constant re-takes on the original shoot as she adapted to the restraints of the costume. Femi got on well with the dancers and, when she finally saw the Special Edition while in San Francisco, liked the results of all the work over the six day shoot.

With her work on the Special Edition complete, Taylor spent some time in the Cayman Islands, followed by a year-long stint in *Jesus Christ Superstar* at London's Lyceum Theatre. ■

REVENGE OF THE BINKS

A DECADE AFTER EPISODE I, ACTOR AHMED BEST RECENTLY WON A MAJOR ANIMATION AWARD FOR PLAYING JAR JAR BINKS. MAYBE HE ALSO GOT THE LAST LAUGH? SCOTT CHERNOFF FINDS OUT!

Respect for Jar Jar Binks? It didn't look likely 10 years ago, when the gangly Gungan made his debut in *Star Wars*: Episode I *The Phantom Menace*. He stood out as the first digitally-animated main character in a major motion picture, and also for being so, well, daffy.

Respect for the character appeared to fall farther in Episode II, when the naïve Naboo native, now a Senior Representative subbing for an absent Senator Amidala, proposed the motion that gave Chancellor Palpatine (Darth Sidious) unlimited political power. Oops!

It seemed that no matter how hard he tried, Jar Jar always ended up doing the wrong thing or looking foolish when he did the right thing—despite the best efforts of the multi-talented and acclaimed actor who brought him to life, Ahmed Best.

Now 35, Best—who, like Jar Jar, made his feature film debut a decade ago in *The Phantom Menace*—is finally feeling the Force function in his favor. He's shot a new film with Samuel L. Jackson and Naomi Watts, welcomed his first son into the world, and collected an Annie Award from the International Animated Film Society for Voice Acting in an Animated Television Program—and that's just in 2009! He won the award for an episode of *Robot Chicken* in which he reprised his most famous role: the goofy Gungan, Jar Jar Binks.

JAR JAR GOES POP!

"I didn't expect to win," Best told *Star Wars Insider* shortly after the ceremony. "I always thought Jar Jar was going to live in infamy."

Even the nomination took Best by surprise—after all, the Annie is prestigious, like an Academy Award for animation, and the competition was fierce—Best was nominated against *Family Guy* creator Seth MacFarlane (for voicing series dad Peter Griffin) and Dwight Schultz, the *A-Team* legend who now plays Mung Daal on the Cartoon Network hit Chowder.

"I beat those two—and neither of them will probably ever hire me again because of this," Best laughs. "I can't speculate on why I won. It sounds such a cliché, but I was honored just to be nominated. I didn't think Jar Jar was ever going to win anything. I didn't write a speech, I thought Seth Macfarlane would win. I was like, 'There's no way I'm winning this award,' and then when they said my name, I thought, 'What? Do you mean me?' It was very surreal. The walk to the stage was a long one, and

I still don't remember what I said. I was just thankful that everyone recognized the work that was done on the show."

Best won for his second Jar Jar bit on *Robot Chicken*, the stop-motion animated Adult Swim series that has now produced two hilarious and hugely popular all-Star Wars specials. In the first one, which premiered in 2007, Best reprised Jar Jar in a brilliant sketch that found the enthusiastic, touchy-feely Gungan thrilled to reunite with a none-too-happy Darth Vader, whom Jar Jar still calls "Annie." He then won an Annie for his performance in a sketch in the 2008 special that found Jar Jar appearing as a celebrity pitchman in a TV commercial spoof. (He's done a few other voices on *Robot Chicken* as well, including an AT-AT driver and voiced a quick line as Darth Maul.)

Best had nothing but praise for the creative team behind *Robot Chicken*, Seth Green and Matt Senreich: "They're doing cutting edge stuff. They're so funny. I think Seth Green is going to be a very big director one day. He said to me, 'I think we're rehabilitating Jar Jar in pop culture.' I said, 'I certainly hope so. I don't get a lot of respect in the sci-fi world for Jar Jar.'"

That wasn't always a great feeling for a guy who grew up a devoted *Star Wars* fan. "I still want to be Han Solo," Best admits. "When I saw *A New Hope*, I was maybe three or four, and I loved the mythology of it, seeing the swords and the fights—I fell in love with that. Then when I saw *Empire*, it was the first epic movie that I was a fan of. I understood the struggle, I understood the

> ## "IT WAS VERY SURREAL. THE WALK TO THE STAGE WAS A LONG ONE, AND I STILL DON'T REMEMBER WHAT I SAID."

Ahmed Best (right) shares a joke with Ewan McGregor, Rick McCallum and George Lucas on the *Star Was* set

characters. I think it stands up as one of my favorite movie of all time."

STOMPING TO SUCCESS!

Being a lifelong *Star Wars* fan, Best was blown away when George Lucas chose him for the first new *Star Wars* movie in 16 years, *The Phantom Menace*. Then 23, he had been performing in the Broadway blockbuster *Stomp* when Episode I casting director Robin Gurland spotted him in the show and summoned him for an audition based on Best's unique and creative physicality onstage. Her hunch— that Best's physicality would be the perfect basis for the digitally animated character her boss had in mind—was confirmed when Lucas cast him after a motion capture audition.

"When I showed up," he recalls, "I was like, 'Do they realize I'm not supposed to be here? I'm just a kid from the Bronx.' The learning curve was pretty big for me, going from a Broadway show to one of the biggest movies of all time. But I couldn't be afraid. I knew I had to completely believe in George Lucas."

That meant believing in Lucas' vision for the character who would be animated literally on top of Best. On the set, the actor wore a makeshift Jar Jar suit and tall headpiece, so his fellow cast mates would have a real actor to interact with, and most importantly, so the artists at ILM would have a human reference. Beyond providing Jar Jar's distinctive

voice, Best's performance was also the inspiration for Jar Jar's movements. Back in the late-1990s, it was something that had never been done before.

"It wasn't just doing *Star Wars*, which was enormous, but it was actually taking this risk," he says. "It was making film history as the first all digitally-animated [main] character in a live-action movie. To set the template for that was the most exciting thing for me. Following that, Andy Serkis did it for Gollum (in *The Lord of the Rings*), but being the first guy to do it was really important to me. I take a lot of pride in that. It's not recognized very much, but I'm very proud that I was the first person to take that risk."

JAR JAR ACROSS THE WORLD

Shooting Episode I in England and Tunisia, near the locations used for the original *A New Hope* was, "very surreal. I never really processed how big things were. I was just going along for the ride, because it was my first major film and it was *Star Wars*. I remember sitting in the dressing room one-day thinking, 'Well, it's all downhill from here. You can't get bigger than this.'"

Indeed, the anticipation for *The Phantom Menace* was massive, and for a while, Jar Jar was everywhere, his smiling visage adorning everything from pillowcases to soda cans. Not surprisingly, Best's personal favorites are the ones he finds

> "GEORGE IS TELLING ME, 'BIGGER, FUNNIER, JUMP HIGHER,' SO I HAVE TO BE ENORMOUS IN THE SCENE AND LIAM [NEESON] IS DOING ALMOST NOTHING."

"WHO WANTS TO EAT A JAR JAR TONGUE FRUIT ROLL-UP?"

the funniest. "There were some that were absolutely ridiculous," he laughs, "like the lollipop thing—do you remember that? It was Jar Jar's face and then as soon as the mouth opens, a lollipop comes shooting out like a tongue. I was thinking, 'This thing is not good, man! Somebody needs to re-think this!'

"There was Jar Jar saturation," he continues, noting a curious amount of Binks merchandise that, like the lollipop, seemed centered around Jar Jar's tongue. "The tongue was a big deal. Some of the merchandise was crazy. Who wants to eat a Jar Jar tongue Fruit Roll-Up?"

But make no mistake: Ahmed Best remains a fan and declares that, a decade on, The Phantom Menace still holds up. "It came on cable the other day, and I was watching it and thinking, 'This movie is a good movie.' As a piece of film, as a story, it works fantastically. It is well done, well thought out, well executed, and it sets up the trilogy very well. My favorite person in the movie is Liam Neeson. He's so good in it—you didn't want Qui-Gon to die."

The Oscar-nominated Neeson was just as impressive on the set—although his co-star didn't realize it at first. "I would watch Liam while we were acting and it didn't look like he was doing very much," Best says. "Honestly, I didn't see him doing anything. Liam has this soft demeanor about him. I had to be huge. George is telling me, 'Bigger, funnier, jump higher,' so I have to be enormous in the scene and Liam is doing almost nothing.

"But when I looked at the playback on the monitor, I thought, 'This is amazing—this guy is doing more stuff than I'm doing with a back flip.' He was like a Film Acting 101 course for me. He'd move his eyebrow and it would mean 10 times more than me doing three flips in the water. He was the person I learned most from on-set—I really enjoyed watching him and learning from him, and hearing his stories. We laughed a lot. It was great."

UNDERWATER ACTION!

Along those lines, Best said one of his favorite Episode I memories is of himself and Neeson, along with Ewan McGregor, filming their scene in the tri-bubble bongo submarine after leaving Otoh Gunga. "That was one of the funniest days," Best recalls. "Your imagination daydreams about what shooting Star Wars is going to be like, and you think, 'Oh, there's going to be a starship, and we're going to walk into it, and there's going to be all this high tech stuff moving around, and ships flying at you.' But we get in the ship, and there are two Englishmen shaking it back and forth on sticks. It was the most low-tech experience that you could have!"

Best said the day devolved into silliness for everyone. "Here was big Liam in the back seat of this big old submarine and Ewan and me in the front seat pretending to swim through the ocean, and so many ridiculous lines that I didn't know what they meant— nobody knew what they meant because it was in gibberish Jar Jar speech. So I go to George and ask, 'Hey George, what does this mean?' And he goes, 'I don't know—just say

be cool with my nephew."

Best has observed that Jar Jar's fans seem to be those who are able to laugh along with the saga, like the creators and fans of Robot Chicken, or Comedy Central's The Colbert Report, on which Best also played Binks. "Jar Jar really works for comedy, which is what it was all about in the beginning. People took it a little seriously. We were just trying to be funny."

Of *Robot Chicken* viewers, he says, "They're like, 'Well, thankfully he can take the self-importance out of the character. But you know, I never really took the whole thing too seriously, even with all the criticism. At the end of the day, I'm an actor who did my job, and if George Lucas is happy, then I am too. It's his vision, it's his story, it's his folklore, and as an actor, I want to make the director's vision a reality. If I did that, I'm happy, period."

Clearly, George Lucas was very happy, inviting Best back for Episodes II and III. In Attack of the Clones, Jar Jar is promoted to Gungan Senior Representative in the Galactic Senate, where he fills in for Senator Amidala and gets used as a pawn by Chancellor Palpatine in a power play that ultimately results in the Emperor taking over the galaxy. "I've always wanted that storyline to get explored," Best muses.

it!' I'm like, 'What? Didn't you write this?' Shooting that submarine scene is one of my fondest memories."

The good times translated to Best's performance as the most overtly comedic character in the *Star Wars* canon. "It felt like a Buster Keaton kind of role," Best says of the beloved silent film comedian who influenced him. "I was trying to channel that kind of energy to the character."

However, some fans and critics were not amused. "They really wanted to see a dark, serious story. They had their expectations."

The backlash hit hard. "It was so shocking because we were all very excited while we were doing it," Best says, adding, "But Jar Jar was never for 35-year-olds. He was for the six-year-olds. So among six-to-10 year olds, I am incredibly popular."

Best notes that when kids find out he played Jar Jar Binks, "They go bananas! They go crazy! Recently, my nephew, who is four years old now, saw Star Wars, and he saw my name on the screen and he asked, 'Why is Uncle Ahmed on the screen? Who was he?' My sister told him that Uncle Ahmed was Jar Jar, and now I'm a hero. He didn't want to have anything to do with me before that. The magic of George Lucas helped me

"SETH GREEN SAID TO ME, 'I THINK WE'RE REHABILITATING JAR JAR IN POP CULTURE.'"

UNMASKED!

Shooting the next two movies was a little easier since the production team had refined the process of creating Jar Jar so that the actor could don a less cumbersome Jar Jar costume while on camera. "They knew how to shoot him. I didn't have to wear as much of the Jar Jar suit —just the arms and the head, and then in Episode III, I didn't even need to wear that. That was just me in a big cloak, and they animated the head on top of it."

But despite Jar Jar's scaled-down role, Lucas paid tribute to Best, along with Anthony Daniels, the Star Wars icon behind C-3PO, by casting them both—unmasked—as denizens of the Outlander Club on Coruscant. His character, named Achk Med-Beq, was soon immortalized as an action figure. "My mom has it," he confesses, adding, "I don't have one and she won't let me have it!"

Best also reprised his role in the eighth episode of the most recent saga incarnation, Star Wars: The Clone Wars. "I really enjoy the episodes on Cartoon Network, and I think Jar Jar is great for that show," he says. "I always thought he should have had his own kids' show, an animated series."

Best is cagey about whether or not he would return to The Clone Wars, considering that another actor, B.J. Hughes, voiced the character in a subsequent episode because Best was busy with other projects. "If they ask me to do it again, I'll think about it. I love doing animation. I love the process. I love the story of Star Wars. I was just at a point where I was like, 'You know what, I did this and let me see what else is out there.'"

MACE WINDU....BINKS?

When Best spoke to Insider, he was still shooting the movie Mother and Child, a drama starring Naomi Watts, Annette Bening, Kerry Washington, and fellow Star Wars alum Samuel L. Jackson.

"I play Sam Jackson's son," Best reveals. "Ironic, isn't it? I should have done that in Episode I. Mace Windu Binks—that would really make some people mad!"

Also appearing in the film is Jimmy Smits of Episodes II and III, making Mother and Child something of a Star Wars reunion. "We pretty much just kind of recognize that we were all in it and chuckle about it," Best says. "I see Sam quite a lot around town and he's real cool. Every time I see him, he introduces me with, 'This is Ahmed, aka Jar Jar!' And I'm like, 'Yo, Sam, you don't have do that anymore,' as much as I dig it."

But while he's done some acting since moving to Los Angeles a year after the release of Episode I, Best has been focusing most of his efforts behind the camera.

"Since I moved out to L.A., I've been

> "PEOPLE TOOK IT A LITTLE SERIOUSLY. WE WERE JUST TRYING TO BE FUNNY."

Clowning around with stunt co-ordinator Nick Gillard!

> ## "I'VE LEARNED A LOT OVER THE LAST 10 YEARS. JUST BEING IN *STAR WARS* OPENS DOORS FOR ME. IT'S A GIFT THAT KEEPS ON GIVING.

doing more producing and directing than anything else," he says. He started by executive-producing the anthology series The DL Chronicles, which ran on the cable network Here! TV in 2005, and spent 2008 working on This Can't Be My Life, a sitcom he directed, produced, and co-wrote for the internet, featuring guest appearances from actresses Rosario Dawson (Sin City) and Tracie Thoms (TV's Cold Case and Wonderfalls). He's shopping the show, starring his friend, comedienne Sheilynn Wactor, to TV but releasing it initially on YouTube.

DREAM PROJECT

Now, Best is working on his dream project. "I'm doing an all-black science fiction show called The Nebula. I'm a huge sci-fi guy. I really love it. I play a captain with the Shatner swagger and the rebel Han Solo attitude."

Best created, produces, and directs the show, which will come in two forms: a web series set on a starship, and a hoped-for TV series in the vein of The Office, about the making of the web

show. Both are comedies, and Best has already shot one episode with guest star Seth Green. "He came and just destroyed us all! He was absolutely unbelievable. And then the next episode is hopefully going to have Levar Burton from Star Trek: The Next Generation which is going to be a very interesting cross-platform Star Wars-Star Trek hybrid. Levar heard about it and wanted to be a part of it. I think it's something really special. I hope George likes it."

The Nebula will also, like his other projects, feature original music by Best himself, an accomplished musician who released three albums with the group The Jazzhole, and currently plays with rock band The United Kings of Scotland and a funk/jazz combo called The Screaming Headless Torsos. "I go under a bunch of different pseudonyms. So you'll hear it and not know it's me. I've found that works really well in my case."

Could that be because some people just won't take Jar Jar seriously? Not according to Ahmed Best, who said he's got nothing but gratitude for his part

in the Star Wars universe. Thinking back on the intimidating Episode I release 10 years ago, he says, "I had a great time with it. I enjoyed going to all the premieres and meeting all the folks. I took it all in my stride. I wanted it to be the beginning of a long career. And it was. And it still is."

Talking to the Insider just five days after his wife Raquel gave birth to their first child, son Marley Ellington, Best continues, "I've learned a lot over the last 10 years. Just being in Star Wars opens doors for me. It's a gift that keeps on giving. I have to thank Jar Jar for my house. I have Jar Jar to thank for the fact that I can support my wife and now my son. If I didn't have Jar Jar in my life, none of these things would have come as quickly, but because George Lucas saw a kid from the Bronx as somebody to make film history, I've got to give thanks. That's pretty huge."

Now that's deserving of some respect. ☺

EXPANDED UNIVERSE >>>

For more information on Ahmed Best's videos and music, go to: myspace.com/ahmedbestmusic.

RETURN OF THE
EWOK

by Scott Chernoff

BOBA FETT HID IN THE SHADOWS OF THE DEATH STAR, undetected. It was there in the dark, lonely corridors, atop the gleaming black floors, that the bounty hunter would wait patiently for his quarry. But unlike the scores of smugglers, scoundrels, and renegades he had captured in his day – from the lowliest Rodian to the elusive Han Solo himself – there was no bounty for this victim, no vicious Hutt waiting to add the hunted to his art collection. No, this time it was personal.

Boba Fett was hunting Ewok.

What brought about this odd opposition? What bizarre series of events could have possibly led an unassuming Ewok into not only confrontations with Boba Fett and Darth Vader but also a primitive and dangerous dance with Jabba the Hutt? What surreal story could possibly involve both a major European soccer match *and* an onscreen meeting between Wicket and Yoda?

The answers lie in a charmingly wacky home movie called *Return of the Ewok*. The hilarious brainchild of *Return of the Jedi* first assistant director David Tomblin, *Return of the Ewok* stars Warwick Davis in the twisting and turning tall tale of how Davis, then 11, got his part as Wicket the Ewok in *Jedi*. Written and directed by Tomblin using his own 16mm camera, and featuring enthusiastic cameos from virtually all the stars of *Jedi*, the 24-minute film was shot in 1982 on lunch breaks and Sundays during the London and California shooting of the film then called "Revenge of the Jedi."

Even though Warwick actually got his part at an open call (see his interview in *Star Wars Magazine 17*), Tomblin's film finds young Warwick wondering what to do with his life when he's inspired by *The Empire Strikes Back* to become a movie star. He raises Boba Fett's ire by considering taking over his part in *Jedi* before settling on Wicket. In the end, of course, he somehow helps save the galaxy.

Crammed with inside jokes and weird moments of farce, infused with Warwick's winning cheerfulness, and enhanced by the strangely successful pairing of John Williams' music with that of late Seventies pop sensation Supertramp, the film is a treasure trove for fans, a mind-blowing array of previously unseen images of favourite characters in new environments. We see Wicket on Dagobah, Chewbacca

on Earth and even Mark Hamill, Harrison Ford, and Carrie Fisher, all in costume, just kicking back in their dressing rooms at historic Elstree Studios.

"Those were their actual dressing rooms where they'd hang out at Elstree," Davis, now 29 and fresh off Episode I, recalls. "We used all the sets we could get into. Everyone who took part did so voluntarily – David is so well-respected and liked they would do it for him on their lunch breaks or day off."

Warwick Davis [centre] with Mark Hamill [right] and Mark's son Nathan [left].

But in fact, the film wasn't always shot during breaks. "While they were shooting the shield generator explosion," Davis reveals, "David said, 'We're going to shoot the bit for our film now as well.' There was David, the first assistant director, running the show for the director of the main movie and he's also making his own movie on the side at the same time! There was this dual shooting going on."

But, Davis pointed out, "It wasn't on the sly. George knew about it. I think the original concept was that it was going to play as a kind of teaser to *Return of the Jedi*, a promotional idea that never really came to fruition in the end. But it was great the way we were allowed to go on and film – I can't see that kind of thing having happened on Episode I."

Return of the Ewok was definitely a looser

production. "David would come up with bits," Davis remembers. "He would scribble something in the middle of the night and we'd do it the next day."

For the young Warwick Davis, starring in this side-project to *Return of the Jedi* was just one more whirlwind experience among many. "The whole experience of *Jedi* was so overwhelming," he says. "At 11, I couldn't comprehend it. I just said, 'This is good fun,' and got on with it. I didn't really realise the significance of everything."

In fact, for years Davis held onto his video copy of *Return of the Ewok* without considering what a hot property he had (not even the Lucasfilm archives had one). He first mentioned it in a 1996 interview, and finally unveiled it for the public in a world premiere at the *Star Wars* Celebration in Denver earlier this year. "It wasn't something we planned to keep under wraps," he says, "just nobody ever talked about it. It's not until you think about *Star Wars* a lot that you realise that within it, there's some unique footage that's really priceless."

Unfortunately, the original 16mm print of *Return of the Ewok* has been lost and all that is left is the very grainy, poor quality video dub from which our "screen-grabs" were taken. Tomblin never finished the post-production. "The charm about it for me now is that raw state it's in," Davis says. "You can see the reel changes – it gives you that real lost-in-the-attic feel."

Warwick Davis in part of his Ewok costume.

Because of the quality of the video, *Star Wars Magazine* is unable to reproduce large-size photos from the film. So we decided to turn the necessity of small pictures into a plus and show you *lots* of shots from this amazing lost treasure, telling the story of the short film comic-book style. So read on, Rebels, for the shocking and exciting tale of *Return of the Ewok*.

Warwick strides through London to the tune of Supertramp's "Take the Long Way Home." Says our hero, "There comes a time in every man's life when he must go out into the world to seek his fame and fortune. But where do I start?"

Warwick ponders his future, considering stints as prime minister or admiral of the Naval fleet, when he comes upon David Prowse's real-life London gym.

Warwick finds the Vaderesque actor/bodybuilder lifting weights and catches a ride from Prowse. Warwick decides weightlifting is "too much competition – but I might have beaten him pound-for-pound." Instead, he tries soccer.

"Now this is more like it! My favorite football team – Chelsea. They certainly need my help!"

For these shots, director Tomblin set up his net just outside the touch line, to the side of the field during an actual soccer match at Chelsea Stadium. By placing his camera behind the net or from an off-field angle, he could make it look like Warwick was really in the game.

Deciding soccer would be too dangerous, Warwick crosses the street and discovers a cinema playing *The Empire Strikes Back*. "Ah," he says, "this looks more interesting."

During a clip of Luke Skywalker's lightsaber battle with Darth Vader on Cloud City, Mark Hamill, in full Bespin fatigues and with makeshift lightsaber, backs out of the cinema, tired. When Warwick asks if he's OK, Mark responds, "I just need a breather."

"Go back! You can do it!"
Inspired by Warwick, Mark charges back inside and the film cuts to Luke in *Empire* returning to fight Vader with renewed vigor. Even though Hamill was actually suffering from a fever the day he shot this scene, his heroics are still enough to inspire Warwick to become a movie star.

Warwick takes a meeting with a talent agent (veteran actor Roy Kinnear, recognizable as Veruca Salt's overly indulging father in *Willy Wonka and the Chocolate Factory*), who happens to be desperate to make a buck off the film then called "Revenge of the Jedi." Skeptical of Warwick, he asks, "What can you do?"

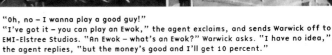

"I can play small parts."

After rummaging through a trunk of costumes, Warwick tries Boba Fett's helmet on for size. The agent asks, "You think you can handle the part?"

"Oh, no – I wanna play a good guy!"
"I've got it – you can play an Ewok," the agent exclaims, and sends Warwick off to EMI-Elstree Studios. "An Ewok – what's an Ewok?" Warwick asks. "I have no idea," the agent replies, "but the money's good and I'll get 10 percent."

A professional from the start, Warwick arrives at Elstree in costume. Admonishing his cab driver that, "Ewoks don't have money," he pays his fare with a banana.

These were the real production offices for "Revenge of the Jedi." Warwick makes his way to a dressing room and knocks on the door.

Warwick: "Please could you tell me where Ewoks have to report?"
Harrison: "What's an Ewok?"
Warwick: "I don't know, but it cost me 10 percent."
Harrison: "I know the feeling. Come on, we'll ask Mark."

"The script's so full of surprises," Mark says. "I mean, it's been top secret. Maybe Carrie knows – let's ask her."

"Oh, I know," Carrie says. "You should report to Jabba the Hutt's palace. It's full of unusual and wonderful things."

A grateful Warwick goes off to find Jabba's palace, with Carrie Fisher telling him, "May the Force be with you." Once Warwick is gone, Harrison Ford asks Mark Hamill, "What'd he say he was?"

A trio of stars (Anthony Daniels as C-3PO, Peter Mayhew as Chewbacca, and a remote-controlled R2-D2) strolls through the Elstree backlot, which was closed in 1993 to make way for a supermarket. The Rebels are no help to Warwick: when he asks for directions to Jabba's palace, they scatter in fear. "Jabba the Hutt can't be a very nice person," Warwick concludes.

"I've come for a job," Warwick tells Salacious Crumb (Tim Rose), who directs him to Max Rebo.

When Warwick hits a key on bandleader Max Rebo's keyboard, an English language version of the classic *Jedi* hit "Lapti Nek" begins, prompting Warwick to break into an impromptu and awesome robot dance.

Warwick interrupts a choreographer and his assistant, who are working with two dancers as Jabba gyrates rhythmically to the music. The choreographer (left) is played by director David Tomblin

Tomblin tells Warwick he has no use for an Ewok in Jabba's palace and sends him to find Frank Oz.

Warwick makes a narrow escape from Jabba's court.

Suddenly, the solitary Ewok finds himself on the Death Star.

Boba Fett (Jeremy Bulloch in costume) emerges from the shadows, shouting (in Tomblin's distinct British brogue, added later), "Ewok!"

Warwick figures Fett for a case of professional jealousy. "Boba Fett – he must have heard I was up for the part!"

Beating a hasty retreat from the bounty hunter, Warwick ends up in the Emperor's gigantic Throne Room. "Wow, if this is Frank Oz's office, I wonder how big Jim Henson's is. It must cost a fortune to heat this place!"

Instead of Oz, Warwick finds someone quite different.

"Ewok! What are you doing in my domain?" demands Vader (it's Dave Prowse in the suit, but Tomblin's voice). Yet again, Warwick gets away.

Warwick finds C-3PO negotiating with *Jedi* co-producer Robert Watts for a private dressing-room for himself and R2-D2. "Artoo's batteries take up a great deal of space," Threepio insists and he won't let the little Ewok get a word in edgewise.
Using a trick he learned from watching *Empire*, Warwick switches Threepio off.

A grateful Watts puts Threepio to better use and promises to lead Warwick to Yoda himself.

"Well, little Ewok, journey a long way. Yes, expecting you was I." Yoda tells Warwick that Ewoks come from the green moon of Endor and issues him his "galactic passport and ticket."

Despite the papers from Yoda, Warwick gets a funny look from a young girl (his sister, Kim). Heathrow Airport officials tell Warwick, "No Ewoks"...

...so he goes incognito...

...and boards a rocket to Endor...

Once on the sanctuary moon, Warwick is reunited with the Rebels, who are hiding from Imperial forces. "Sorry to startle you," Warwick says, "but I'm still lost – could you please tell me where the Ewok village is?" Han replies, "I'm sorry kid, but we're in big trouble ourselves right now."

Alone, Warwick stops for a rest. "I'm getting very hungry. I wonder what Ewoks eat. I wish I hadn't given that man my banana."

A swarm of Ewoks rushes in from the forest, surrounding Warwick and embracing him as John Williams' *Star Wars* end titles music swells.

As the music plays, we see a montage of clips depicting the Endor battle. This shot, featuring Wicket struggling with a large blaster, was also shot (with a different camera) for *Jedi*, but didn't make the final cut. Sixteen years later, a similar bit with Jar Jar Binks was featured during Episode I's Naboo ground battle.

Tomblin shot Wicket throwing a bomb into the Endor shield generator right before it blew up, shooting from a different angle at the same time as *Jedi* director Richard Marquand shot the explosion for the final film.

Warwick bids a cheerful farewell to his new friends. "Well, Warwick, it wasn't easy," Mark Hamill says, "but we couldn't have done it without you." Carrie Fisher plants a kiss on Warwick's cheek and he skips off, shouting, "Give my love to the Ewoks!" A wistful, melancholy Mark Hamill replies, "Sure will."

You can barely see them, but Warwick's real-life mom Sue and dad Ashley arrive to take him home. They don't believe him at first when he tells them of his adventures – that is, until they encounter Yoda (offscreen), who tells Warwick's father, "May the Force be with you, Dad."

STAR WARS LIBRARY

- *ROGUE ONE: A STAR WARS STORY* THE OFFICIAL COLLECTOR'S EDITION
- *ROGUE ONE: A STAR WARS STORY* THE OFFICIAL MISSION DEBRIEF
- *STAR WARS: THE LAST JEDI* THE OFFICIAL COLLECTOR'S EDITION
- *STAR WARS: THE LAST JEDI* THE OFFICIAL MOVIE COMPANION
- *STAR WARS: THE LAST JEDI* THE ULTIMATE GUIDE
- *SOLO: A STAR WARS STORY* THE OFFICIAL COLLECTOR'S EDITION
- *SOLO: A STAR WARS STORY* THE ULTIMATE GUIDE
- *THE BEST OF STAR WARS INSIDER* VOLUME 1
- *THE BEST OF STAR WARS INSIDER* VOLUME 2
- *THE BEST OF STAR WARS INSIDER* VOLUME 3
- *THE BEST OF STAR WARS INSIDER* VOLUME 4
- *STAR WARS:* LORDS OF THE SITH
- *STAR WARS:* HEROES OF THE FORCE
- *STAR WARS:* ICONS OF THE GALAXY
- *STAR WARS:* THE SAGA BEGINS
- *STAR WARS* THE ORIGINAL TRILOGY
- *STAR WARS:* ROGUES, SCOUNDRELS AND BOUNTY HUNTERS (SEPT '19)
- *STAR WARS* CREATURES, ALIENS, AND DROIDS (NOV '19)
- *STAR WARS: THE RISE OF SKYWALKER* THE OFFICIAL COLLECTOR'S EDITION (DEC '19)

STAR WARS
ROGUES, SCOUNDRELS AND BOUNTY HUNTERS

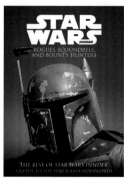

STAR WARS:
THE RISE OF SKYWALKER
(DEC '19)

MARVEL LIBRARY

X-MEN
THE DARK PHOENIX SAGA (MAY '20)

NOVELS
- **ANT-MAN** NATURAL ENEMY
- **AVENGERS** EVERYBODY WANTS TO RULE THE WORLD
- **AVENGERS** INFINITY (NOV '19)
- **BLACK PANTHER** WHO IS THE BLACK PANTHER?
- **CAPTAIN AMERICA** DARK DESIGNS (OCT '19)
- **CAPTAIN MARVEL** LIBERATION RUN (OCT '19)
- **CIVIL WAR**
- **DEADPOOL** PAWS
- **SPIDER-MAN** FOREVER YOUNG
- **SPIDER-MAN** HOSTILE TAKEOVER
- **SPIDER-MAN** KRAVEN'S LAST HUNT
- **THANOS** DEATH SENTENCE
- **VENOM** LETHAL PROTECTOR
- **X-MEN** DAYS OF FUTURE PAST

MARVEL STUDIOS:
THE FIRST TEN YEARS

MOVIE SPECIALS
- MARVEL STUDIOS' *ANT MAN & THE WASP*
- MARVEL STUDIOS' *AVENGERS: ENDGAME*
- MARVEL STUDIOS' *AVENGERS: INFINITY WAR*
- MARVEL STUDIOS' *BLACK PANTHER* (COMPANION)
- MARVEL STUDIOS' *BLACK PANTHER* (SPECIAL)
- MARVEL STUDIOS' *CAPTAIN MARVEL*
- MARVEL STUDIOS' *SPIDER-MAN: FAR FROM HOME*
- MARVEL STUDIOS: THE FIRST TEN YEARS
- MARVEL STUDIOS' *THOR: RAGNAROK*
- *SPIDER-MAN: INTO THE SPIDERVERSE*

ARTBOOKS
- MARVEL'S *SPIDER-MAN* THE ART OF THE GAME
- MARVEL: *CONQUEST OF CHAMPIONS* THE ART OF THE BATTLEREALM
- *SPIDER-MAN: INTO THE SPIDERVERSE*
- THE ART OF *IRON MAN* 10TH ANNIVERSARY EDITION

DISNEY LIBRARY

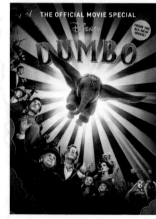

DISNEY *DUMBO*
THE OFFICIAL MOVIE SPECIAL

DISNEY•PIXAR *TOY STORY 4*
THE OFFICIAL MOVIE SPECIAL

DISNEY *THE LION KING*
THE OFFICIAL MOVIE SPECIAL

DISNEY *FROZEN 2*
THE OFFICIAL MOVIE SPECIAL
(OCT '19)

AVAILABLE AT ALL GOOD BOOKSTORES AND ONLINE

TITAN-COMICS.COM | TITANBOOKS.COM

Copyright © 2019 Disney/Pixar. All Rights Reserved.
© 2019 Lucasfilm Ltd. and ™. All Rights Reserved. Used Under Authorisation.
© 2019 MARVEL.